Fugitive Slaves
and the Unfinished
American Revolution

Fugitive Slaves and the Unfinished American Revolution

Eight Cases, 1848–1856

GORDON S. BARKER

For Fred & Ann

with my very
best wishes

G. S. B.

McFarland & Company, Inc., Publishers

Jefferson, North Carolina, and London

LIBRARY OF CONGRESS CATALOGUING-IN-PUBLICATION DATA

Barker, Gordon S., 1952–
    Fugitive slaves and the unfinished American Revolution :
eight cases, 1848–1856 / Gordon S. Barker.
        p.   cm.
    Includes bibliographical references and index.

    ISBN 978-0-7864-6987-1
    softcover : acid free paper ∞

    1. Fugitive slaves—United States.   2. Fugitive slaves—
United States—Biography.   I. Title.
E450.B25 2013
306.3'620922—dc23
    [B]   2013015551

BRITISH LIBRARY CATALOGUING DATA ARE AVAILABLE

Front cover: Federal and state troops returning Anthony Burns
(1834–1862) to slavery after his fugitive slave trial at the courthouse
in Boston, Massachusetts, May 1854, line engraving, 19th century
(Granger Collection)

Manufactured in the United States of America

McFarland & Company, Inc., Publishers
    Box 611, Jefferson, North Carolina 28640
        www.mcfarlandpub.com

For Charles Scott Barker and Florence Enid Eaves
My parents, my teachers

Table of Contents

Preface   1

Introduction: Fugitive Slaves and American Revolution   2

1. William and Ellen Craft: "Running a Thousand Miles" for Inalienable Rights   21

2. Rescuing Shadrach: The "Noblest Deed in Boston Since the Boston Tea-Party of 1773"   37

3. Thomas Sims: Renewing the Revolutionary Struggle for American Liberties   54

4. William Parker and Revolutionary Heroes at Christiana   77

5. The Jerry Rescue: Breaking Bondage and Saving America in Syracuse   96

6. Rescuing Joshua Glover and Guarding American Liberties   118

7. Anthony Burns: "Resolution to Strike the Blow, for Freedom or the Grave"   136

8. Margaret Garner: Tragedy and Revolutionary Resistance in Cincinnati   160

Epilogue: An Enduring Revolution   181

Chapter Notes   185

Bibliography   207

Index   213

Preface

This work focuses on several truly remarkable African Americans and their struggle for freedom in late antebellum America. My hope is that their stories will help academic and public historians recognize the major contributions of these fugitive slaves and the people — black and white — who shared their dreams for freedom and a more perfect Union.

This work could not have come to fruition without the help of many wonderful people and organizations. Melvin Patrick Ely, the William R. Kenan, Jr., Professor of Humanities in the Lyon G. Tyler Department of History at the College of William and Mary kindly arranged for me to be a scholar-in-residence at the Earl Gregg Swem Library during the summer of 2011. I am also grateful for the assistance that I have received from the librarians and staff at the Bishop's University Library, McGill University Library, the Library of Congress, Syracuse University Library, the James A. Gibson Library of Brock University, the American Antiquarian Society, the Boston Public Library, the Massachusetts Historical Society, the Boston Athenaeum, and the Wisconsin Historical Society. The Bishop's University Research Office and Michael Childs, Bishop's University's Vice-Principal Academic, provided funding and support for this project; Bishop's University's Crossing Borders Research Cluster provided a forum for insightful discussion and debate. Valerie Martin made arrangements for the illustrations, prepared the index, and carefully read through the manuscript. Dana Broadbent did the final proofreading. Finally, this work would not have seen the light of day without the patience and support of my partner Christiane and my daughter Nadine. Not only did they put up with a disorganized, organized historian on a daily basis and on several heavily charged research trips, but they often provided advice and insight as well as loving support and encouragement. To them I say a very special thank you.

Introduction: Fugitive Slaves and American Revolution

The Antislavery struggle is for the freedom of man, without distinction of race or color.... No matter who the man may be that shall try his hand against this movement, he will fail in the end. No matter what party may attempt to put it down; that party will be dashed in pieces. It is a rock; and "whosoever shall fall thereon shall be broken, but on whomsoever it shall fall, it shall grind him to powder." — Wendell Phillips

If it is the "cradle of liberty," they have rocked the child to death ... one-sixth of our countrymen are clanking in chains upon the very soil which our fathers moistened with their blood. — William Wells Brown

You and I prefer the peaceful method [to abolish slavery]; but I, at least, shall welcome the violent, if no other accomplish the end. So will the great mass of thoughtful good men at the North; else why do we honour the heroes of the Revolution. — Theodore Parker

On July 4, 1826, the fiftieth anniversary of the Declaration of Independence, Americans mourned the loss of Thomas Jefferson and John Adams, who along with George Washington had come to symbolize the birth of the Republic and the struggle for nationhood. For many Americans, their coincident deaths exactly fifty years after the Declaration symbolized the passing of the Revolutionary Generation. In the North and South, Americans expressed reverence for these men who had been instrumental in establishing America in the community of nations and guided the young country through the turbulent years of the Revolution, the framing and ratification of the Constitution, and the Federalist Era when the United States experienced troubles at home and abroad, including a quasi-war with France.

The passing of the second and third presidents, however, seemed also to usher in a new era, another phase in the republican experiment. The nation had recovered from the Panic of 1819; internal improvements, including the Erie Canal, linked once disparate regions; and the country even enjoyed some renewed "Good Feelings" after Henry Clay brokered the Missouri Compromise bringing Missouri and Maine into the Union, thus preserving balance between slave and free states. Many white Americans surely believed the trying times that the Revolutionary Generation had wrestled with were giving way to an epoch of prosperity and harmony, which would allow the new nation to expand westward from "sea to shining sea" as the Democratic editor John O'Sullivan later put it when he coined the term "Manifest Destiny." Certainly from the perspective of white males, who voted in increasing numbers after electoral reform in the 1820s, the Revolution had established a veritable Empire of Liberty, something James Monroe confirmed with his message to Congress in 1823, later dubbed the Monroe Doctrine. Written by Secretary of State John Quincy Adams, the Monroe Doctrine acknowledged the new nation's uniqueness and instituted an American foreign policy for the Western hemisphere. It told Old World powers that the Americas were for Americans, the United States would tolerate no further European colonization on this side of the Atlantic, and hence European imperialists better stay away.

But on the Fourth in 1826, as Americans mourned two heroes and looked forward optimistically, they also turned to their Revolutionary legacy seeking guidance to ensure that they would walk fittingly in the footsteps of exemplary founders. Therein lay an urgent need for a grand master narrative, a history that acknowledged their heroes' accomplishments and positioned the republican experiment within the broader story of human progress. Responding to this requisite, George Bancroft wrote his *History of the United States* portraying the Revolution as a truly heroic struggle of liberty-loving white American merchants, planters, and yeomen farmers who sought to throw off the yoke of tyranny.[1] Bancroft's narrative served as a pillar for a new historical academy and, in fact, many Americans still embrace his periodization of the Revolution, ending it with the cessation of the military conflict. From Bancroft, Americans learned that the Revolution finished with Lord Cornwallis's surrender at Yorktown in 1781 or with the Treaty of Paris in 1783. The Founding Fathers then resolved the problems of the Critical Period and ensured the republican experiment by the framing and ratifying of the Constitution. Afterward, their enlightened leadership guided the Republic through its tumultuous Federalist years. With the passing of Jefferson and Adams on the venerated Fourth, post–Revolutionary white Americans felt they had the duty to carry the country forward. The New National Era had begun; the Revolution moved "into history" and white Americans sought ways to appropriate it — often, unfortunately, to the exclusion of others.[2]

Although twentieth-century historians of the progressive and imperialist schools criticized Bancroft's romantic Whig interpretation of the Revolution as they pointed to the Founders' material interests or the inefficiencies of imperial political and economic management, few scholars questioned his periodization until the 1980s when social history shifted the focus to ordinary Americans. For example, in *Shays' Rebellion: The Making of an Agrarian Insurrection*, David P. Szatmary described ordinary folk in the 1790s still in search of benefits in the new social and political order. About the same time, Mary Beth Norton and Linda Kerber published seminal works addressing challenges confronting late eighteenth-century women. Not long after, in *Race and Revolution*, Gary Nash examined the Revolutionary Generation's failure to extend liberties to black Americans, implicitly demonstrating that the Revolution had yet to be completed.[3]

As the 1990s progressed, such concerns loomed larger, further undermining acceptance of Bancroft's periodization. In *Radicalism of the American Revolution*, Gordon S. Wood argued that the Revolution must be interpreted as a deep-rooted social, political, and cultural transformation that spanned some one hundred years from the 1740s through to the Age of Andrew Jackson. The Revolution, contended Wood, represented more than the military conflict that began with shots fired at Lexington and Concord and ended with the Treaty of Paris. Even Wood's critics who voiced concerns in the *William and Mary Quarterly*'s forum on his work agreed with him on this point.[4] So also did the radical historians Peter Linebaugh and Marcus Rediker. In "*Many Headed Hydra*": *Sailors, Slaves, Commoners, and the Hidden History of the Revolutionary Atlantic*, Linebaugh and Rediker viewed the Revolution as a pan–Atlantic movement that swept the Atlantic world driven by labor's embrace of ideologies rejecting traditional hierarchies. The Revolution was not confined to the Thirteen Colonies nor was it limited to the time frame usually associated with the Anglo-American imperial crisis. Linebaugh and Rediker also have a different set of heroes as they underscore the agency of workers and seamen, including free black sailors and slaves, who transmitted revolutionary undercurrents throughout the Atlantic littoral.[5] The Revolution, they stress, reflected the determination of ordinary sorts to shape their world; the revolutionary die had not been cast by virtuous, enlightened white merchants, planters, and yeomen farmers.

In many ways, it is surprising that scholars of African American history did not contest Bancroft's periodization earlier. In the nineteenth century, William Cooper Nell, William Wells Brown, and George Washington Williams focused primarily on the heroic contributions of African Americans who "partook of the 'Spirit of 76.'" The African Americans' "splendid behavior on all the battlefields of the Revolution," wrote Williams, proved that "the Negro soldier fought his way to undimmed glory, and made for himself a magnificent record in the annals of American history."[6] Emphasizing black feats, the early chroniclers downplayed defections of African Americans to the British after the emancipation proclamations of Lord Dunmore in 1775 and Sir Henry Clinton in 1779, which promised freedom to slaves who rallied to the British. Simply put, these scholars sought to write blacks into a patriotic history of the Revolution.[7] Until then, as Benjamin Quarles noted, Bancroft and other whites published histories suggesting "that the British and Americans fought for seven years as if a half-million African Americans were magically whisked off the continent."[8] As black writers took up their pens, they also contended with racism evincing arguments that "the celebration of the Fourth of July belong[ed] exclusively to the white population of the United States."[9]

Twentieth-century African American historians concerned with the collective experience of blacks rather than individual heroism also did not challenge the usual periodization, even as they stressed blacks' continuing search for freedom, a quest not confined to the Revolution's traditionally defined time frame. Herbert Aptheker shifted from addressing the contribution of black patriots to studying enslaved blacks who fled to the British with "one set purpose — the achievement of liberty" but he did not contest the Revolution's periodization. Neither did John Hope Franklin or Benjamin Quarles in his masterful work, *The Negro in the American Revolution*. Writing in the Civil Rights Era, Quarles, argues Douglas R. Egerton, was still "understandably anxious to demonstrate the black contribution to America's victory" and show that African Americans "quickly caught the spirit of '76."[10] Although advancing nuanced interpretations of the black experience during the Revolution, Sylvia Frey and Joyce Lee Malcolm did not call for revisions to its periodization. Focusing on strategic interests, Frey highlights the "triagonal nature" of the conflict involving patriots, loyalists, and the enslaved black population. Malcolm examines unique contexts that influenced blacks as they evaluated their options and shows how different circumstances pushed individuals to align with the patriots or the loyalists.[11]

Today, however, we need to reconsider the periodization of the Revolution, particularly as Americans recognize their diversity and demand a more inclusive master narrative. Acceptance of Bancroft's periodization yields a flawed view of a uniform beginning and end of the Revolution for all Americans that fails to acknowledge that Americans defined *their revolutions* differently. Americans' interests differed and they realized their goals at different times. Although a white planter or a New England merchant utilized the rhetoric of enslavement, his rejection of the legislative authority of a political entity across the Atlantic differed immensely from an American slave's aspirations to be free. The transfer of political sovereignty the planter or merchant demanded took place in Paris in 1783, if not before at Yorktown in 1781; white elites could interpret either year as the end of the Revolution — as Bancroft did. This was not the case for a slave who remained in the "iron house of bondage"; in the Paris negotiations, enslaved blacks were dealt with "in the same category with horses and other articles of property."[12] Recent African American scholarship demonstrates that slaves did not regard the Revolution as over; their struggle continued whether it found expression discreetly or overtly, individually or collectively.[13]

We also need to recognize that Bancroft's periodization supports an implicit appropriation of the Revolution by white merchants and planters, the groups it favors. In the 1780s, these elite white males achieved their goal. For them, the Revolution was over and in the 1820s they sought to appropriate it, write it into history, and embark on the expansion of the New National Era, even as others still struggled for their American liberties. For the blacks, the Revolution continued; it was a battle against slavery. For them, the Revolution ended — at the very earliest — with the ratification of the Thirteenth Amendment.[14]

Slave revolts prove that blacks believed the Revolution still raged in the antebellum period. Leaders of major uprisings, notably Gabriel Prosser, Charles Deslondes, Denmark Vesey, and Nat Turner, were men with broad revolutionary visions and intent on transformation — not just on resistance. Gabriel thought that slaves, free blacks, and white workers with whom he rubbed shoulders in Richmond's hiring-out market and grog shops shared his natural rights ideologies and would join his movement.[15] A decade later in Louisiana, "conversant in the doctrines of the French Revolution, and aware of the powerful example of the Haitian revolutionaries," Charles Deslondes, Kook, Quamana, and their followers "came well armed for battle with a powerful set of revolutionary ideas, well honed skills, and a complex organization of insurrectionary cells."[16] Like Gabriel before, or Vesey and Turner after, these men sought to reshape their worlds through revolution.[17]

So also did other antebellum Americans who joined them in striving for a better republic — indeed for that "more perfect Union." Unlike Bancroft, their revolutionary goals had not yet been achieved and they were not yet willing to rest with what the Founders had realized. The Unitarian minister Theodore Parker, for example, stressed that "the expectation of the people, in 1787," of forming "a more perfect Union" to secure "the blessings of liberty" and abolish slavery had not been achieved.[18] Like Parker, the Reverend Samuel Joseph May believed that "the fathers of our Republic never meant to perpetuate slavery."[19] Such antebellum Americans sought to extend the Revolution. The fugitive slave crises of William and Ellen Craft, Shadrach Minkins, Thomas Sims, William Parker, Jerry, Joshua Glover, Anthony Burns, and Margaret Garner reveal many Americans longing and fighting for "a more perfect Union," just like their forbears. As they did so, they strove in the name of the Revolution.

"GIVE ME LIBERTY, OR GIVE ME DEATH." During the late antebellum fugitive slave dramas, the fugitive slaves and their abolitionist allies, black and white, embraced Patrick Henry's Revolutionary American motto, "Give me Liberty, or Give me Death!" (Library of Congress).

In these mid-nineteenth century dramas, the fugitive slaves themselves embraced revolutionary ideology that invariably found expression in Patrick Henry's hallowed words, "Give me Liberty or Give me Death." They appropriated and acted out Patrick Henry's motto, thereby elevating their cause to that of "heroic resistance and republican virtue" and transforming themselves into American Revolutionaries.[20] When Anthony Burns heard rumors of plots to return him to "the prison-house of slavery," he swore that "should [someone] attempt to deprive me of my liberty as before, then I would enforce the motto of Patrick Henry, *Liberty or Death*."[21] Describing slavery as the "sum of all villainies," William Parker vowed that he was prepared to "fight until death" for freedom. Jerry too declared "he would die rather than go back to slavery."[22] When returned to bondage, Thomas Sims repeatedly "pleaded for a knife with which to free his soul."[23] Most dramatic was Margaret Garner's murder of her daughter Mary. She acted out the principle of liberty or death as she took her infant's life. She was not the first to protect a loved one from slavery in this way. "The [slave] mother has taken the life of her child, to preserve that child from the hands of the Slave-trader. The brother has taken the life of his sister, to protect her chastity," lamented the fugitive slave William Wells Brown. "As the noble Virginius seized the dagger, and thrust it to the heart of the gentle Virginia, to save her from the hands of Appius Claudius of Rome," said the man often considered to be the first African American novelist, "so the father [has] seized the deadly knife, and taken the life of his daughter to save her from the hands of the master."[24] Antebellum newspapers took Garner's murder as proof of the liberty-or-death principle. The headline, "ARREST of FUGITVE SLAVES — A Slave Mother Murders her Child rather than see it Returned to Slavery!" seemed to say it all. A life without liberty was no life at all.[25]

The fugitive slaves' allies, of course, also embraced Patrick Henry's powerful ideology. On the eve of William and Ellen Craft's flight, Lewis Hayden, a key actor in the Shadrach, Sims, and Burns dramas, presided at a meeting in which black Bostonians assailed the Fugitive Slave Law. "We prefer *liberty to life*, we mutually pledge to defend ourselves and each other," resolved Hayden and his brethren. African Americans across the North and from Canada shared this vision. Josiah Henson, co-founder of the Dawn Settlement in Ontario, joined his former countrymen in Boston in endorsing "Patrick Henry's immortal sentiment, *Liberty or Death!*"[26] In New York City, blacks rose in convention to ask, "Shall we resist oppression? Shall we defend our liberties? Shall we be FREEMEN or SLAVE?" They promised to fight for freedom at all costs "with the surest and most deadly weapons including bowie knives and revolvers."[27] According to the Reverend Jermain W. Loguen, Syracuse blacks believed that "it's our duty to protect ourselves at the expense of life, if need be."[28] Striking out against pacifist whites as he supported Jerry, the Reverend Samuel Ringgold Ward exhorted blacks to put their lives on the line. "If white men won't fight," declared Ward, "let fugitives and black men smite down Marshals and Commissioners — any body who holds Jerry — and rescue him or perish."[29] Denouncing a slave catcher in Pittsburgh, Martin Delany swore, "If he crosses the threshold of my door, and I do not lay him a lifeless corpse at my feet, I hope that my grave may refuse my body a resting-place, and the righteous Heaven my spirit a home."[30] Frederick Douglass portrayed fugitive slaves as "heroic defenders of the just rights of man." Speaking of William Parker and his allies, Douglass reminded Americans that fugitive slaves pursued freedom with resolve. "What they [Parker and his compatriots] had already done at Christiana, and the cool determination which they showed [in the name of liberty]," wrote Douglass, "left no doubt in my mind that their deeds would equal their words."[31]

As blacks asserted themselves in life-and-death struggles for freedom, they claimed the right to share in America's Revolutionary heritage. Charles Lenox Remond told audiences that, even if racist whites said Bunker Hill was "no place for niggers," every glorious feat from Lexington and Concord to Yorktown was also a black triumph.[32] But unlike their white neighbors, these antebellum blacks did *not* consider the Revolution finished and called on Americans to "complete the [R]evolution."[33] With so many of their brothers and sisters still enslaved, the Revolution was not over. As Frederick Douglass said, "slavery ha[d] a right to go any where in this Republic and Liberty no where except where Slavery will let it."[34]

As mid-century fugitive slave dramas unfolded, many whites proved they still lived by Henry's motto and that they too were ready to use force to extend American liberties to their black neighbors. Enraged by the Fugitive Slave Law, Gerrit Smith called on abolitionists to defend fugitive slaves "by every means possible." He encouraged the Syracuse Vigilance Committee to rescue Jerry by force and spirit him to Canada *before* Commissioner Joseph Sabine ruled on his case. He reasoned that the "moral effect" of Sabine ruling in favor of Jerry could be "nothing [compared] to a bold and forcible rescue"—a struggle of liberty or death. Samuel Joseph May, also a member of the Syracuse Vigilance Committee, discarded his pacifist beliefs during the Jerry drama. He asked antislavery militants in New York's "citadel of upstate antislavery" if they stood ready to defend the freedom of fugitive slaves "with their lives." His audience responded with a resounding "Yes."[35]

Despite his pacifism, William Lloyd Garrison used Patrick Henry's hallowed words. Speaking to the Massachusetts Anti-Slavery Society, he declared, "[T]he voice of God in the soul cries aloud, 'Give me liberty, or give me death.'"[36] Other editors also adopted the Virginian's famous words to sanction fugitive slave rescues. After the Christiana riot, the editor of the *Pennsylvania Freeman* made sure that readers understood what was at stake. "Had not Americans claimed 'Liberty or death,' 'Resistance to tyrants is duty to God,' as their National Creed?" he asked. If that was so, he reasoned, "What wonder that the Negro fugitives think it is no crime ... to defend their liberties by the same means for which the 'Revolutionary heroes' of our own and other countries are glorified." John Andrew, later governor of Massachusetts, defended the daring rescue of Shadrach Minkins saying that "he would rather one hundred men should die in defense of freedom than one slave go back to be trodden down."[37]

Theodore Parker often justified his radical abolitionism on the basis of his Revolutionary heritage. Describing his reaction to slave catchers attempting to seize William and Ellen Craft, he declared, "I have had to arm myself. I have written my sermons with a pistol in my desk, — loaded, a cap on the nipple, and ready for action." He felt a duty to defend them. "I was born in the little town where the first bloodshed of the Revolution began," explained Parker. "My grandfather drew the first sword in the Revolution. With these memories in me, when a parishioner [Ellen], a fugitive from slavery, a woman, pursued by kidnappers, came to my house, what could I do less than take her in and defend her to the last?"[38] Likewise, the Reverend Thomas Wentworth Higginson, later also a member of John Brown's Secret Six, revealed how he was moved on Revolutionary grounds.[39] For him, the Fugitive Slave Law had permitted slavery's tentacles to reach into the free states, making freedom a life and death struggle. He said, "Freedom needs defenders." Stating that "life is something more than dress and show," he thought that he could "only make [his] life worth living for, by becoming a revolutionist." He certainly justified and remembered the rescue of Burns on this basis. "The strokes on the door of the Court House that night," said Higginson, "went echoing from town to town, from Boston to far New Orleans, like the first drum beats of the Revolution — and each reverberating throb was a blow upon the door of every Slave-prison of this guilty Republic."[40]

Samuel Gridley Howe too invoked his Revolutionary heritage when he supported militant action to save Burns. Calling for Bostonians to be "united in the glorious sentiment of our Revolutionary fathers," he shouted, "Resistance to tyrants is obedience to God." The Declaration of Independence underpinned his condemnation of slaveholders "who den[ied] the natural right of a man to his own body — of a father to his own child — of a husband to his wife." Like Wendell Phillips, Howe wanted Bostonians to prove that they were "not bastards" but "the children of Adams and Hancock."[41] Writing in his journal, Bronson Alcott also shared such beliefs. When he saw a manacled fugitive slave in the streets of Boston, he felt the "indignation of every one in whom sentiments of justice and humanity yet survive" and demanded "redress at any hazard."[42] During the Burns crisis, the Reverend James Freeman Clarke called for a renewal of "the spirit of '76" and declared that it was time for "the tocsin of liberty to sound out again from Faneuil Hall."[43] These were Josiah Quincy's sentiments when he saw Thomas Sims sent back from Boston to slavery; referring to Lexington and Concord, he demanded a return to "the Boston of 1775."[44]

Joining their fathers, husbands, sons, and brothers in espousing Henry's motto, women also drew on their Revolutionary heritage in fugitive slave crises. Helping Frederick Douglass guide William Parker across the Genesee River to freedom, Julia Griffiths heralded the "watchword, 'Liberty or Death.'"[45] In Boston, radical female abolitionists invoked their earlier sisters' Revolutionary example as they rallied for Burns. Some, like Sarah Pellet, admonished women who did not live up to past standards. "Had the ladies acted up to the dignity of true women," she proclaimed, "they might have saved Anthony Burns. Had the women of Boston turned out *en masse*, and placed themselves before the cannon's mouth, would any man have dared to fire at them?" Abby Kelley Foster too saw fugitive slave crises as Revolutionary fights for freedom. "[T]he *war exists already*, and has been waged unremittingly ever since the slave has been in bondage," she exclaimed. "Four millions of slaves are disarmed warriors today; and all the evils of war, violations of life, liberty, property and every other right, are *now going on,* and *increasing.*" She concluded — ominously — "Certainly every friend of liberty here would rejoice to hear to-night that slaves of Louisiana or of Tennessee had risen against their masters." Little Charlotte Forten agreed. Horrified by Marshal Watson Freeman, his deputies, and the military who were ready "to shoot down" any defender of Anthony Burns, the young black girl wrote, they were "without mercy"; she saw the Burns affray as a life or death struggle.⁴⁶ The Margaret Garner crisis caused some women to discard pacifism for more militant means. Touched by the horror of a child-murder, Sarah Ernst, a Garrisonian pacifist in Cincinnati, said it proved that it was time for Americans to act in earnest. "We feel we *can not, dare not* relax in our endeavors ... when a *mother* kills one child...." Within weeks of the child-murder, Hattia M'Keehan penned a novel based on the sorrowful tale; she titled it *Liberty or Death!; or, Heaven's Infraction of the Fugitive Slave Law.*⁴⁷

As these mid-century fugitive slave crises fueled tensions on a political and social landscape imbued with natural rights ideology and moral beliefs in Higher Law, especially after the Second Great Awakening and Harriet Beecher Stowe's publication of *Uncle Tom's Cabin* in 1852, anti-slavery militants challenged the appropriation of the Revolution by Americans who supported or compromised with slavery and sought to conserve the Union as it was. Arguing the Revolution was unfinished, abolitionists positioned their cause in the broader story of advancing freedom, often marrying it with their goal of achieving "a more perfect Union." Addressing the Massachusetts Anti-Slavery Society, Wendell Phillips concluded that "the American Union ... [had] proved a sad and total failure, having, from its formation to the present day, directly tended to the moral degradation and ruin of the American people, and the extension and perpetuity of the most dreadful form of bondage now known to mankind."⁴⁸ Invoking history, he urged Massachusetts to welcome and protect fugitive slaves whom he described as "brave men and tender women, feeling the breath of hounds upon their naked limbs, bearing musket shot in their still bleeding flesh, risking death by angry floods, or frozen rivers, by starvation, in boxes, on railroad cars, deep in the hold of heavy laden ships." Accentuating the plight of fleeing bondswomen, Phillips spoke of "mothers bringing the little child's body who has sunk to death in their arms—daughters flying from a fate worse than death." They demonstrated valor that "only the highest hours of history can equal." Phillips argued that there was not a more noble "exile" than the fugitive slave and reminded his audience that "in 1641, our fathers, just landed, proclaimed that Massachusetts had open arms for all exiles, all fugitives from tyranny and oppression." Phillips wanted Massachusetts to be "worthy of its ancient name." He concluded, saying "Let history tell that on our soil to say, 'I am a man,' unlocked every chain and shriveled unholy parchments to ashes, while the emancipated head flashed the mailed arm of the Commonwealth with its protecting legend, 'SUB LIBERTATE QUIETEM.'"[49] With such fervor, Phillips believed he had "Set the nation on fire"—the fire of revolution. After the Garner crisis in Cincinnati, he told an audience, "If a Negro kills his master tonight, write his name by the side of Warren; say that he is a William Tell in disguise, or a John Hancock in eclipse. I want to accustom Massachusetts to the idea of insurrection; to the idea that every slave has a right to seize his liberty on the spot." For Phillips, the antebellum antislavery cause was Revolution.[50]

Black Americans too sought to appropriate the Revolution as they embraced its legacy. They did so increasingly forcefully after David Walker published his *Appeal in Four Articles* in 1829. Walker's "militant statement of racial pride hurled against white assertions of black inferiority" and overtly challenged exclusive white appropriation of the Revolution. He also assailed African colonization schemes, saying "Let no man of us budge one step ... and let slave-holders come to beat us from our country. America is more our country, than it is the whites'—we have enriched it with our *blood and tears*."[51] Walker appealed to the "first principles of the Declaration of Independence, especially to the right of revolution," which later underpinned African American agency when 180,000 blacks fought for the Union, transforming the Civil War into a war of liberation.[52]

Antebellum blacks used the Declaration, often in conjunction with Patrick Henry's motto, in very ingenious ways. After Congress enacted the Fugitive Slave Law, black Bostonians issued the "*Declaration of Sentiments of the Colored Citizens*," which stated, "The example of the [R]evolutionary Fathers in resisting British oppression, and throwing the tea overboard in Boston Harbor, rather than submit to a three-penny tax, is a most significant one to us when MAN is likely to be deprived of his God-given liberty." They appropriated the Revolution by honoring Crispus Attucks, the black killed in the Boston Massacre, as the Revolution's "first Martyr." They also declared, "The battle cry of Patrick Henry of Virginia—'GIVE ME LIBERTY, OR GIVE ME DEATH'—and that of General Warren, 'MY SONS SCORN TO BE SLAVES' are immortalized, and we are proud in not being exception[s] to that inspiration." They vowed to "DIE freemen, rather than LIVE slaves." The black Bostonian

Joshua B. Smith remarked that he did not want to hear anyone "preach *Peace*, for as Patrick Henry said, *'There is no Peace'*"; Josiah Henson reasoned that anyone condemning the black fight for freedom would have to denounce, by analogy, the "examples of WASHINGTON and JEFFERSON, and all Martyrs of Liberty."[53] These blacks repeated an earlier message of the slaves of William Whipple, the signer of the Declaration of Independence from Portsmouth, New Hampshire. Having imbibed the Declaration's equal rights ideology, Prince Whipple, Windsor Moffat, and twenty other African Americans petitioned for American liberties on November 12, 1779—"just as Whipple and others had signed the Declaration."[54]

WILLIAM COOPER NELL. William Cooper Nell and other leading black Bostonians penned the Declaration of Sentiments of the Colored Citizens of Boston. They said, "the battle cry of Patrick Henry of Virginia—'GIVE ME LIBERTY, OR GIVE ME DEATH,'—and that of General Warren, 'MY SONS SCORN TO BE SLAVES,' are immortalized, and we are proud in not being an exception to that inspiration."

Blacks and their white allies often elevated fugitive slaves to the status of Revolutionary heroes. Henry Bibb, the literate runaway who edited the *Voice of the Fugitive*, summed up black sentiments after the Christiana riot when he welcomed William Parker to Canada. "This man in our estimation deserves the admiration of a Hannibal, a Toussaint L'Ouverture, or a George Washington. A nobler defense was never made in behalf of liberty on the plains of Lexington, Concord, or Bunker Hill than was put forth by William Parker at Christiana," wrote Bibb.[55]

In Syracuse, Samuel Ringgold Ward, perhaps the most eloquent black orator, claimed the Declaration for himself and his black brethren. After witnessing the brutal treatment of Jerry when the latter failed on his first attempt to escape, the fugitive slave preacher asked, "Why did my fathers fight the British, if one of their poor sons is to be treated this way?" He answered his own question, also emphasizing Jerry's biracial heritage. "In the name of our common nature — in the name of the Declaration of Independence — in the name of the law in the Bible ... do break these chains, and give me the freedom which is mine because I am a man, and an American," exclaimed the black preacher. And of Jerry, he cried, "What a sight!... A slave, in a free Northern city chained as a felon would be chained, with the blood of Anglo-Saxons in his veins. Still a slave: the son of a wealthy planter in Tennessee, and still a slave."[56]

Fugitive slave dramas catalyzed debates between Americans about the Revolution and its meaning, fueling — as we have seen — the discourse of antebellum America's most outspoken abolitionists who unleashed their own interpretations of the republican experiment and demanded "a more perfect Union." As ordinary Americans joined these conversations, they sometimes demonstrated that they held notions of continuing revolution as well. As I have argued in *The Imperfect Revolution: Anthony Burns and the Landscape of Race in Antebellum America*, ordinary folk often played instrumental roles in fugitive slave crises. Edward Magol suggests they were the real "source of republican virtue."[57] Bruce Laurie certainly implies this of Martin Stowell, an active participant in both the Jerry and Burns crises.[58] Fugitive slave dramas set many average Americans on fire. C.M.K. Glen, a resident of Macedon, New York, wrote to Frederick Douglass approving of William Parker's militancy at Christiana. Referring to the killing of the slaveholder Edward Gorsuch, Glen said he "hope[d] that the bloodshed, may be a good investment for freedom" and declared "that the right of Revolution belongs to every man, to *black, as well as white,* that these men had as perfect a right to fight for their liberty as our revolutionary fathers did for theirs." He also thought William Parker "should be placed side by side with Lafayette."[59] Jabez D. Hammond of Cherry Valley, New York felt the same way. Writing to Gerrit Smith, he said, "I am most pleased with the bold and manly announcement you make of the physical force which will probably be put in requisition for the abolition of slavery. I have long been of opinion that slavery will never be abolished by moral suasion alone," he wrote, adding that emancipation could only be achieved "by means of blood and slaughter"— in short by revolution.[60] After the Garner murder, an Illinoisan named Glover assailed pacifism.

Writing to Garrison, Glover observed, "if there is a reasonable prospect that the slaves of the South can gain their liberty by insurrection, non-resistants [*sic*] could aid them in doing so." Contending Southerners had only themselves to blame if "the bloody ghost of insurrection" still petrifies them, Glover concluded "revolution is the only hope of the slave," and the "great American Juggernaut will be broken in pieces, and an emancipated nation will be prepared to worship the true God. Revolution, peaceably if we can, but — *Revolution!*"[61]

If it was revolution, it had to be popularized. Strikingly, the mid-nineteenth-century "revolutionists"— to use Higginson's term — deployed the same tactics and strategies as Patrick Henry had during the struggle for Independence. Appealing to ordinary Americans, the great Virginia orator had attracted small farmers and dissenters to the resistance of Tidewater planters and New England merchants. Likewise antebellum Revolutionaries mobilized ordinary people.[62] The abolitionist editor Sherman Booth rode through the Wisconsin countryside crying "Freemen to the rescue" to rally popular support for Joshua Glover.[63] Inside or outside churches, in small meetings or large conventions, in assemblies or legislatures, in private homes or public places, in printed pamphlets, books, biographies, newspapers, and broadsides, or in diaries and personal correspondence, activists seized upon fugitive slave dramas to use time-proven tactics— especially oratory — to popularize their cause.[64] Fugitive slave crises stirred speakers and they stirred audiences. "Smarting" after the enactment of the new Fugitive Slave Law, Ward embarked on an extensive speaking tour visiting in one summer "numerous districts of New York, Pennsylvania, Ohio, Illinois, Wisconsin, Michigan, and Indiana as well as Connecticut, Rhode Island, Massachusetts, and New Hampshire."[65] Ward's words, like those of Henry, became the language of revolution and his struggle was as earnest as that of Lexington and Concord, Bunker Hill, or Yorktown.

Few invoked the Revolutionary heritage more strongly than Theodore Parker. Thundering that his "father fired the first shot [against the British]" and that "the blood which flowed there [Lexington and Concord] was kindred to this which courses in my veins to-day," Parker sought to emulate his forefathers' example.[66] The Boston dramas of William and Ellen Craft, Shadrach, Sims, and Burns heightened his oratory; his fiery sermons and impassioned speeches became the stuff of revolution. He reached his zenith after Burns's return to Virginia, when he pronounced that the "great cause of Human Freedom in America and the world ... has seldom been in more danger," and he emphasized that "a great political revolution" was now underway. Indicted for "a speech in Faneuil Hall against kidnapping [fugitive slaves]," Parker reminded the grand jury that his appearance on March 5th marked the "eighty-fifth anniversary of the Boston Massacre," when the first blood of a black Revolutionary spilled on Massachusetts soil. The fifth of March, 1770, he declared, ranked with the Fourth of July, 1776, the day that gave expression to the principle that all men are endowed by their Creator with certain inalienable equal rights to life, liberty, and the pursuit of happiness. Under slavery, stated Parker, "There are no natural, unalienable, and equal rights ... no natural, unalienable, and equal right to life, liberty, and the pursuit of happiness."[67]

Other abolitionists adopted similar rhetoric. Thomas Wentworth Higginson asserted, "I tell you the conflict with Slavery is not reform, it is Revolution" as he advocated violence after the Craft crisis. Higginson explained, "We abhor bloodshed, and they are terrible times when it becomes necessary to speak of bloodshed; yet when it comes to the actual case, it is hard to say where a man must stop in defending his inalienable rights."[68] Fugitive slave dramas convinced Parker Pillsbury to call "for the true completion of the American Revolution." By mid-century, he concluded "that the time for ballots has past, and the time for bullets has come."[69] Likewise, the spectacle of a chained Jerry convinced Samuel Joseph May that "it was necessary to bring the people into direct conflict with the Government" and he condoned any measures "necessary to fight for the rescue of any black man from the horrors of a return to slavery."[70]

In the antebellum fugitive slave dramas, antislavery militants—like their late eighteenth-century forefathers or even their seventeenth-century ancestors who sailed into Massachusetts Bay—sought also to make America an example to the world. After Sims was returned to Georgia, the Massachusetts Anti-Slavery Society lamented, "Times have changed since Boston was the gaze and admiration of the world for her heroic resistance to tyranny. Seventy years ago she was a little town, in comparison with her present dimensions, yet she would not submit to insult from constitutional authorities set over her when they were violating what she esteemed 'a higher law.'" In their annual report, the members demanded a return to Massachusetts' glorious past, noting "[S]he defied the physical force of the most powerful empire in the world, when it presumed to invade her rights. Then she could stand against the world." The society underscored that Massachusetts had not done so in bowing before slave power to return Sims.[71] Ward stressed that America tarnished its placed in the history of human freedom when President Millard Fillmore signed the Fugitive Slave Law "on the eighteenth day of September, lacking but one day of six hundred and twenty-four years and three months from the signing of [the] Magna Charta." Rather than a beacon of freedom to the world, the slave power–driven Republic, he said, was "horrifying all Europe."[72] Higginson, too, spoke of America's example. "Needed was braveness without ignorance," declared Higginson, "the moral courage of the Puritans ... that we may show the world that a community may be educated in brain without being cowardly in body; and that a people without a standing army may yet rise as one man, when Freedom needs defenders."[73] Perhaps, however, the female English abolitionist Harriet Martineau best summarized the message American fugitive slave dramas sent to the world. She portrayed the effort to save Burns as a "revolutionary deed," and described it as a fight for the "privileges which had been transplanted from the field of Runnymede into the valleys of Massachusetts." She thought Massachusetts was poised "to fight the battle of Independence over again," and hoped English liberties would win. "It is surely impossible," she said, "that republicans, descended from Englishmen, should not preserve, in the 19th century, personal liberties which were obtained by their ancestors in the 12th."

Nevertheless, at home and abroad, the most powerful "revolutionists" in the fugitive slave dramas were the fugitive slaves themselves, especially as they appealed to Patrick Henry's motto or the Declaration.[74] Anthony Burns assailed his excommunication by the Baptist Church in Fauquier County, Virginia, "on the charge of 'disobeying both the laws of God and men,' in absconding from the service of [his] master." Claiming his freedom, he vowed, "I was stolen and made a slave as soon as I was born. No man had any right to steal me. That manstealer who stole me," stressed Burns, "trampled on my dearest rights. He committed an outrage on the law of God.... God made me a man — not a slave.... I utterly deny that those things which outrage all right are laws."

Burns summed it up saying, "To be real laws they must be founded in equity."[75]

If it is remarkable how mid-nineteenth century fugitive slaves turned to the Declaration and Patrick Henry's motto to justify their cause and define themselves as Revolutionaries, it is also striking that some wrote their autobiographies or told stories, thus following the examples of such exemplary American Revolutionaries as Thomas Jefferson and John Adams who penned memoirs and letters for the record knowing they were making history. In this regard, the achievement of William Craft, a man who could not read or write when he escaped bondage, is astonishing. Writing from England, he challenged the Republic that still sought to enslave him using its own Revolutionary heritage. He began his autobiography saying:

> Having heard while in Slavery that "God made of one blood all nations of men," and also that the American Declaration of Independence says, that "We hold these truths to be self-evident, that all men are created equal; that they are endowed by their Creator with certain inalienable rights; that among these, are life, liberty, and the pursuit of happiness"; we could not understand by what right we were held as "chattels." Therefore, we felt perfectly justified in undertaking the dangerous and exciting task of "running a thousand miles" in order to obtain those rights which are so vividly set forth in the Declaration.[76]

In the 1850s, the American Revolution raged and African Americans and their allies saw themselves as Revolutionaries. Fugitive slave dramas were part of the American Revolution.

William and Ellen Craft
"Running a Thousand Miles"
for Inalienable Rights

Slavery is detested, — we feel its fatal effects, — we deplore it with all the pity of humanity.... It would rejoice my very soul that every one of my fellow-beings was emancipated.— Patrick Henry

The spirit of the pilgrim fathers, which was manifested at Bunker Hill, at Saratoga, and at Yorktown, still exists in the North.... The spirit which overthrew the British Crown will submit to no force that shall compel it to comply with the odious provisions of this enactment [Fugitive Slave Law].— *London Morning Advertiser*

The Fugitive Slave Bill ... has already in hot haste commenced its bloody crusade o'er the land, and the liability of ourselves and families becoming its victims at the caprice of Southern men-stealers, imperatively demands an expression, whether we will tamely submit to chains and slavery, or whether we will, at all and every hazard, LIVE and DIE freemen.— *Declaration of Sentiments of the Colored Citizens of Boston*

On May 1, 1851, the world's gaze turned toward London, where Queen Victoria officially opened her beloved Prince Albert's carefully planned Great Exhibition of the Works of Industry of All Nations at the special Hyde Park exhibition hall that observers quickly dubbed the Crystal Palace. For many English, the Crystal Palace and London's hosting of the first world's fair stood as testament to England's superiority in a nineteenth-century European-led world. When the Great Exhibition ended five months later, more than six million visitors had viewed the technological and cultural wonders of their time. Visitors marveled at a variety of English achievements, including scientific instruments, state-of-the-art power looms, and new printing presses that reflected the nation's industrial leadership. But they also admired contributions from such rival states as their great continental neighbor France and their former rebellious Thirteen Colonies. The French showcased "sumptuous tapestries, Sevres porcelain and silks from Lyons, enamels from Limoges and furniture." Americans proudly displayed their scientific and industrial prowess with such innovations as Samuel Colt's repeating firearms and McCormick's grain reaper, which had been instrumental in transforming the American heartland into a breadbasket for the world.[1]

Visitors also reveled at a continuing stream of dignitaries who took in the sights and enjoyed concerts at Hyde Park — the Queen, the Prince Consort and other royalty, Lords, Members of the House of Commons, European aristocrats, wealthy landowners, leading merchants and bankers, diplomats, as well as Western Europe's most celebrated artists. Famous Americans were there too. In the summer of 1851, many of the new nation's industrial and financial leaders, politicians, wealthy planters, and such famous writers as Lewis Carroll crossed the Atlantic. But William and Ellen Craft, two fugitive slaves who had suddenly achieved celebrity status, made their presence felt as well. In late 1848, less than three years earlier, they had fled more than a thousand miles to Philadelphia to escape from the their Georgian masters Dr. Robert Collins and Ira Taylor — men whom Massachusetts Free Soil senator Charles Sumner called "Lords of the Lash."[2] After recovering from their arduous journey at the home of a Pennsylvanian Quaker named Barkley Ivens, the Crafts traveled to New England and settled in Boston. In the Old Bay City, they carved out new lives on free soil until two slave-hunters, John Knight and Willis H. Hughes, best known as "the jailer of Macon," arrived to return them to bondage under the Fugitive Slave Law that had been enacted as part of the Compromise of 1850. Although initially protected in Boston's tightly knit black community and supported by such radical white abolitionists as Ellis Gray Loring, who "concealed" a frightened Ellen, and the Reverend Theodore Parker, who armed himself and wrote his "sermons with a pistol in [his] desk," ready to defend his fugitive slave parishioners at all costs, William and Ellen Craft eventually had to seek refuge in Canada. After a few weeks in Halifax, Nova Scotia, they boarded a steamer destined for Liverpool and the

Boston Vigilance Committee paid the $250 cost of their transatlantic passage.[3]

Only in their mid-twenties, these remarkable fugitive slaves who could neither read nor write when they escaped bondage quickly became literate and began to mingle in some of England's most respected social circles. In mid–1851, the Crafts, already well-positioned among England's leading abolitionists and determined to help free their brothers and sisters enslaved in the American South, took their antislavery campaign to the grandest global stage ever created — the Great Exhibition at the Crystal Palace. Intent on being seen and heard, William and Ellen Craft arranged "a mock slave auction" exposing the horrors of the South's Peculiar Institution. They made sure that Crystal Palace revelers left the fair grounds with vivid images of America's "dark underside," not just the new nation's fine technology and industrial achievements.[4] Juxtaposing the harsh realities of Southern slavery — chaining, whipping, exploitation, poor nourishment and shelter, buying and selling of people, separating families, and sexual abuse of human property — against the nineteenth-century wonders of science, art, and industry, the Crafts were definitely both seen and heard. Visitors arriving to celebrate the advancement of civilization came face-to-face with human suffering that still blemished the American South, an enduring scar on humanity that reflected early modern Europeans' revamping of the ancient institution of slavery to reap profits from the transatlantic slave trade and New World plantation staples. William and Ellen displayed it as a wound that Southern slaveholders, overseers, traders, and slave-catchers reopened daily.[5]

The Crafts' "spectacular story" clashed with late antebellum America's goal of rivaling, if not surpassing, Europe as the symbol of human progress. Not surprisingly, the couple's ordeal was a story that English and Continental Europeans, seeking to retain their position at the apex of western civilization, seized upon as they made their way through the exhibition grounds. One English abolitionist sardonically exclaimed "What an anomaly that such persons [as the Crafts] should be compelled to flee from republican America to monarchical England, for personal safety!" Such comments accentuated white Americans' embarrassment with having to share the limelight with two African Americans who had been born into slavery in Georgia and still fled from it. The Crafts' seeking safe haven on English soil also raised questions about America's recent acquisition of Texas and resounding victory in the Mexican War, which had permitted the annexation of California and the territories of New Mexico and Utah. Indeed, as Europeans and English hosts welcomed the white descendants of George Washington, Thomas Jefferson, Patrick Henry, and their compatriots, the Crafts' mock slave auction made them wonder whether the United States had waged "war against Mexico ... solely to extend and perpetuate slavery; to increase the profits of the slave trade, and to give efficiency to slave breeding."[6] Outspoken abolitionists, including African Americans Charles Lenox Remond and Robert Purvis, who joined the Crafts at the world's fair, fueled such speculation as they asked whether future histories would regard the late president Zachary Taylor, America's Mexican War hero, in as favorable a light as William and Ellen Craft or Frederick Douglass.[7] In this context, white American dignitaries also seemed to pale against the dark, noble-looking William and his striking, almost white wife Ellen, the daughter of a female slave who had been raped by her master. Evincing valor and virtue on the world stage, the Crafts stirred emotions as they recounted how they had overcome almost insurmountable obstacles to flee the "iron heel of despotism" in the American South.[8] At the Crystal Palace, William and Ellen Craft—courageous, virtuous, cultured, and now literate—stood proudly before the world as they exposed the evils of Southern slavery. "Very intelligent" and attractive, the "fair-skinned" Ellen represented much more than a "chief attraction of a ball-room," declared one observer; she was a "heroine" who had escaped "prostitution" at the hands of a ravishing tyrant—her "heathen" master.[9] William, "erudite and witty" and an "accomplished writer" after only a few months of instruction, symbolized what some antislavery observers regarded as true "manhood." The Reverend Theodore Parker thought that William put to shame the proslavery whites who refused to extend to him the American liberties that they took for granted for themselves.[10]

The moral contrast between the Crafts and the upholders of slavery led one visitor departing the Hyde Park fair grounds to conclude that leading "representatives of the civilized world," including the Queen, Prince Albert, the royal children, the Duchess of Sutherland, the Duke of Wellington, and many European aristocrats, had now been introduced to that abhorrent, "peculiar staple of America—Slavery."[11] In the aftermath of Parliament's passage of the Imperial Emancipation Bill in 1833, abolishing slavery throughout the empire, and Britain's signing of treaties with most European nations to eliminate remnants of the transatlantic slave trade, British abolitionists felt well-positioned to criticize Americans. Moreover, when President Millard Fillmore reaffirmed his commitment to enforce the Fugitive Slave Law of 1850, British and American antislavery activists delighted in making the England-based Crafts the subject of lively transatlantic correspondence and speculation. Francis Bishop raised the specter of an American attempt to reclaim the two fugitive slaves. "Can it be true, as the papers report, that President Fillmore has written to Dr. Collins ... stating that, if necessary, the whole force of the Union shall be put into operation to bring back the fugitives?" wrote Bishop to William Lloyd Garrison. "If so," he exclaimed, "what a spectacle [this would be] for the world!"[12]

If the Crafts' tale kindled sentiment on the far side of the Atlantic, it also resonated with a growing number of Americans who cherished Patrick Henry's motto "Liberty or Death" as part of their heritage. Standing before audiences in Boston or London, were not William and Ellen Craft living testimony to the great Virginian's words? Wendell Phillips, the antislavery Golden Trumpet, thought so. One might "look in vain through the most trying times of our Revolutionary history for an incident of courage and noble daring equal to that of the escape of William and Ellen Craft," declared Phillips after the couple had arrived in Boston, where William joined Lewis Hayden and other blacks in swearing an oath to "LIVE and DIE freemen."[13] The Crafts moved into Hayden's famous colored boardinghouse at 66 Southac Street in an area that racist white Bostonians called "Nigger Hill." Hayden ran a successful clothing store and his "happy and industrious wife," who was also a fugitive slave, took care of the boardinghouse. William Craft started a business as a carpenter and cabinet-maker. He eventually set up his own shop on Cambridge Street, acquired a range of tools for his trade, and built an inventory of wood, glue, and other materials. Ellen worked as a seamstress.[14] Having been deprived of a legal wedding in the South, William and Ellen were married by Theodore Parker. John White Chadwick, Parker's biographer, recounts that there were two tables in the room in which Parker married them — on one lay a Bible and on the other a bowie knife. After the ceremony, the preacher spontaneously placed them in William's hands, saying that one was to defend the body and "the other [was] for the soul's defense."[15]

On the world stage, the very striking Ellen became a powerful symbol on account of her gender, her race, and her fugitive slave status. As an enslaved woman, she represented a person whose "rights as mother, daughter, or laborer, [had n]ever received full legislative protection."[16] Contesting her status as human property at the Crystal Palace, she demanded empowerment according to "America's principles of social equality and freedom" and poignantly underscored the hypocrisy of slavery as an enduring contradiction. On the eve of Harriet Beecher Stowe's publication of *Uncle Tom's Cabin*, which through the experiences of the slave mother Eliza exposed the horrific plight of female slaves, Ellen proved to be just as capable as William of taking on anyone who advocated slavery or compromised with it. One observer called her a "missionary among grandees" who did not shrink from challenging "the enemies of her people" even if they were aristocrats or occupied positions of power. Another described her as "polished" and added that "her conversation stamps her as being possessed of high intellectual attainments."[17]

But what also set the Crafts apart was their tale, one that Wendell Phillips thought ranked with "the most thrilling in the nation's annals."[18] Along with other abolitionists and Northern blacks, Phillips made the Crafts' "singular escape from slavery" a veritable staple in the antislavery fight. Ellen had pretended to be a sickly young white male planter who sought to leave Savannah in search of a healthier climate to regain his strength. Destined for Philadelphia, the "invalid gentleman" made believe that he was too weak to travel alone so he had arranged to have William, his personal slave, accompany him. The frail young planter not only mingled with white slaveholders on trains and steamers but actually stayed in hotels frequented by such well-known slaveholders as South Carolina's proslavery champion John C. Calhoun. Antislavery militants quickly labeled later ingenious fugitive slave escapes as being "*a la William and Ellen Craft*" and the couple's notoriety soared. Prior to their transatlantic crossing, they were featured speakers on the antislavery tour, particularly in New England where they entertained audiences with descriptions of how they had prepared their disguises. They had bound the illiterate Ellen's right arm in a sling so that she would not be asked to sign hotel registers. They thrilled listeners recounting such narrow escapes as when a white cabinet-maker for whom William had worked appeared at the railway station from which they departed or when a friend of Ellen's master boarded the train car in which they were seated and failed to recognize her. They described their luck when a Maryland railroad official allowed them to travel on to Philadelphia from Baltimore even though the sickly young planter did not have proof of ownership of William, which typically was required for travelers crossing the Mason Dixon line.[19]

The Crafts sometimes shared the podium with other fugitive slave orators, including Frederick Douglass, the novelist William Wells Brown, or Henry "Box" Brown, the ingenious fugitive slave who shipped himself from Richmond to Philadelphia in a crate to escape bondage.[20] After one of the couple's first public appearances at a packed hall in Abington, Pennsylvania, Lewis Ford wrote to William Lloyd Garrison saying that William Wells Brown and the Crafts had made the gathering "one of the most heart-stirring meetings" the community had ever seen and the speakers had

WILLIAM AND ELLEN CRAFT. Less than three years after their legendary escape from slavery in Georgia, William and Ellen Craft mingled in London social circles and took their antislavery campaign to the grandest global stage ever created — the Great Exhibition at the Crystal Palace. They arranged a mock slave auction to expose the horrors of slavery in the American South (Boston Athenæum).

admirably advanced "the cause of freedom."[21] At Newburyport a few weeks later, the Crafts spoke to a hall "filled to its utmost capacity" with some eight to nine hundred people to whom William told the couple's incredible story "in so simple and artless a manner, as must have carried [antislavery] conviction to the mind of every one present."[22] In Springfield, Massachusetts, he spoke of the couple's experiences in slavery and then again described their escape "for about one hour with thrilling interest."[23]

In an era of expanding print culture and growing demand for sensational entertainment, the Crafts' tale struck a chord with a wide range of antebellum Americans. Their thousand-mile escape was filled with drama and good guy–bad guy stories of close calls in which the virtuous and ingenious Crafts emerged as heroes. Like Harriet Beecher Stowe's soon-to-be-published heart-wrenching images of Eliza, child in arms, jumping ice floes to cross the Ohio River to escape slave-catchers, the Crafts' story was a truly gripping account that only the most cold-hearted could dismiss. Some two years before the publication of *Uncle Tom's Cabin*, the Crafts' story "destroyed the [moral] middle road" of slavery.[24]

Before antislavery audiences imbued with religiosity after the Second Great Awakening, William recalled how as a slave child he had watched his father, mother, and sister sold away to different masters; he never saw them again. Ellen described how her master and father — a man who had forced himself on her mother — tore her "from her mother's embrace in childhood." She confirmed that the sexual abuse of slaves was "common practice" for Southern slaveholders who fathered mulatto children and "with the greatest impunity" sold the fair-skinned girls, the preferred concubines of southern planters, into the horrible fancy trade. Nineteenth-century audiences viewed Ellen as a heroine who had narrowly escaped, and her husband painted her as one of many. He told the story of a slave girl named Antoinette, "the flower of [her] family, a girl who was much beloved by all who knew her, for her Christ-like piety, dignity of manner, as well as her great talents and extreme beauty." Craft remembered her being purchased for two thousand dollars by a "drunken slave-dealer" and her tale ended in tragedy. When the tyrant sought to defile her, she fought to the bitter end before she "pitched herself head foremost through the window," living and dying by Patrick Henry's motto "Give me liberty or give me death."[25]

With such vivid images, the Crafts transformed their tale from an "interesting narrative" into a compelling attack on slavery as an evil institution. Although Ellen had run a thousand miles to escape the nightmare of being forced to be a tyrant's "slave and paramour," just as her mother and so many other female slaves had been, she also stressed that the Crafts had fled to realize their love for each other and to avoid being separated by sale. As Frederick Douglass so aptly put it, "freedom or death became their joint language," one sealed by their love and devotion to each other. The Crafts explained that for them the fear of separation was worse than the "meanest drudgery," even torture or whipping. Their message resonated with Northerners as well as audiences in Edinburgh, Liverpool, Bristol, Plymouth, Taunton, Bridgewater, Gloucester, Cheltonham, Bath, and with the multitudes at Prince Albert's Crystal Palace. Ellen reminded "virtuous ladies" that she represented one of "nearly two millions of their own sex" who were deprived of their children by sale, stirring resentment in England, Europe, and America of an institution that legitimated violence against women and children. After Ellen spoke in Bristol, the Bristol and Clifton Ladies Anti-Slavery Society immediately passed resolutions supporting the Crafts and assailing anyone who compromised with slavery.[26] William's plight also touched both women and men in audiences. "[Y]e who love the wife of your affections," wrote an Edinburgh journalist who had listened to William lecture on the separation of families and other horrors of slavery could only have "warm sympathies" for enslaved bondsmen. Such sentiments translated into celebration when Ellen gave birth on England's free soil to their first child. One of their English friends informed William Lloyd Garrison that the "happy event took place at Oakham, where W. and E.C have been for some time residing and enjoying the advantages of the Educational Institution at that place."[27] Even before the staged slave auction at the Crystal Palace, the Crafts had achieved "signal success" in exposing slavery's nightmares; as "specimens of American property," said Garrison, "they taught terrible lessons in Europe of the United States of America."[28]

The Crafts' story heightened calls for resistance to the Fugitive Slave Law on moral, religious, and humanitarian grounds. William proved unrelenting in his attacks on the law as he constantly reminded English audiences of how slavery spread its tentacles to free soil and terrorized blacks. Speaking at Crosby Hall in London shortly after Millard Fillmore arrived on a visit, he denounced Fillmore as the one who signed the "iniquitous" bill into law.[29] English churchmen embraced the Crafts' arguments and criticized American churches that did not take a decisive stand against bondage. Welcoming the Crafts, an assembly of Bristol clergymen passed a series of resolutions denouncing proslavery churches and demanded that American clergymen distance themselves from the South's Peculiar Institution. The ministers in the city that had once thrived on the transatlantic slave trade declared that the Fugitive Slave Law was "inconsistent with the claims of Christianity, and with the duty of ministers of the Gospel towards the oppressed." The clergymen spoke of "the fierce contest between freedom and oppression, conscience and law" and declared support for those who "announced their determination to obey God rather than man."[30]

In many ways, the English response to the Crafts reflected the anti-slavery feelings they had sparked when they arrived in Boston where William joined abolitionists attacking the Fugitive Slave Bill. He reminded audiences that despite Northerners' "boast of freedom," the Fugitive Slave Law guaranteed there was no American soil "not given up to slaveholders to hunt him and his wife upon, and drag them again into slavery." After one of William's speeches, a listener penned a letter to the *Liberator* noting, "Oh! is it not a burning shame, that our dear New England cannot be free to give shelter and protection to two such noble persons as Mr. and Mrs. Craft, who have proved themselves as great heroes as any our country has produced."[31] Recognizing the couple's popularity, Wendell Phillips used them as an example to attack Daniel Webster, the Fugitive Slave Law champion, saying "And weightier than the Constitution, stronger than laws, is one Ellen Craft, to open the hearts of Northern freemen that door which Daniel Webster wishes to shut."[32]

From their arrival in the free states until their flight to England, the Crafts ignited the radical abolitionist campaign demanding that Northerners leave proslavery churches and disengage from the Union that allowed slavery to flourish. For example, along with Henry "Box" Brown, William and Ellen Craft catalyzed the Seventeenth Annual Meeting of the Massachusetts Anti-Slavery Society in 1849. When the Crafts were invited to the platform, "they were received with cheers," and the assembly immediately passed three resolutions declaring that nobody present would help return a "slave to his bondage"; that nobody present would "stand still and do nothing" to help a fugitive slave; and that all "would aid in protecting, receiving, and saving" a fugitive from slavery.[33]

After William described the couple's escape and Henry "Box" Brown sang, the Reverend Samuel May vehemently attacked proslavery churches. Stephen Foster spoke next, again underscoring "the guilty character and position of American ministers and churches" that allowed bondage to persist. Noting that slavery also flourished in the nation's capital, Foster denounced the Free Soil Party as a vehicle for "maintaining the compromises with slavery."[34] The assembly then considered a resolution to dissolve the Union — something that such abolitionists as Wendell Phillips had already called for as a means of ending an immoral association with slaveholders. Sympathizing "deeply and warmly with ... [their] outraged and enslaved brethren," and aroused by Phillips "eulogizing" fugitives from bondage, notably the Crafts and Henry "Box" Brown, the convention resolved "that the best way we know of to express efficiently our sympathy and respect, is to labor for the overthrow of that Union which builds the dungeon, and that Church which bolts its door."[35] In reporting on the meeting, Frederick Douglass sought to build upon the wave of antislavery sentiment it had produced and reprinted the resolution "That as the American Church has been fully proved to be the bulwark of slavery, we believe the time has come when it should be destroyed root and branch, as of no use to the people, and a curse to every moral reform." He also supported Wendell Phillips's "petition to the Massachusetts' Legislature ... for secession from the Union" and Garrison's call for "THE IMMEDIATE DISSOLUTION OF THE AMERICAN UNION— a Union based on the prostrate bodies of three millions of the people, and cemented with their blood."[36] Douglass singled out the Crafts, once again, as living testimony to the horrors of slavery.

It was in this explosive context that slave-catchers John Knight and Willis Hughes arrived in Boston to reclaim William and Ellen Craft. They had been hired by the wealthy Collins. The latter, a Unionist-Whig from Macon, Georgia, sought to recover his human property but also to test the enforcement of the new Fugitive Slave Law, which most Southerners considered to be the one and only concession to the South in the Compromise of 1850. Collins also doubted that Northerners would respect the law.[37] When the slave hunters arrived in the city, the Boston Vigilance Committee, which had "increased rapidly" to 250 members, "swung into action" distributing broadsides and handbills supporting the Crafts and denouncing slave-catchers.[38] The Reverend Theodore Parker, in whose congregation the Crafts worshipped, donated "a thousand dollars" to his parishioners' cause and initiated a "relentless campaign" against the slave hunters that led to their arrest for having slandered the Crafts and damaged William's business. The slave catchers had to pay $10,000 to free themselves on bail only to be taken again into custody "on a charge of attempting to kidnap Craft and wife."[39] Their second arrest generated intense excitement in Boston as some 1500 blacks and 500 whites converged on Court Square, where they "hissed" at Hughes and Knight and called them "bloodhounds." The *Boston Daily Atlas* reported that one black Bostonian arrived at the scene on horseback promising that "he would be the first man to shoot Hughes." After paying bail and returning to their hotel, Hughes and Knight confronted antislavery militants. Visited by Parker, who warned them that he "did not think he could suppress the mob any longer," Hughes and Knight accepted the preacher's demand that they "leave the city instantly."[40] The agitation attracted attention throughout the nation, North and South. *The Cleveland Herald* reported that the "Fugitive Slave excitement continues" in Boston and described the abolitionists' strategies to get Hughes and Knight out of the city, including having the slave hunters charged with kidnapping. In Philadelphia, the *North American and United States Gazette* also described events, noting that Parker and his allies requested that the owner of the United States Hotel in Boston "turn Messrs. Hughes and Knight out" as part of the abolitionist scheme to force them out of the city.[41]

The Craft drama incited Lewis Hayden and other leading black Bostonians to pledge to use all means to resist the "God-defying and inhuman" Fugitive Slave Law, and radical white abolitionists quickly joined them.[42] Stephen and Abby Kelley Foster, Lucy Stone, and the Reverend Samuel Joseph May renewed their attack on proslavery churches. Stone reiterated the demand that Americans leave churches that demonstrated "enmity to humanity and freedom" by not taking a stand against bondage and she was particularly harsh on Boston churches. "Probably not a church in this town," proclaimed Stone, "would open its doors to

William and Ellen Craft, and suspend its services for a single half-day to allow them to tell the thrilling story of their escape from slavery, and its crucial wrongs." May continued to brand American churches "bulwarks" for slavery and asked conscientious Americans to "stand outside" those that failed to denounce slavery. The Fosters too contributed to the chorus "exposing the corruptions of the false and Anti-Christian Church of this land."

Equally interesting was how New England antislavery leaders used William Craft's status as a respected artisan and cabinet-maker to promote antislavery sentiment among working-class men. At the same Massachusetts Anti-Slavery Society convention that called for disunion and disengagement from proslavery churches, Charles Stearns sponsored a resolution aimed at northern white workers. "Whereas the rights of the laborer at the North are identified with those of the Southern slave, and cannot be ob-

ABBY KELLEY FOSTER. **During the William and Ellen Craft drama, Abby Kelley Foster and her husband assailed proslavery churches. Under the cover of darkness, Thomas Wentworth Higginson often led fugitive slaves to the Fosters' farm and the abolitionist couple spirited them to freedom in Canada.**

tained as long as chattel slavery rears its hydra head in our land," resolved Stearns, "it is equally incumbent upon the working-men of the North to espouse the cause of the emancipation of the slave and upon abolitionists to advocate the claims of the free laborer." The convention adopted Stearns's motion. Subsequent fugitive slave dramas saw an increasing number of artisans and workers embrace the antislavery cause.[43]

If the Craft drama heightened abolitionist sentiments and fueled the antislavery press in the North, it had a much different impact south of the Mason Dixon line. In Greenville, South Carolina, a newspaper editor contended that the agitation in Boston, especially the abolitionists' clash with the slave hunters Hughes and Knight, demonstrated Northerners' disrespect of legislation ensuring Southerners' rights to reclaim their human property. He published Hughes's sordid tale of how the slave catchers had been forced out of the free states empty-handed under the headline "Inefficiency of the Fugitive Slave Law" and, like Hughes, he emphasized that the Crafts affair sent a secessionist message to the South. "Every man who has a Southern heart in his bosom and would maintain the honor of his country," wrote the editor, "should sustain the Southern Rights cause."[44] In North Carolina, abolitionists' heavy-handed treatment of the slave-hunters evoked a similar reaction and, in fact, some outraged businessmen initiated a boycott of Northern goods. Stopping all northern purchases, John H. Leary of Edenton vowed to "bestow his patronage on Norfolk, and other Southern cities."[45] In Mississippi, Hughes's story of the failed enforcement of the new Fugitive Slave Law also found an attentive audience. *The Mississippian* published the slave hunter's entire account and concluded that abolitionism had infected the North to such an extent that fugitive slave legislation had become a dead-letter. Under the headline "The Crisis: The Fugitive Slave Law at the North," the paper described how antislavery militants had expelled Hughes and Knight from Boston. It also underscored the militancy of black Bostonians noting that during the affray William Craft had been "guarded by no less than two hundred of the colored citizens of Boston, all of whom were 'armed to the teeth,' and pledged to defend William and his wife as long as life lasts."[46] Interestingly, these Southern newspapers paid little attention to Northern sentiment in favor of the Fugitive Slave Law. They ignored the views of Knight who in contrast to Hughes believed that many Bostonians, particularly the so-called Cotton Whigs who did substantial business with the slaveholding South, supported the enforcement of the legislation. "From all I saw, and heard, and experienced while in Boston," said Knight, "I am convinced that public opinion there, in regard to the Fugitive Slave Law, is undergoing a change." He thought more white Bostonians, including "business men, and men of property," favored enforcement and one of the reasons causing this shift was that they "wished to get rid of the Negroes." Knight was sure if enforcement of the Fugitive Slave Law ever "came to a trial of strength, the Negroes and Abolitionists would be put down."[47]

Although Hughes and Knight slinked out of Boston without the

Crafts, Frederick Douglass, Theodore Parker, Wendell Phillips, William Lloyd Garrison, and other abolitionists did not celebrate. They were perturbed by the confusing crosscurrents in public opinion and the Crafts' forced exile to Canada and England to avoid being returned to bondage. For them, the drama proved that the republican experiment in American liberty had been undermined by Southern planters. The law served "SLAVE CATCHERS" and "Southern Nabobs," exclaimed Garrison. "How long will we suffer ourselves to stand in the ignoble relation to them?"

The outspoken editor of *The Liberator* also wondered how long a people, professing to believe in principles enshrined in the Declaration, could countenance such fugitive slaves as the Crafts being "deprived of their birthright" and treated as "outlaws amongst us, yet without having committed any crime." He abhorred the hypocrisy of Bostonians who supported Daniel Webster's defense of the Fugitive Slave Law as a compromise of the Constitution.[48] The editor of Boston's *Emancipator & Republican* shared Garrison's sentiments; he wrote that the leader of Massachusetts Cotton Whigs "would return Henry Box Brown, [William and] Ellen Craft, William Wells Brown, Lewis Hayden, Henry Bibb, and the gifted Frederick Douglass and their worthy associates who have escaped from bondage."[49]

The Crafts' relationships with antislavery activists in the North enhanced their impact. Having settled in Boston and lectured on the antislavery circuit, they forged strong ties with the tightly knit black com-

THEODORE PARKER. Proclaiming Shadrach Minkins's rescue the "noblest deed" in Boston since the Tea Party in 1773, Theodore Parker said that the day Thomas Sims was returned to bondage in Georgia was "the saddest day" the Old Bay City had ever seen. Parker said the kidnapping of Sims confirmed the triumph of slavery "over the graves of our revolutionary ancestors, and on the hallowed soil of Bunker Hill" (Boston Athenæum).

35

munity and radical white abolitionists in the Old Bay City, which increased antislavery militancy when Knight and Hughes arrived to reclaim them. As Boston Vigilance Committee members "shadowed" the Southern slave hunters and turned the force of the law against them, they defied the Fugitive Slave Law. Such radical abolitionists as Theodore Parker and Lewis Hayden were ready to both hide and arm them. When Parker married the Crafts, he had become absolutely "intrepid in his hostility" to slave power and the new fugitive slave legislation; his friend Bronson Alcott, the famous transcendentalist, wrote in his diary that "Parker keeps pistols ready for service in his study."[50]

What was most striking among those who rallied behind the Crafts, whites and blacks, was not just their willingness to shelter the couple and defy the Fugitive Slave Law but also how they justified their support of the Crafts on the basis of their Revolutionary heritage and God-given rights. Like his forbears, Parker saw the struggle as one for "Liberty or Death." "[B]ut what could I do?" he remarked, emphasizing that he had been born in the town where the American Revolution began and his grandfather had drawn "the first sword." For him, it was a fight against tyranny just as it had been a few generations earlier at Lexington, Concord, and Bunker Hill. William Craft and his black brethren also framed their stance in this way as they signed the "Declaration of Sentiments of the Colored Citizens" and endorsed Patrick Henry's motto, declaring "God willed us free" and "We will as God wills: God's will be done." Meeting in Boston's Belknap Street Church and inspired by Charles Lenox Remond's outstanding oratory, black Bostonians swore "that our oft repeated determination to resist oppression is the same now as ever — and we pledge ourselves at all hazards, to resist unto death, any attempt on our liberties." William Craft took the pledge and it was one that reflected the growing militancy that he and Ellen helped to fuel in Boston before taking it to the global stage at the Crystal Palace, proving that they too were American Revolutionaries for liberty.[51]

CHAPTER 2

Rescuing Shadrach

The "Noblest Deed in Boston Since the Boston Tea-Party of 1773"

... [The Fugitive Slave Law of 1850] was passed last September ... [it] would have been atrocious two hundred years ago.— Theodore Parker

Thus did the originator [Senator James Mason of Virginia] of that barbarous and inhuman enactment, the Fugitive Slave Law, seize the occasion of the inauguration of the statue of General Warren, to lecture the freedom-loving people of Massachusetts on their *duty* to permit, without molestation, the soil of the Old Bay State to be made a hunting-ground for the panting fugitive from Southern despotism, and on the obligation we are under, according to *his* understanding of the requirements of the Constitution, to join in the chase, with Slavery's bloodhounds, over the graves of our Revolutionary ancestors, and on the hallowed soil of Bunker Hill itself ... in order to return ... Shadrach.—*The Liberator*

That Sunday night in Concord in mid–February 1851 was damp, still, and almost heavy; it was neither cold nor peacefully snowing as so often is the case at that time of year in Massachusetts. It had rained for almost a week throughout New England and the night's pitch darkness must have seemed eerie for Francis Edwin Bigelow who was already on edge with the illness of his beloved wife Ann. At three o'clock in the morning, the hard-working blacksmith heard a horse-drawn carriage pull into his yard. These were unnerving times for an "abolitionist couple" like the Bigelows. In September, as part of the Compromise of 1850, Congress had passed a stringent Fugitive Slave Law, which replaced the previous legislation enacted in 1793 during George Washington's presidency. Viewed as a major concession to the South, the new act circumvented the personal liberty laws passed in several free states that entitled alleged fugitive slaves to writs of habeas corpus, prohibited state jails from being used to detain runaways, and prevented state officials from being involved in capturing fleeing bondspersons. The new Fugitive Slave Law set up special federal tribunals to help slaveholders reclaim their human property in the North, deprived alleged runaways of rights of habeas corpus or trial by jury, and even prohibited them from testifying in their own defense. Particularly alarming for abolitionists were the heavy fines and jail sentences that the new law imposed on individuals who assisted fugitive slaves in their flight and the double fees paid to commissioners when they ruled in favor of masters claiming their human property. Antislavery militants denounced the law as the "most disgraceful, atrocious, unjust, detestable, heathenish, barbarous, diabolical, man-degrading, woman-murdering, demon-pleasing, Heaven defying act ever perpetrated."[1] For the Bigelows and their antislavery friends who helped fugitive slaves escape to Canada what made things worse was that many law-abiding New Englanders supported the legislation as a necessary compromise to preserve the Union. These upstanding citizens agreed with the outspoken Massachusetts senator Daniel Webster that those who defied the new legislation engaged in "TREASON."[2] In early 1851, such views seemed so widespread that Webster believed that his championing of the Compromise of 1850 and call for New Englanders to stand by the Fugitive Slave Law had positioned him to run for the presidency the following year. President Millard Fillmore too considered the act "absolutely necessary" for the Union's survival and, having received praise for his speeches on the Compromise of 1850, he said he felt relieved that "public opinion opposed to the enforcement of the Fugitive Slave Law had begun to subside." When Bigelow stepped to the window to see who arrived in his yard in the dead of night, he also knew that "at least sixty" fugitive slaves had been arrested since the new act had passed Congress on September 18, 1850, and the Fillmore administration was more intent than ever on enforcing the legislation.[3]

But the men who stepped from the shadows were friends who shared his contempt for laws that extended the tentacles of slavery to free soil. Bigelow recognized John J. Smith, a black Bostonian barber and a militant abolitionist whose barbershop had become the headquarters for "secret councils" of organized resistance to the Fugitive Slave Law. Like his namesake, Joshua B. Smith, another black Bostonian who "advised every fugitive [slave] to arm himself with a revolver" and live by the motto "*if Liberty is not worth fighting for, it is not worth having,*" John J. Smith stood ready to fight for the freedom of fugitive slaves, believing also that "when he could not live here in Boston, a FREEMAN," it would be evident that "*he had lived long enough.*"[4] Lewis Hayden, the remarkable Kentucky fugitive slave who moved to the Old Bay State in 1846 also stepped from the carriage. A radical abolitionist, he became the leading black on the Boston Vigilance Committee and a member of its executive committee. It was Hayden who had asked John J. Smith to arrange a team of fleet horses and a carriage to spirit Shadrach Minkins from Cambridge to Concord. Shadrach was the third man to disembark; Hayden and some twenty other black Bostonians had rescued him, sending shock waves across a very divided nation. They had snatched the fugitive slave from the Boston courthouse around two o'clock the day before just after Commissioner George T. Curtis agreed to a request by Shadrach's attorneys Charles G. Davis and Robert Morris, the city's first black lawyer, to postpone hearings on John Debree's claim to have Shadrach returned to Virginia as his slave. Hayden, the architect of the rescue, and his black compatriots boldly barged into a second-floor courtroom just as Davis and the antislavery *Commonwealth* editor Elizur Wright exited the room. Federal authorities later charged Wright for having aided and abetted Shadrach's escape, claiming that as he opened the courtroom door, the antislavery editor "raised his right hand" as a signal for the rescuers to charge in. A witness claimed Wright turned to Hayden's band of blacks saying "Come in now! now!" as he also pressed his foot against the door to stop guards Calvin Hutchins and Edward Jones from closing it.[5] The rush pushed Wright and Davis back into the courtroom and apparently they watched happily as the rescuers overpowered startled guards, seized Shadrach, lifted him "into the air," kicked Deputy Hutchins "in the stomach," and then "stampeded" out of the courtroom with their prize. Yelling "tear him away," the triumphant gang carried Shadrach "pell-mell" down a flight of stairs and out into a square suddenly crowded with blacks and whites of both sexes and all ages.[6] Onlookers reported that the mob outside the courthouse grew rapidly as the disturbance attracted more and more bystanders. Pushing aside the "jubilant" throngs with cries of "stand by," Hayden's determined black band, "looking daggers" as one observer put it, shuttled Shadrach with "his clothes half torn off" away from the building. Seeking to reassure the alarmed fugitive slave, one black rescuer shouted "Don't be afraid; we will stand by you ... till death." Another vowed that he was ready to "spill the last drop of blood" he had in his body to stop the fugitive from being returned to bondage. Shadrach, a man "of dark copper complexion, about five feet eight inches high, [and] stout[ly] built," apparently responded, "If I die, I die like a man."[7]

When the radical black abolitionist Henry C. Wright wrote to William Lloyd Garrison shortly after the rescue, he reported that Shadrach cried out "*I will never be a slave*" as the rescuers carried him out of the

JOHN J. SMITH. The militant black abolitionist John J. Smith's barbershop became the headquarters for "secret councils" of organized resistance against the Fugitive Slave Law. Smith said that "when he could not live here in Boston, a FREE-MAN," it would be evident that "he had lived long enough" (Boston Athenæum).

courtroom. Wright said he also defiantly uttered Patrick Henry's famous line — "*Give me liberty or give me death.*" The militant rescuers bore Shadrach through the crowded court square and "thence to Howard street, where a cab was in readiness." The multitudes closed in behind Hayden's band blocking any pursuit by deputy marshals. The biracial crowd kept yelling "to the rescue," "tear him away," and "we'll stand by you." Hustling Shadrach to the waiting carriage, the rescuers wore "sou'wester [caps] and oilskin garb" that suggested some worked as sailors or longshoremen. As they put Shadrach in the wagon, newspaper reporters said the "crowd of Negroes ... joined instantly by the whole concourse of the street & Square" surrounded the carriage and cheered the rescuers.[8] Another observer, who estimated the number of blacks at "several hundred," said the rescuers bore Shadrach "away in triumph" in the direction of "Nigger Hill." The throng, which had frustrated the pursuing deputies, apparently moved off "like a black squall" and authorities had no idea where the band of rescuers had taken the fugitive slave.[9]

Only a handful of Boston's blacks actually knew Shadrach had been whisked to the home of Hayden's neighbor, Elizabeth Riley. The elderly black widow "safely lodged" him in her attic while the radical abolitionist arranged for an Irish cabbie named Thomas Murray to carry the fugitive slave to the Reverend Joseph C. Lovejoy's place in Cambridge. The latter was the brother of the legendary abolitionist editor Elijah Lovejoy, killed by a proslavery mob in Alton, Illinois, in 1837.[10] In the late afternoon, Murray crossed the Charles River Bridge with Hayden and the man whom he "later learned was Shadrach Minkins" seated in the carriage behind him with "pistols lying on the seat between them."[11] Murray testified later that Hayden paid him double the normal fare for the ride to Cambridge.

The courthouse disturbance and subsequent disappearance of Shadrach happened so quickly that one journalist said it was the "work of a minute." The rescue had been executed with such precision that he concluded it was planned "beforehand" by antislavery militants intent on resisting the federal government's Fugitive Slave Law. "[T]he seizure having been so sudden and unexpected," authorities had not had any chance to recover the fleeing bondsman.[12] *The Boston Daily Atlas*'s reporter penned a similar description of the events in an article entitled "A High-Handed Act — Rescue of an Alleged Fugitive Slave from Custody," which suggested that he had witnessed the entire drama at the courthouse. He too noted the suddenness of the assault, the officers' inability to resist the attack, and the convergence of bystanders, but he also wondered about how quickly the mob that surrounded the building had disappeared. He found it strange that "fifteen minutes after the rescue, all was quiet in and around the Court House."[13]

If he had covered antislavery activities in the city for even a short period of time, the *Boston Daily Atlas* reporter must have suspected that Hayden and John J. Smith, renowned throughout the Old Bay State as black freedom fighters, had somehow been involved in the rescue. When Bigelow, "a core member" of the Concord Underground Railroad, recognized the duo in his yard, he would immediately have known the urgency of the undertaking. Bigelow's involvement in spiriting fugitive slaves to freedom had probably taken him to Smith's Boston barbershop, which rivaled Hayden's legendary boardinghouse at 66 Southac Street as a rendezvous for militant black Bostonians and fugitive slaves. Hayden had the reputation of a man who never backed down; he had the respect of black Bostonians and everyone engaged in Underground Railroad activities in New England. "[W]e should think from the spirit and bearing of this Hayden," wrote Frederick Douglass after the Shadrach drama, "[that] he would be among the last to stand idly by, when a brother man guilty of no crime, was about to be robbed of his liberty. It would be just like him, [a] warm-hearted, fearless man, to sing out, stand back gentlemen, I must have a hand in this."[14]

In contrast to Hayden and Smith, Shadrach was known to only a handful of Americans before the "Great Excitement" on February 15, 1851. Born between 1814 and 1822 to a female slave owned by Thomas Glenn of Norfolk, Virginia, Shadrach was between 29 and 37 years old on the day of his "sensational" rescue.[15] Initially known as Sherwood, Shadrach became the property of Glenn's widow after her husband's death. She sold him to her neighbors, the Hutchings, but not long afterward, Martha Hutchings who inherited the family's business and slaves, ran into financial difficulties and sold him again — this time to John A. Higgins, the son-in-law of John Debree, a U.S. Navy purser stationed in Norfolk. Higgins and his wife lived with Debree and, in November 1849, Higgins transferred his ownership of Shadrach to his father-in-law for a nominal sum of $300, presumably to settle some debt. During the 1840s, the proud bondsman discarded the name Sherwood and began calling himself Shadrach, a change that may well have reflected "his own quiet act of independence and rebellion" against the institution of slavery. Six months after becoming Debree's slave, Shadrach decided that he would no longer be the property of another person. On May 3, 1850, when the slave curfew bell in Norfolk chimed, it "no longer tolled for Shadrach Minkins, and it never would again."[16]

How Shadrach fled that day remains unknown, but he likely stowed away on one of two merchant ships that left Norfolk for Massachusetts during the first week of May — the *Alvaro Lamphir* or the *Vesper*. Alternatively, he may have boarded a mail packet heading north to Baltimore or New York City.[17] By late May, he was in Boston; he had joined the city's Methodist Church and obtained "a job working as a waiter" at Taft's Cornhill Coffee House in the heart of the city. The Cornhill was but a stone's throw from the State Hall, Boston Courthouse, and Fanueil Hall, often known as the Cradle of Liberty. Ideally located for lawyers, merchants, and politicians, the Cornhill ranked as "one of the city's finest restaurants" at the time.[18] It was there on February 15, 1851, that slave-catchers, having obtained an arrest warrant for Shadrach under the Fugitive Slave Law "the night previous," captured the runaway bondsman. The slave hunters grabbed him as he unsuspectingly served breakfast to Cornhill patrons. Led by the deputy marshal Patrick Riley, they carried him "with his waiter's apron still on" to the nearby courthouse where he appeared before U.S. Commissioner George Ticknor Curtis.[19] News of Shadrach's arrest spread "as if with wings" among Boston blacks and either Hayden or the Reverend Leonard Grimes of Boston's Twelfth Baptist Church informed the Boston Vigilance Committee and trusted antislavery lawyers, notably Davis and Morris, who could act on Shadrach's behalf. When Debree's attorney Seth Thomas appeared before Curtis demanding Shadrach's immediate return, "considerable numbers" of blacks had already made their way to the courthouse, setting the stage for the daring rescue that President Millard Fillmore repeatedly denounced as a "flagitious" outrage but antislavery folk considered a majestic deed of "the Sword of Justice."[20]

In the early hours of February 16, 1851, Bigelow welcomed Shadrach, fed him, and provided him with a bed for a few hours of sleep. The same day, he drove him to Leominster, some thirty miles away, where Shadrach, disguised in women's clothing, apparently attended his first antislavery rally with Frances Drake, an abolitionist friend of the Bigelows. Shadrach told the Drakes that if he was taken by slave-catchers at the rally, they "should have nothing but a dead body to carry from the state." From Leominster, Shadrach went to Fitchburg, an important rail connection to Montreal, the largest city in Canada, which had become free soil after the Imperial Parliament passed the Emancipation Bill in 1833 abolishing slavery throughout the British Empire, effective August 1, 1834. Shadrach crossed the Canadian border on Thursday, February 20, 1851, only five days after Hayden's band whisked him from the courthouse.[21] Shadrach, like so many fugitive slaves and free black migrants who followed the North Star, became a British citizen, legally free and protected by English Common Law. As he crossed the St. Lawrence and landed on the Island of Montreal, he may have known that no fugitive slave, even one who had committed a serious crime, had been extradited to the United States from Canada since British authorities returned Nelson Hackett in 1837 for having stolen his master's gold watch.

In Montreal, Shadrach embarked on a new life of liberty, took an Irish bride, had children, and opened a restaurant on St. Paul Street in the area now known as the Vieux Port or Old Montreal. He never forgot his rescuers. "I am at a loss for words to express the gratitude I feel to those kind and dear friends in Boston, and believe me," promised Shadrach in a letter sent from Montreal, "I shall always consider it my duty to pray for their health and happiness." Shadrach never returned to the United States, even after the American Civil War and the Thirteenth Amendment abolished slavery in December 1865. Shadrach died of a "disease of the stomach" ten years later "in the middle of a long hard winter" and he was buried in Montreal's Mount Royal Cemetery, which today covers much of the mountain overlooking the island city at the entrance to the St. Lawrence Seaway.[22]

Coming on the heels of the William and Ellen Craft drama, Shadrach's rescue was a watershed and it changed a troubled nation and the way many Americans, black and white, dealt with slavery. Theodore Parker thought the rescue was "the most noble deed done in Boston since the Boston Tea-party of 1773." Ralph Waldo Emerson, confessing to be "ashamed" of Boston after the passage of the Fugitive Slave Law, said the rescue put him in "better spirits." Frederick Douglass believed the saving of Shadrach was "cheering evidence that the love of Liberty and reverence for [Higher] Law have not died out in the land." Participants at a Weymouth antislavery convention shortly after the drama declared "the recent peaceful deliverance of the fugitive Shadrach out of the hands of his ruffian persecutors, is a cause for high and just congratulations among the friends of freedom on earth." The religiously inclined concluded "there is joy in heaven among angels of God, over any one slave that escapeth."[23] Dr. Henry Bowditch too saw the rescue as a "holy" cause while Henry C. Wright wrote to William Lloyd Garrison saying "I am wild with joy." In Worcester, Thomas Wentworth Higginson admired Hayden's all-black band and mused that "it would have been a great pleasure to me to have lent a hand in the Shadrach affair." He also praised the "Concord blacksmith" for having delivered Shadrach from the "fiery furnace." Abolitionists everywhere proclaimed "a man had been saved from Hell."[24]

But, as noted, the rescue set in motion myriad shock waves across America that sparked views that differed sharply from those in evidence at Weymouth, Concord, Leominster, 66 Southac Street on the other side of Beacon Hill, or in the offices of Elizur Wright's antislavery newspaper *The Commonwealth*, which printed a special Sunday edition bearing a headline that read, "KIDNAPPERS DISAPPOINTED."[25] Reverberations were felt "all the way to Washington" and throughout the South. In the Senate chamber on the Tuesday after the rescue, an astonished Senator Henry Clay of Kentucky denounced the deeds of the previous Saturday in the "most indignant terms." The rescue was "altogether wrong," he stated, contending that it reflected mob rule, the very "worst kind of tyranny." The Kentucky slaveholder found it appalling that a federal law had been violated "by Negroes; by African descendants; by people" who as far as he was concerned had no rights in what he referred to as "our political system."[26] Demonstrating strident racism, he asked the Senate "whether the government of white men ... [would] be yielded to a government of blacks."[27] Other white Southerners were equally disturbed and their reactions were also tinged with racism. Senator Jeremiah Clemens of Alabama said that if the abolitionist-infected North rendered the Fugitive Slave Law "a dead letter, the day for dissolution of the Union had arrived." He challenged his fellow Southerners who judged the fugitive slave legislation not to have been enforced to "immediately advocate a dissolution of the Union." He also called on legislatures in the North to pass legislation to exclude blacks, saying exclusionary legislation would be more effective than the Fugitive Slave Law. If blacks were "not allowed to enter free States," reasoned Clemens, "the slaves could not run away" and the South's Peculiar Institution could be sustained in a Union in which slavery and freedom coexisted.[28]

On the following day, Wednesday, February 19, 1851, some twenty-four hours before Shadrach actually crossed the Canadian border, Fillmore responded to what he now viewed as a mounting crisis and issued a proclamation that both he and Secretary of State Daniel Webster signed. They suggested that a revolution seemed to be in the making and they warned it might be "too powerful to be overcome by the civil authority." Fillmore told Americans that he had advised the secretaries of war and navy to order "their forces to Boston to be available to the federal marshal."[29] Demanding that "all well-disposed citizens rally to the support of the laws of their country," Fillmore said his priority was to "maintain the authority of the laws" and to put down any insurrection.[30] Responding to law-and-order sentiments among Northern whites who condemned the rescuers' "high-handed and unlawful act," Fillmore said Shadrach's rescue was a manifestation of "MOB LAW" and he directed the federal district attorney to charge anyone who had "aided, abetted, or assisted" Shadrach's escape. Following the advice of Webster and Curtis, Fillmore also declared that the band of rescuers were guilty of "levying war" or "treason" against the Union. Disregarding Massachusetts personal liberty laws, Boston's Board of Aldermen, obviously agreeing with the president, told Mayor John P. Bigelow to "direct the city marshal to assist agents of the state and federal government in the execution of their duty when obstructed by a mob."[31]

Not surprisingly, a number of Boston's leading merchants and industrialists supported such a stance. Denouncing reckless abolitionists, Cotton Whig Robert C. Winthrop thought it "lamentable to have such triumph given to [what he considered] Nullification and Rebellion." Believing that the rescue undermined law and order as well as compromises of the Constitution necessary to preserve the Union, the wealthy Amos Lawrence questioned whether "we [shall] stand by the laws or shall we nullify them?" Americans, he thought, had a choice to make — "Shall we uphold the Union or shall we break it up?"[32] Conservative newspapers contributed to such concerns. The *New York Journal of Commerce* published a report about "[N]egro insurrection" in the Old Bay City and the editor of the *Boston Courier* said that he felt obliged to uphold the city's reputation and restore the "Commonwealth's dignity." He railed against the "mischief which mad Abolitionism ... wantonly perpetrate[d]."

Welcoming evidence of support from law-and-order constituencies and what he saw as a "spirit of reconciliation," Fillmore declared that he had confidence that "our liberty and our Union may subsist together for the benefit of this and all succeeding generations." By the end of February 1851, Garrison complained that "all the Hunker papers" in Boston had censured the act of saving a fugitive slave from being returned to bondage and Henry C. Wright lamented that several newspapers in Ohio and the West "condemn[ed] Shadrach's rescue.[33] With these sentiments prevailing, federal officials carried out a series of arrests. Over a two-week period, they charged a number of Boston abolitionists, white and black, with having aided and abetted the rescue. The antislavery attorney Charles G. Davis and *Commonwealth* editor Elizur Wright, the men who left the courtroom as the assault began, were among the first arrested. Authorities also quickly indicted a black barber from Salem named Alexander P. Burton, a black truckman known as John Foye (or Noye), the white superintendent of Tremont Temple, Joseph K. Hayes, Shadrach's colored attorney Robert Morris, and four black clothing merchants—Lewis Hayden, James Scott, Thomas Paul Smith, and John P. Coburn. The charges against Davis, Foye, and Burton were withdrawn and not one of the others was convicted.[34]

While Mayor Bigelow, the Board of Aldermen, and leading Cotton Whigs thought they needed to defend their city's reputation, some Southerners deemed it beyond repair. Bostonians had allowed "a horrible crime" to be committed on "the afternoon of the 15th" and now, according to some slaveholding Southerners, a "dire calamity hung over the land." Even if some law-abiding Bostonians turned over a new leaf and admitted that although the "Fugitive Slave Law is not a popular one," it still needed to be "observed as all other laws must be," many whites below the Mason Dixon line felt that irreparable damage had been done.[35] A correspondent for the *Boston Courier* reported that "the heart of the South was stirred with the bitterest feelings—that the mortification and chagrin of Southern men were extreme—at the high-handed rescue of Shadrach." By not enforcing the Fugitive Slave Law, which guaranteed the protection of Southerners' property as well as their right to reclaim it, and allowing such an outrage to occur, Bostonians, they said, "were trampling down the sacred constitutional rights of sister states."[36]

In response, Southern Nationalists resurrected the Georgia Platform framed by Southern rights advocates during the Great Debates of 1850 less than a year before. That platform stated that Southern states would support the Compromise of 1850 on the condition that the Fugitive Slave Law would be faithfully executed. For many slaveholders, the Shadrach rescue represented a glaring violation and the time had come for the slaveholding states to leave the Union. "If we are to judge from the tone of the Southern press, and the complaints that reach us through more private channels," said the *Boston Daily Atlas* in a lengthy report entitled *AN UNDERSTANDING*, "the North is regarded with less favor than heretofore." The paper's editor stressed that "the wrath of Southern gentlemen" was now especially aimed at Boston where many slaveholders believed "mad abolitionism" reigned. The Shadrach rescue represented what one Southern paper labeled "the most outrageous violence and rebellion." The *Savannah Republican* summed it up saying, "The city of Boston is a black speck on the map — disgraced by the lowest, the meanest, the blackest kind of nullification."[37]

If the *Savannah Republican* suggested the Shadrach rescue had angered Southerners, the *Georgia Citizen*'s demands for the punishment of Bostonians and other Northerners who failed to respect the Fugitive Slave Law indicated some Southerners wanted retribution; they thought Fillmore's proclamation had not gone far enough. "The President," stressed the *Citizen*'s editor, "should also order a naval and military force to that point, sufficient to batter down the walls of Boston and lay it in utter ruin, unless Massachusetts will do her duty, as a member of the great confederacy of States, and enforce the laws and Constitution of the Union." He thought the first step in redressing the situation was to rid the Old Bay State of abolitionism, root and branch. "[H]ang the ringleaders in the riot, white and black," he declared and he singled out Elizur Wright, Charles Davis, and Theodore Parker. He reminded his readers that capital punishment was warranted for treason and he said Shadrach's rescue was just that. He concluded with a warning obviously intended to evoke memories of the Continental Association boycotts in 1774. "If the State of Massachusetts does not purge itself of the iniquity practiced within her borders," he advised that the South should "have her ports blockaded and her commerce cut off."[38] This Southerner wanted to conserve the order that the Revolution had produced — and that order included Southerners' rights to reclaim and hold their human property.

But to others in antebellum America, the Shadrach affair proved that Americans still faced tyranny, which called for continuing revolution to throw off its yoke and extend rights to all antebellum Americans— blacks included. It was from this perspective that such militants as Theodore Parker, Henry C. Wright, Samuel Joseph May, Lewis Hayden, and Elizur Wright criticized Fillmore's commitment to enforce the Fugitive Slave Law and his administration's proslavery stance after the Shadrach rescue. Antislavery editors shared these men's views and they too invoked America's Revolutionary heritage. The *Hartford Republican*'s editor thought that the enforcement of the Fugitive Slave Law and Fillmore's proclamation were "hastening a dreadful catastrophe"; he said the administration's response was "a deliberate attempt to repeat the policy of George III, and thrust offensive and tyrannical laws upon a free people by brute force." He reminded readers of the many petitions that Northerners had sent to Washington. "When the Fugitive Slave Law was pending in Congress, the people of the free States gave distinct and timely notice that it was abhorrent to their moral sense, and they could not in conscience obey it." In light of this, Fillmore's knee-jerk reaction in issuing his odious proclamation was abusive, especially as it confirmed Clay's pronouncements the day before to the effect that "THE LAW WILL NOT BE REPEALED" and "YOU SHALL SUBMIT TO THIS LAW."[39] Another Northern paper, the *Dover Morning Star* printed a letter entitled "THICK DARKNESS," which concluded that "national tyranny has become so rampant" and "law and authority so completely at its service."[40]

Theodore Parker, guided as always by the Revolutionary principles handed down to him by his father and grandfather, led his congregation in a prayer for Shadrach, openly defying the Fugitive Slave Law and Fillmore's proclamation. He called on "all Christian people, to aid him [Shadrach] in his efforts to escape from the hands of the slave-hunters now seeking for his life." With characteristic flourish, the radical abolitionist ended his prayer imploring "God's mercy for a hunted fugitive, and justly solicit[ed] the aid of Heaven to overrule and avert the horrible doom that awaits the captured fugitive."[41] In nearby Worcester, Thomas Wentworth Higginson also turned to the examples he had received "from my two soldier and sailor grandfathers" and framed his militancy with the revolutionary fervor that later found expression in his famous *Massachusetts in Mourning* sermon. "[I]f men array brute force against Freedom — pistols, clubs, drilled soldiers, and stone walls, then the body has its part to do in resistance," reasoned Higginson. After the Shadrach drama, Parker, Higginson, and other militant members of the Boston Vigilance Committee organized a "minute man" band — just as their forbears had done — to stand in readiness to help "on any emergency."[42]

Henry C. Wright also invoked the legacy of the American Revolution. When he joined Garrison in celebrating Shadrach's rescue, he applauded Hayden's group of twenty or so blacks, referring to them as "that heroic, God-directed band of free, noble spirits that dashed down the *wooden* obstacles that stood between a man and liberty, and bade the slave be free, the chattel be a man." Echoing remarks of Parker and Higginson, he said that storming into the courthouse, Hayden's group proved they were "Brave men and true! Patriots, heroes, friends of God and Humanity!" In them, he recognized "the spirit of Washington, of Warren, of Hancock, of Adams, and of all who, in this or other lands, have vindicated the cause of the oppressed, animated your hearts, and led you on to the *bloodless*, noble deed."[43] Shadrach's rescuers were heroes and ranked with the Republic's greatest patriots.

These black patriots' deeds signaled a new, increasing militancy in black communities throughout the North, which reflected their disillusionment with the federal government's enactment and stringent enforcement of the Fugitive Slave Law of 1850. Indeed, in the Shadrach rescue and after, blacks played "a prominent part in almost every instance where a fugitive slave was rescued or where attempts were made to effect a rescue." Black agency and leadership in fugitive slave dramas reflected Northern blacks' increasing impatience with pacifism in white-led antislavery movements, which often shaped law-abiding tendencies that prevailed among the property-owning middle classes. Black impatience loomed large in the days after the rescue, notably when authorities indicted several blacks for involvement. "Within an hour [of John Noye's arrest] a crowd of several hundred was milling around the Court House." A day later, another crowd "quickly materialized" when authorities charged James Scott.[44] That Shadrach's rescue catalyzed Northern blacks into action is not surprising. From the time slave catchers seized James Hamlet, the first runaway returned to the South under the new Fugitive Slave Law, blacks found many white Northerners' responses to the plight of fleeing bondspersons woefully lacking — if not irksome when inaction also seemed imbued with white racism. Moreover, fugitive slave crises often sparked racism and Fillmore's denouncement of Hayden's band as "sundry lawless persons, principally persons of color, combined and confederated together for the purpose of opposing by force execution of laws of the United States" was a striking example. Black abolitionists, including Frederick Douglass, also had less patience with whites who believed that Northerners had a "duty" to return fugitive slaves or others who regarded those deputized as marshals under the Fugitive Slave Law as "heroic warriors" defending the compromises of the Constitution supposedly needed to preserve the Union.[45] Douglass's remarks suggesting that the best way to resist the Fugitive Slave Law was to have "a half dozen or more dead kidnappers" and "Thank God, Shadrach is where no republican Haynau can molest him more!" reflected the new militancy and blacks' determination to enjoy American liberties, even if they confronted a landscape imbued with racism and law-and-order attitudes that prejudiced them as well as their enslaved brothers and sisters.[46]

Black Bostonians and their white allies did not get to celebrate Shadrach's

LEWIS HAYDEN. Lewis Hayden never backed down when defending fugitive slaves. "[W]e should think from the spirit and bearing of this Hayden," wrote Frederick Douglass after the Shadrach drama, "[that] he would be among the last to stand idly by, when a brother man guilty of no crime, was about to be robbed of his liberty. It would be just like him, [a] warm-hearted, fearless man, to sing out, stand back gentlemen, I must have a hand in this" (Boston Athenæum).

rescue for long. After Fillmore's proclamation, law-abiding whites in the North seemed to heed warnings about "the danger of mob rule" and

51

such disillusioned antislavery activists as Samuel Gridley Howe found not "a blush of shame, not an expression of indignation at the thought that a man [such as Shadrach] must fly *from* Massachusetts to the shelter of the red cross of England to save himself from the bloodhounds of slavery." Emerson's spirits sagged once again and he thought "Boston was a base place just now."[47] Slave hunters seemed to prowl everywhere, instilling fear in the hearts of fugitive slaves and "filling them with dismay." Although white abolitionists ridiculed Fillmore's proclamation and some like Garrison denounced it as "simply an insult," black Bostonians who had fled from bondage knew they were now very much at risk. Some 100 blacks left Boston in the days after the Shadrach affair, rivaling the number that had departed immediately following the enactment of the Fugitive Slave Law the previous September. This time, many were women. Abby Alcott wrote that she had "sent 20 colored women to service in the country — where for the present they will be safe." She was as determined as any of Boston's male abolitionists and ready to face the consequences. After the Shadrach indictments, she stated, "[I] may yet have to meet the penalties of the law — I am ready."[48]

Although discouraged by the "general acquiescence" of their neighbors to the Fugitive Slave Law, several of Alcott's friends on the Boston Vigilance Committee and her allies in the country remained steadfast in their refusal to surrender to federal law. Meeting at Weymouth in March 1851, one month after the Shadrach rescue, they passed a series of resolutions — the first being "That if ever 'Resistance to tyrants is obedience to God,' it is when tyrants usurp the authority of God." They denounced the Fugitive Slave Law "a daring outrage on the laws of Nature and Nature's God" and declared that it was "the duty of the people, to tread it under their feet." They also attacked the Free Soil Party, saying "we have no Free Soil — no spot where the slave can stand, secure from the claim of his master."[49]

Gerrit Smith and the English abolitionist George Thompson presided at another meeting in March, at Peterboro, New York. They addressed concerns that Samuel Joseph May and other New York activists had raised during the William and Ellen Craft drama, concerns that resurfaced in the Shadrach affray. Describing the Fugitive Slave Law as "a compound of meanness, tyranny and atheism," Smith, Thompson, and the assembled antislavery folk declared that "the church and ministry which will sustain the government of the United States, as at present administered, is not the church and ministry of Jesus Christ" and they called on Northerners to abandon churches that did not take a stand against slavery. The meeting's third resolution juxtaposed the Shadrach affair against Revolutionary principles. "The recent rescue, in the city of Boston, of an alleged fugitive slave, was not the act of a mob, but a lawful, Christian and patriotic use of force in support of the great cause of justice, humanity and civil liberty, warranted by the Gospel and the Declaration of Independence." For them, the Shadrach drama was part of their Revolutionary legacy. "We hail it," they said, "as a cheering proof that the spirit which resisted the British Stamp Act and threw the tea into Boston harbor, still lingers in the bosom of the descendants of the Pilgrims."[50]

In Massachusetts a group of impassioned abolitionists that included Samuel Gridley Howe, Samuel Sewall, and Horace Mann also sought to fuel the fires previously kindled during the William and Ellen Craft crisis and re-ignited by Shadrach's rescue. They announced a state convention to be held in April at Worcester with the striking slogan "No Union with Slaveholders." They also called for a national convention at Buffalo on the Fourth of July, inviting all who shared their "abhorrence" of the "unconstitutional and nefarious [Fugitive Slave] Law."[51] They did not know that the city of Hancock and Adams was about to become the scene of another remarkable fugitive slave crisis—that of Thomas Sims. It too would resonate across antebellum America and cast a dark shadow over the landscape of a troubled and increasingly divided country.

CHAPTER 3

Thomas Sims

Renewing the Revolutionary Struggle for American Liberties

Souls of the patriot dead,
On Bunker's height who bled!
   The pile, that stands
On your long-buried bones—
Those monumental stones—
Should not suppress the groans,
   This day demands.

For Freedom there ye stood;
There gave the earth your blood;
   There found your graves;
That men of every clime,
Faith, color, tongue, and time,
Might, through your death sublime,
   Never be slaves.

Over your bed, so low,
Heard ye not, long ago
   A voice of power,
Proclaim to earth and sea,
That, where ye sleep, should be
A home for liberty,
   Till Time's last hour?

Hear ye the chains of slaves,
Now clanking round your graves?
   hear ye the sound
Of that same voice, that calls
From out our Senate halls,
"Hunt down those fleeing thralls,
   With horse and hound!"
     — The Reverend John Pierpont

On a cool New England night in early March 1851, the North Star shone brightly above Thomas Sims as he stealthily rowed the skiff away from the brig *M & J.C. Gilmore*. Gentle waves in Boston Harbor rocked the small boat and lapped at the sides of the larger vessel, drowning the noise of the oar hinges grating with every stroke the twenty-three-year-old fugitive slave from Georgia took as he pulled closer to free soil. Some two weeks earlier on February 21, 1851, the "slender," "good-looking," "very bright" mulatto, a bricklayer by trade, had stowed away in the bow of the *M & J.C. Gilmore*, leaving behind his free-born wife and "several children in Savannah." "Perhaps he had heard of Boston ... even of

54

Faneuil Hall, of the old Cradle of Liberty," the Reverend Theodore Parker remarked a few weeks later. Because of his demeanor, one contemporary observer suggested that the well-mannered, young bondsman who made "arrangements" for his family to join him in the North would not normally have been "taken for a slave."[1]

Sims demonstrated remarkable perseverance in his flight northward. After being turned down by the steward of the *M & J.C. Gilmore* when he asked if the vessel needed "a cook," Sims lurked about the ship for several days before sneaking aboard and hiding just before it left port. He endured a "wintry" voyage after the vessel rounded the southern tip of Florida and moved up the coast, lurched by the increasingly cold waves that crashed on America's Mid-Atlantic and New England shores. Sims remained "undiscovered by the crew" until March 6th when the lights of South Boston flickered across the bay, beckoning to him. Perhaps no longer able to contain himself at the prospect of touching the land of liberty and breathing free air for the first time in his life, the bondsman came out on deck and excitedly asked a sailor, "Are we up there?" The seafarer's answer was not what Sims wanted. The man seized him and called for help from his shipmates. They beat the young slave as they dragged him before Captain Eldridge who, along with Cephas J. Ames, the ship's surly mate, interrogated him.[2] Sims swore that he was a free black from Florida; he claimed that his father had purchased his freedom "when he was six months old." He maintained that he had lived in Savannah for only "twelve or thirteen months" and had decided to flee to the North to avoid the $100 fine imposed on unregistered free blacks who migrated to the city. Sims said that he had left his free papers behind.[3] The ill-humored captain did not believe his story; he "cursed" the young black and ordered him locked up in a cabin where Eldridge thought he would remain secure for the night. But Sims was not to be so easily subdued or confined—especially so close to free soil. Using a pocket-knife that the crew had not taken from him when they collared him, Sims escaped from his prison by "unscrewing the lock on the door"; he then quietly made his way on deck, furtively launched the vessel's life-boat, and rowed toward what he believed was free shore.[4]

Once there, he undoubtedly heard black Bostonians complain about the Fugitive Slave Law extending slavery's clutches to the North, but for Sims Massachusetts was free soil—at least for the four weeks or so that he walked about Boston's streets "freely during the day and night." He "took lodgings in a colored seamen's boarding house at 153 Ann Street" operated by a man named Aitken. He then wrote to his wife in Savannah and received a return letter from her at the beginning of April.[5] Unbeknownst to him, their correspondence had been intercepted by his owner James Potter, which set the stage for his recapture after the wealthy rice planter from Chatham County in Georgia became busily engaged arranging to bring Sims back. Potter sent his agents John B. Bacon and M.S. DeLyon to the Old Bay City to claim and capture Sims. The prosperous slaveholder was known to be a very cold-hearted soul who cared little about the loss of a slave, but "he felt that it was his duty to prosecute his rights" to uphold the South's Peculiar Institution. Like many other Southern Nationalists, Potter embraced the so-called Georgia Platform, which stated that the slaveholding states would remain in the Union only if federal fugitive slave legislation was faithfully executed. Believing that claiming his slave — now that he knew his whereabouts — was an opportunity to "vindicate and test the rights of the South under the Fugitive [Slave] Law," Potter also paid for a white bricklayer named Edward Barnett to travel to Boston to identify Sims beyond any shadow of doubt. During hearings the following week, Barnett did exactly that; he testified that he worked "on the same scaffolding" with Sims, who had informed him that "he belonged to James Potter" and "paid his wages to Mr. Potter monthly." To ensure that his case would not be set aside on any technicality related to his ownership of Sims, Potter also arranged for a court transcript to be duly signed by Henry R. Jackson, Judge of the Superior Court of the Eastern District of the State of Georgia, affirming that "one Thomas Sims escaped from the State of Georgia while owing service" to him. Showing this certificate of ownership to federal officials, the rice planter's agents quickly obtained a warrant for Sims's arrest from George T. Curtis, one of three United States slave commissioners in the Boston area.[6] Directed "To the Marshal of our District of Massachusetts," the warrant was dated April 3, 1851, and it boldly stated, "In the name of the President of the United States of America, you are hereby commanded forthwith to apprehend Thomas Sims now alleged to be in your District, a colored person, charged with being a fugitive from service in the State of Georgia."[7]

Although armed with such a powerfully worded missive, the arresting officers—City Marshal Tukey, Asa O. Butman, and Alfred Sleeper, another policeman who "had been on the prowl for Sims"—did not use it when they charged the fugitive slave as he walked along Richmond Street toward Endicott with his "companions" on Thursday evening, April 3, 1851. Despite the fact that Massachusetts personal liberty laws prohibited state and local officials from participating in apprehending alleged runaways, Tukey positioned a posse of policemen "close at hand, ready for action at a moment's notice."[8] Fearing resistance from Sims or antislavery Bostonians who might witness the arrest, and aware that state and local officials were not allowed to act under the Fugitive Slave Law, the deputies carried out "instructions from the Mayor [John P. Bigelow] to preserve the peace of the city" and they charged Sims with disorderly conduct. Sims contested his arrest for "making a disturbance in the street." When they also falsely accused him of having "stolen a watch," he realized their intentions and called them "kidnappers"; he also stabbed Butman with his pocket knife as he sought to free himself. Overpowered, handcuffed, but still shouting, "I'm in the hands of kidnappers," he was taken to the Boston courthouse, which United States District Marshal Charles Devens turned into a federal jail—again in violation of Massachusetts personal liberty laws.[9]

Some Southern newspapers rejoiced that Tukey and his men had arrested Sims with such "celerity." They asserted that "law, order, and good government can be carried out in Boston" and triumph over mobs, fanatics, and wild abolitionists—men like William Lloyd Garrison, Wendell Phillips, Thomas Wentworth Higginson, Lewis Hayden, and Theodore Parker. Such statements reflected Southern Unionists' hopes that Boston would redeem itself after the fanatical abolitionism so evident during the Shadrach rescue. Some Northerners shared these wishes. For example, Garrison singled out an extract from the *New York Herald*, which took a strong law-and-order stand and reported that "the eyes of the whole country have been riveted on Boston since the arrest of Sims," a claim that was obviously not far off the mark, as a few days later Savannah's *Daily Morning News* reaffirmed the Georgia Platform in an editorial under the heading of "The Boston Fugitive Slave Case." Ominously the paper's editor declared that "the fate of the Union depends" on Sims's return and the enforcement of the Fugitive Slave Law. He wrote, "If there is conservatism, honesty, patriotism, and justice enough at the North to put down the fanatics who are making war upon the South, the Union, and the Constitution, then our Confederacy may be perpetrated." But the editor warned readers that "should abolitionism be permitted to rule the day — if, as a political power, it should obtain the ascendancy — then will come troubles of which we have only had a foretaste, and the doom of the American Union will be irrevocably sealed."[10]

In the nation's capital, President Millard Fillmore and his officials also gazed nervously toward Boston, especially as the local press reminded them how precarious the situation really was. "The authorities of the City [of Boston] and the Federal Government cannot again be taken by surprise," said the editor of Washington's *Daily National Intelligencer*, even as he noted "the local police are empowered to support the Marshal in keeping safe custody of the party claimed, and are already on the *qui vive*, so that no suddenly-conceived and unopposed rescue, as in the case of Shadrach, can be accomplished in this case." Like many other antebellum Americans, black or white, in the North or South, he considered the Sims case of great historical importance and a critical test for the fate of the nation.

When Devens locked Sims in a third-floor jury room at a courthouse "full of armed men," news of the arrest spread to Boston's black community and leading antislavery whites, two groups that challenged what Fillmore called "general acquiescence" to the Fugitive Slave Law. One report said that "a strong excitement pervaded the city."[11] The Boston Vigilance Committee began to move into action, although divisions between radical abolitionists and those Higginson called "'non-resistants' [*sic*] or 'political Abolitionists'" hampered decision-making. Higginson, Parker, Hayden, and the more radical vigilance committee members recommended overt defiant resistance; more conservative members favored limiting the Boston Vigilance Committee's role by adhering to past policies of only extending "legal assistance and the provision of shelter and transportation."[12]

The first vigilance committee member to act on behalf of Sims was the antislavery attorney Samuel E. Sewall, and he did so on his own. Fearing that Sims might be denied a hearing with counsel and quickly shipped to the South, he hastened to the courthouse where the deputy marshal Patrick Riley, considered by abolitionists as one of Boston's "chief bloodhounds," refused to let him in. After Sewall insisted on his right to act as "counsel for the fugitive" and Riley continued to block him, tempers flared and the deputy marshal ordered a nearby "*posse of watchmen*" to slap the attorney in a holding cell to cool off. Although Riley released Sewall soon afterward, he instructed him to "leave Court Square" immediately.[13] Two other outspoken Boston Vigilance Committee members, "the trenchant editor" of the antislavery *Commonwealth* newspaper Elizur Wright and Theodore Parker, also made their way to the courthouse that evening. Parker later denounced what he had seen in the heart of Boston, exclaiming, "[T]he manstealers are here; the commissioner issues his warrant; the marshals serve it in the night ... when odious beasts of prey, that dare not face the light of heaven, prowl through the woods— Those ruffians of the law seized their brother-man."[14]

But Sewall, Wright, and Parker were not alone in Court Square that night. Ordinary Bostonians gathered too as the arrest, according to Wendell Phillips, sparked the "burst of popular indignation" that city officials had expected and sought to avoid by having the slave-catching officers "disguise themselves" and "lie" when they arrested Sims. Phillips contended that if the deputies had exposed their real intentions, Sims would have been "torn from their grasp" and he was probably correct as alarmed onlookers followed the wagon carrying Sims all the way to the courthouse. The growing crowd fueled the authorities' apprehensions "that the peace of the city would be disturbed" and supposedly justified ordering out the militia.[15] Memory of Shadrach's rescue accentuated the angst of federal officials and also convinced Bigelow to act firmly. One reporter who witnessed the "feverish state of excitement" in Court Square wrote that "whites and blacks thronged in great numbers, highly excited and impatient." Putting it in historical context, he wrote that it was "a scene of intense interest, and hardly paralleled in the history of a city so full of startling incidents as that of Boston."[16]

The next morning, the agitation continued. "[S]everal hundred people," including black Bostonians who arrived "in considerable numbers," milled around the courthouse creating a commotion. The multitudes displayed varying sentiments; some appeared to be drawn there out of "idle curiosity"; others revealed support for the "authority of law" and defended the enforcement of the Fugitive Slave Law; antislavery white and black Bostonians voiced their opposition to the law they hated.[17] The profile of protesters changed abruptly during the morning, however, when authorities got heavy-handed with black males whom they deemed to be the most likely to attempt a rescue. To show that they were "determined there would be no more escapes," deputies arrested black men "walking back and forth in front of the courthouse," which forced black males, including Hayden and other militants who had been involved in the Shadrach rescue, to keep their distance and made black women and children, along with antislavery whites, more prominent near the courthouse.[18] When "two or three" blacks continued to express their contempt of the deputies, they were charged with having "indulged in language with policemen" but many blacks and whites still showed disapproval, even if it was from a distance, as they "jeered" and "scolded" the deputies for holding Sims.[19] Some abolitionists were seen "pointing" at individuals accused of being "slave hunters," which led Savannah's *Daily Morning News* to complain that some "ill-disposed" persons lay in wait for Potter's agents while others of the antislavery persuasion vehemently protested "the large posse of police officers" surrounding the courthouse.[20]

Overnight, City Marshal Tukey had also called out the militia and rounded up several hundred volunteers to reinforce Devens's guards. Wendell Phillips estimated that "no less than five hundred" police and volunteer deputies formed a column around the courthouse and he said they were heavily armed and ready "to repel any attack." Reports suggested that the mayor had arranged for "eleven companies" of militia to be "stationed at Fanueil Hall" as additional reinforcements. Abolitionists quickly dubbed the burgeoning forces of law and order the "*Sims Brigade.*" Surveying the troops and chains in Court Square, Charles Sumner branded the Boston Courthouse the "Bastille of the Slavocracy."[21]

Indeed, the look of Court Square shocked many Bostonians and the city seemed "under martial law or in a state of siege." Bostonians who prided themselves on being descendants of such liberty-loving patriots as Paul Revere and John Adams deemed it time to act on their Revolutionary heritage. Wendell Phillips exclaimed, "[T]his is the first time hostile soldiers have been seen in our streets since the red-coats marched up Long Wharf" and he asked Northerners to resist the enforcement of the Fugitive Slave Law on the Old Bay City's hallowed ground.[22] Bronson Alcott was equally disturbed and wrote, "The Court House is surrounded with chains and armed police to hold the prisoner in custody." The transcendentalist added, "It is a novel spectacle to our people, and excites the indignation of every one in whom sentiments of justice and humanity yet survive." He mused that the sad scene "visibly answered" what slavery now meant for the North. For these Bostonians, "the truth was out; Massachusetts justice lay enchained at the mercy of the Slavocracy."[23]

As the crowd mingled around the building, Theodore Parker gained permission as a clergyman to see Sims. Describing what he saw inside, the abolitionist preacher said, "Ruffians mounted guard at the entrance, armed with swords, fire-arms, and bludgeons" and all interior doors

CHARLES SUMNER. Charles Sumner, the Massachusetts Free Soil senator who was later caned nearly to death in the Senate by congressman Preston Brooks for criticizing Senator Andrew Butler of South Carolina, branded the heavily guarded Boston Courthouse during the Thomas Sims crisis the "Bastille of the Slavocracy" (Library of Congress).

were barred and locked. "Inside the watch was kept by a horrid looking fellow, without a coat, a naked cutlass in his hand and some twenty others, their mouths nauseous with tobacco and reeking also with half-digested rum paid for by the city." Parker deplored that it was in these circumstances that he was forced to console "the first man Boston ever kidnapped."[24] Higginson seethed as hearings commenced before the federal commissioner. "[S]ix men were at the door of the court-room," complained Higginson and he also noted that "two strong men" sat at the prisoner's sides and "five more in the seat behind him."[25]

Not everyone shared these men's concerns—certainly not a white Southern visitor. Having seen Parker and Higginson, as well as the large number of women protesting Sims's confinement, one Southern slaveholder who walked around the Boston courthouse that week commented that "the Ministers ... are doing all in their power to create feelings hostile to the Constitution and the South, and the women are following their example." He quoted a French *philosophe* as having said, "What cannot priests and women do?" He sardonically answered his own question, saying "We see what they can do."[26]

Early Friday afternoon, April 4, the Boston Vigilance Committee announced they would hold a rally in support of Sims and requested approval from the Massachusetts Legislature to convene it in the State House Yard or at Faneuil Hall. Fearing "treasonously violent" speeches, legislators denied them both locations, which forced the abolitionists to assemble on Boston Common and later at Tremont Temple. Theodore Parker, Samuel Gridley Howe, Francis Jackson, Wendell Phillips, and the Reverend Nathaniel Colver aroused the gathering with powerful rhetoric and "inflammatory appeals" calling for resistance to the Fugitive Slave Law. On the Common, Wendell Phillips asked his audience to prevent Sims from being returned to bondage. He wanted the "Common [to] resound to the declaration that law or no law, constitution or no constitution, chains or no chains, this law shall not be enforced." Phillips had come to believe that forcible resistance was now necessary. "Block the locomotives, tare [*sic*] up the rails, follow the fugitive to the borders of the State, if possible, to rescue him," shouted Phillips. It was time for Bostonians to rise up. Alarming his law-abiding neighbors, Phillips informed the audience that he had "counseled every colored man who had ever felt the chains of Southern oppression, to fill his pockets with pistols" and he denounced federal and state authorities more firmly than before for having cowed before Southern interests. He said, "The people must take up the reins."[27] And move his audience he did. After the meeting, Bronson Alcott spoke of the "true feeling" of those who had assembled on the Common. In his diary, he wrote, "Redress in some way, but redress at any hazard, and a rescue, not of this prisoner perhaps, of one fugitive, or several, but of the consciences and constitution of Massachusetts, the vindication of the rights of freemen." In a burst of emotion, Alcott concluded, "What is a republic, taking sides against itself?"[28]

Later at Tremont Temple, an estimated "one thousand" people listened to Colver condemn the fugitive slave legislation as "so obnoxious and inhuman that he would trample it under his feet." He vowed that if resisting the Fugitive Slave Law meant leaving both his church and profession, "he would unfrock himself" before the gathering. He too resolved that "Constitution or no constitution, law or no law — no fugitive slave shall be carried out of Massachusetts" and he announced another meeting in support of Sims on Saturday, April 5.[29] Bigelow and Tukey considered the speakers' rhetoric so threatening that they ordered out the City Guards, the New England Guards, and the Boston Light Guards, telling them to be ready to suppress any disturbance. Federal authorities were also not about to take any chances; "two hundred and fifty United States troops, with two pieces of ordnance, were kept on alert at the Charlestown Navy Yard" all Friday evening.[30]

The Saturday afternoon meeting took place once again on Boston Common and antislavery enthusiasm soared, especially as Wendell Phillips's oratory reached new heights. Phillips's speech, observed Austin Bearse, the famous Boston Vigilance Committee doorkeeper and captain of the fugitive slave vessel *Moby Dick*, matched "those of [James] Otis and [John] Adams in patriotic fervor, and must hold its due place in the eloquent story of Boston Streets." Again Phillips called for action. If Sims was returned to bondage, the Golden Trumpet wanted it to be done "in the presence of as many indignant hearts as possible." He said the marshal and his deputies "should be obliged, in taking that unhappy man away, to walk over our heads." He promised that he would use "all means that God and nature" had given him to stop the return of Sims and Boston from being disgraced. When the meeting adjourned, participants resolved to assemble on the day that Curtis rendered judgment on Sims's case. The impassioned listeners invited "the good people of the Commonwealth of Massachusetts" to join them. They said that together Massachusetts citizens would "witness the last sad scene of the State's disgrace, if it shall be found impossible to avert it." Their resolution reflected sentiments Henry Wadsworth Longfellow penned the day before. "O city without a soul! When and where will this end? Shame that great Republic, the 'refuge of the oppressed,' should stoop so low as to become the Hunter of Slaves."[31]

Before the fateful day arrived, the Boston Vigilance Committee — "in almost constant session"—focused on numerous initiatives to prevent Sims's return to the "iron house of bondage."[32] Leading Boston attorneys, men of "first eminence," joined Samuel Sewall in Sims's

WENDELL PHILLIPS. Austin Bearse thought that Phillips's speech on Boston Common during the Thomas Sims affair rivaled "those of [James] Otis and [John] Adams in patriotic fervor." The famed Boston Vigilance Committee doorkeeper thought that Phillips's speech should have a "place in the eloquent story of Boston Streets" (Boston Athenæum).

defense. Robert Rantoul and Charles G. Loring represented the bondsman before Curtis, confronting Seth J. Thomas, known as "the legal pimp of the slave catchers," who acted for Potter.[33] Sims's lawyers took an array of legal actions at both the federal and state levels seeking to save him from "imminent peril." Claiming that Sims was unlawfully detained and challenging the constitutionality of the Fugitive Slave Law, the attorneys filed habeas corpus motions before Massachusetts chief justice Lemuel Shaw. Shaw, however, denied the writs and upheld the constitutionality of the fugitive slave legislation, citing the ruling of United States Supreme Court associate justice Joseph Story in *Prigg v. Pennsylvania* as a precedent. Shaw said that the Massachusetts court lacked jurisdiction in the case and declared that the Fugitive Slave Law was constitutional; he supported "comity between states." Before the aging Massachusetts chief justice, Sewall also "introduced an affidavit attesting to the prisoner's free status." When Sewall declared that Sims "never knew such a person as James Potter," Shaw refused to listen.[34]

On Monday, April 7, 1851, an even more determined Sewall requested a postponement of the fugitive slave hearing, hoping to gain time to strengthen Sims's defense. When Curtis refused, the bondsman's lawyers filed a writ of personal replevin, which would have removed the prisoner from "the custody of the United States Marshal Devens" and provided him with a right to a trial by jury under the 1836 Massachusetts law entitled "An act to restore the trial by jury on questions of personal freedom." When the sheriff served the writ on Devens, however, the marshal refused to respect it. In another attempt to free Sims from the federal authorities, the lawyers arranged for a criminal complaint against him for having assaulted Asa Butman "with the intent to kill." Arguing that the criminal charge took precedence over the fugitive slave claim, a civil action, they contended that Devens should hand over Sims to state authorities. The Southern press assailed the motion as "an impudence unparalleled even in this age of audacity." Devens, however, had foreseen the maneuver and he had obtained a similar warrant against Sims beforehand under federal law from U.S. Commissioner Benjamin F. Hallett, which effectively blocked the antislavery attorneys' scheme. On Thursday, April 10, Sims's legal team filed another habeas corpus motion that was rejected — this time by Judge Peleg Sprague. When Devens also failed to bring Sims before the federal tribunal to be tried on the criminal charge, the prisoner's lawyers filed yet another habeas corpus motion before Justice Woodbury, who set a hearing for Friday, April 11, the same day on which Curtis was scheduled to announce his ruling.[35] When Charles Sumner and Sewall appeared before Woodbury on Sims's behalf, Curtis had already considered Sims's lawyers' arguments and determined the fugitive slave's fate.

Rantoul and Loring argued five key points before the commissioner. First, they contested the constitutionality of the Fugitive Slave Law on the grounds that a commissioner deciding the fate of a fugitive slave assumed "judicial power," which according to the Constitution could be "exercised only by a judge of the U.S. Court duly appointed." A slave law commissioner was "not such a Judge." Second, they claimed that the Sims case represented a suit involving "an alleged right of property" and "a right of personal liberty," which both entitled the parties involved to a trial by jury. They deemed any law denying parties this right to be "unconstitutional and void." Third, they questioned the competence of the transcript of record of the Georgia court as evidence in "a suit pending, or to be tried in another State [Massachusetts]." They also said that the transcript should not be used as evidence because Sims had not been represented in the proceeding that the transcript covered. Rantoul concluded Sims's defense arguing again that the Fugitive Slave Law was "unconstitutional and void" and "not within the powers granted to Congress by the Constitution."[36]

Despite the lawyers' seemingly powerful defense, most Boston Vigilance Committee members remained pessimistic. After observing Rantoul's closing arguments, Alcott thought that Curtis, a supporter of Webster, "seemed to have made up his mind." The transcendentalist was correct, as behind closed doors, Webster actually "personally supervised arrangements" for Sims's trial.[37] Other observers also guessed that "despite the ravings" of the likes of Garrison, Phillips, and Parker, authorities would "discharge their duty to the Constitution, the Union, and their Southern fellow-citizens." In Washington, the *Daily National Intelligencer* confidently predicted that Sims "will be remanded to his owner."[38]

In light of such expectations, the Boston Vigilance Committee developed an impressive array of other strategies, legal and non-legal. Seeking to hamper Potter's claim, they charged Bacon and Delyon with kidnapping and had them taken into custody. The slave hunters were forced to pay bail of $5000.[39] The abolitionists also had an arrest warrant issued for the *M. & J.C. Gilmore*'s mate Ames for having assaulted Sims. Seeking other means to support the fugitive slave, they arranged for Senator Keyes to petition the Senate on behalf of Sims demanding that the Massachusetts judiciary issue a writ of habeas corpus and that a law also be enacted to authorize an inquiry into Sims's "right to a trial by jury and [also ensure] that the petitioner 'may not be surrendered, exiled, or returned to bondage, until proven to be a slave' by due course of law." Keyes told the Senate that because of Shaw's earlier decisions "the noble writ of habeas corpus lay a dead letter at the feet of the Fugitive Slave Act." The antislavery senator failed to get the legislation but the Senate did vote to appoint a committee to investigate whether "the freedom of any inhabitant of this Commonwealth is in danger" and whether the

City Marshal or state officials had violated "any law for the security of personal freedom."[40]

Such measures, along with the array of pamphlets, broadsides, and posters that the vigilance committee distributed throughout the city, publicized Sims's plight and stirred antislavery sentiment. One poster also cautioned blacks to be careful dealing with police officers, noting that "since the recent ORDER OF THE MAYOR & ALDERMEN, they are empowered to act as KIDNAPPERS and SLAVE CATCHERS." As the day for Curtis's decision approached, the Boston Vigilance Committee posted "immense placards" calling all citizens to Court Square on Friday, April 11.[41] In a meeting chaired by Horace Mann at Tremont Temple, Samuel Gridley Howe thought passions had reached such a level that the community was "on the verge of revolution." Mann and other "rising antislavery politicians" such as John G. Palfrey and Henry Wilson sought to advance their careers and build notoriety by capitalizing on the "popular resentment aroused by the fugitive slave issue."[42] The vigilance committee also used churches as a means of building support for Sims. The Sunday after the fugitive slave's capture, Sewall circulated a letter from Sims to Boston's houses of worship stating "the undersigned, a freeman, and in peril, desires the prayers of this congregation that God may deliver him from his oppression, and restore him to freedom."[43]

Recognizing the likelihood of Curtis remanding Sims to Potter, Boston "revolutionists"—to use Higginson's expression—also devised more radical rescue strategies; they were far from "cowed" as some Southerners and proslavery Northerners suggested they were. Higginson and "a few kindred spirits" advocated "a physical assault on the courthouse." When the law-abiding majority of the vigilance committee blocked the scheme, the Worcester preacher complained that some members of the Boston Vigilance Committee had a "great want of preparation ... for this revolutionary work." He thought more fugitive slave dramas were required to radicalize some of his middle-class fellow committee members. Raised as they had been, he said, it would take "the whole experience of one such case to educate the[ir] mind[s] to the attitude of revolution." But this did not stop "the impetuous young minister" from devising a remarkable plan whereby Sims would "escape confinement by leaping out of a courthouse window" onto mattresses placed below before being whisked to a waiting carriage, which would carry him out of town. Even the most conservative vigilance committee members bought into Higginson's scheme and the Reverend Leonard Grimes visited Sims to apprise him of it. Everything was set to go but, just before the time planned for the escape, Higginson scouted out the scene and found that somebody had betrayed the plot and metalworkers were "busily at work fitting iron bars" on the window of the room in which Sims was held.[44] Although crestfallen, radicals like Higginson and Parker remained determined to save Sims and they continued to hatch plans until Sims had been returned to Georgia. Perhaps the "most daring" scheme was concocted at Theodore Parker's house. "It contemplated nothing less than the seizure" on the high seas of the ship called the *Acorn* that federal authorities had consigned to carry Sims to Savannah. Parker and his co-conspirators selected Austin Bearse, whom everyone recognized as a skilled sailor and Higginson considered "one of our best men," to carry out the maneuver. Again, in the end the timid majority of the Boston Vigilance Committee, arguing that the plan was impracticable, vetoed it in favor of the idea, which Wendell Phillips proposed, of bribing the *Acorn*'s captain, Henry Coombs. That plan "failed to work" as Coombs refused to be bought off.[45]

On Friday morning, with multitudes about the courthouse, Curtis rendered his decision. He acknowledged that the Sims case, a controversy between parties, involved judicial power but he said it was "for Congress to decide in what mode, to what extent, and under what form of proceeding that judicial power shall be called into exercise in order to give effect to the right of the owner claiming a fugitive slave." Rejecting Rantoul's argument that a commissioner usurped authority that the Constitution gave only to judges, Curtis asserted that there was "a class of inquiries, judicial in nature, and special in their purpose, which may be confided to the determination of officers who are not judges." He said slave commissioners, similar to such other government officials as patent officers, assumed ministerial roles that gave them a right to rule on certain questions. Responding to the argument that Sims had a right to a trial by jury, Curtis referred to Story's opinion in *Prigg v. Pennsylvania* and added that the Sims case was "a summary ministerial proceeding, in aid of a right of removal, and that the liberty of the party is not in contestation here, for final adjudication" — in essence implying that final adjudication would be left to courts in Georgia, an altogether farcical ruling since a state court had already certified Potter's claim. Denying Rantoul's contention that Congress did not have the power "to legislate on the subject of the surrender of fugitive slaves at all," Curtis pointed to Article IV of the Constitution. He considered also that "the object of this provision was to prevent State legislation from interfering with or impairing the right of the master to the service or labor of his slave" and, for this reason, he said personal liberty laws did not take priority over the Fugitive Slave Law. Congress, declared Curtis, had the authority to enact fugitive slave legislation and he believed the only outstanding question was whether the prisoner before him was James Potter's slave, the man described in the transcript of record from the Georgia court. On this, he said that he regarded the evidence of Potter's agents and the bricklayer Barnett as conclusive and quickly remanded Thomas Sims to the slaveholder saying "it is my duty to grant the claimant the certificate which he demands."[46]

Just before Curtis finished his remarks and it was clear that he would authorize Sims's return to bondage, Sims exclaimed, "I will not go back to Slavery. Give me a knife, and ... I will stab myself in the heart, and die before his eyes!" For Sims, it was "Liberty or Death." When Judge Woodbury rendered judgment on the last habeas corpus suit later that day, basically the last chance for Sims, he too ruled against the fugitive slave. Though not surprised, the bondsman's supporters were devastated and they assembled in despair that evening in Washington Hall. "The Boston of 1851 is not the Boston of 1775," declared Josiah Quincy. "Boston has now become a mere shop — a place for buying and selling goods; and I suppose, also, of *buying and selling men*."[47]

Theodore Parker thought that the Sims decision transformed Massachusetts into "a hunting-ground for the panting fugitive" and confirmed the triumph of slavery "over the graves of our revolutionary ancestors, and on the hallowed soil of Bunker Hill." Expecting federal officials to remove Sims under the cover of darkness because of their fear of public indignation, Parker led some one hundred Bostonians in a vigil at the courthouse that night. The preacher guessed correctly — between three and four o'clock in the morning guards began to drill in Court Square, a signal that something was afoot. Just before 5 o'clock, a posse of some three hundred men formed "a hollow square" into which they led Sims. "[H]is sable cheeks were bathed in tears; and although

AUSTIN BEARSE, REMINISCENCES OF FUGITIVE-SLAVE LAW DAYS IN BOSTON. Austin Bearse joined Theodore Parker and other abolitionists in a vigil outside Boston's courthouse the night Thomas Sims was returned to slavery in Georgia. When marshals marched Sims to Long Wharf, onlookers asked, "Is this Boston? Is this Massachusetts? Is that Charlestown and Bunker Hill?" (Boston Athenæum).

he evinced the deepest grief and sorrow, he marched with a firm manly step, like a martyr and a hero, to his fate," remembered Austin Bearse. "The anguished spectators uttered cries of 'Shame! shame!' and questions such as 'Is this Boston?' 'Is this Massachusetts? 'Is that Charlestown and Bunker Hill?'" The Cape Cod sea captain believed that early morning stealth was the only way the U.S. marshal could have marched Sims to Long Wharf. "The whole proceeding was too cowardly to be undertaken [even] under the pale beams of the moon, so the leader of the work waited until her silver light faded behind the western hills," wrote Bearse. The federal marshal "then marched ... his shameful band over the sacred ground consecrated to liberty and sealed by the blood of our revolutionary fathers." Dr. Henry Ingersoll Bowditch agreed with Bearse. As he and other abolitionists watched the procession pass over the ground where Crispus Attucks died in the Boston Massacre, Bowditch asserted "none dared carry [Sims down State Street] save at that early hour."

Parker, Channing and the hundred abolitionists who followed the procession denounced the deputies as they treaded over the "holy spot."[48] They spontaneously convened an emergency vigilance committee meeting "to agitate for the repeal of the Fugitive-Slave bill, or to make it a dead letter." Later that morning they sent a public message:

To the Citizens of Massachusetts: —

The Committee of Vigilance of Boston, at a meeting held at half past five this morning, passed a resolution respectively asking the people of Massachusetts to toll the bells in their several towns as the intelligence reaches them of the return of a fugitive slave from this Commonwealth.[49]

When Sims's escort reached the end of Long Wharf and put him aboard the *Acorn*, "a man standing on the wharf cried out, 'Sims! preach liberty to the slaves!'" U.S. deputy marshals Riley and Byrnes, accompanied by officers Dolliver, Clark, Sawin, and True, quickly embarked with the prisoner, joining "a crew of eight men, two mates and the captain." To defend against any rescue at sea, the *Acorn* had "two cannon" as well as a number of guns and much ammunition. Late in the day, the brig was seen at anchor off Nantucket Roads; at about half past eight in the evening, it hoisted sail and "with a fair wind" headed southward just in time to prevent Boston police officer Lawton and Deputy Sheriff Adams of Norfolk County, arriving off Nantucket Roads on a chartered steamer, from serving another criminal warrant that would have allowed them to take Sims into their custody — "by force if necessary."[50]

When Sims arrived in Savannah one week later, he received "thirty-nine" lashes in a public square before spending two months in the city jail. Potter later sold him at auction to a Vicksburg mason from whom he escaped in 1863 as Union forces triumphed on the Mississippi. Sims finished his life in Washington, DC, working as a bricklayer and a messenger for the United States Department of Justice.[51]

When the Sims drama ended, proslavery advocates in the South initially praised Bostonians who had "redeemed" their city only a few months after the Shadrach rescue. The *Savannah Republican* said "it was a pleasant duty to accord to the authorities and people of Boston great credit for the firm and energetic manner in which they have demeaned themselves." Fillmore agreed, and he let Webster know. "I congratulate you and the country upon a triumph of law in Boston," wrote the president, "She has done nobly. She has wiped out the stain of the former rescue and freed herself from the reproach of nullification [of the Fugitive Slave Law]." Some Bostonians, notably leading Cotton Whigs and others doing business with the slaveholding South, rejoiced as well. The *Boston Herald* proclaimed "our city is redeemed from the opprobrious epithets which have been denounced against her," and even the *Boston Transcript*, a Whig paper, reported that "the temper of the military has been equally commendable."[52]

But it was not long before angst crept in, especially in the South but also in Washington and among some law-abiding Northerners, who favored compromise with Southern slaveholders. Within a week of Sims's departure from Boston, the editor of Savannah's *Daily Morning News* stressed "the extreme difficulty" with which Potter's slave catchers had reclaimed Sims and how "narrowly the agents had escaped with their prisoner." The editor thought that the exorbitant cost of returning Sims and the fact that a Southern slaveholder had been forced "*to steal his property in the dead of night*" proved the Fugitive Slave Law could not be faithfully executed. Indeed, he concluded that "the law is not worth the parchment on which it is written," and the following day reiterated his concerns, estimating that the cost of recovering Sims had reached some $10,000, an enormous sum at the time. That "much vaunted Fugitive Slave Law," he wrote, "proves to be a rather uncertain and very expensive business." Responding to such concerns, the *Daily National Intelligencer* suggested that the Sims case underscored again the troubled nation's sectional divide on the Fugitive Slave Law, noting that "Disunionists at the South will persevere in denouncing the law as inefficient," and "Abolitionists at the North will still continue their dirty work."[53]

Though the sectional rift remained the same, the Sims drama changed things in Boston, significantly so for some — particularly the city's blacks. Disillusioned in the autumn of 1850 with the enactment of stricter fugitive slave legislation, many blacks in the free states, who feared kidnapping under a law that prohibited them from testifying in their own defense, fled to Canada seeking safe haven. In Boston, two months after rejoicing over Shadrach's rescue, blacks revealed deep resentment about how state and local officials had colluded with federal authorities to return Sims to servitude. They criticized whites who professed to be antislavery yet refused to take a stand to stop Sims's return from free soil. The Sims case, declared Frederick Douglass, "created the deepest feeling against the law and its upholders." Moved in this way, Boston's black clergymen — men such as the Reverend Leonard Grimes — became more militant, assumed new leadership among abolitionists, transformed their churches into "institutional centers for the antislavery movement," and started to take initiatives independently of their white allies. After Sims's return to Savannah, Grimes, on his own, raised $1800 to purchase the unfortunate bondsman's freedom. Although he failed to strike a deal with Potter, his actions demonstrated blacks' new determination to exercise agency. The Sims case further raised the profile of blacks, including the militant Lewis Hayden, the architect of the Shadrach rescue. His determination that no fleeing bondspersons arriving in Massachusetts be returned to slavery heightened antislavery militancy and energized vigilance activity. From 1851 onward, many Boston Vigilance Committee meetings took place at Hayden's house; he was instrumental in assisting "sixty-nine fugitives" achieve their freedom in the months following Sims's rendition. Records for this period also show increased direct involvement of blacks in the city's antislavery activities as seen by the Boston Vigilance Committee remuneration of some forty-nine black Bostonians "who harbored fugitive slaves."[54] Black orators, including Frederick Douglass, William Wells Brown, Charles Lenox Remond, and Samuel Ringgold Ward, increased their speaking after the Sims crisis. Ward, for example, embarked on the legendary speaking tour that took him to "numerous districts of New York, Pennsylvania, Ohio, Wisconsin, Michigan, and Indiana as well as Connecticut, Rhode Island, Massachusetts, and New Hampshire" — all in a few months without the conveniences of modern travel.[55]

The Sims case touched whites as well. "The times," lamented Bowditch, "are horrible." Ralph Waldo Emerson looked at slavery as a veritable "calamity" that he said "darkens my days." Writing of a North scarred by slavery, he contended that the Peculiar Institution had transformed the "most triumphant escutcheon the sun ever shone upon into a jail or a barracoon" for the slaves of Southern slaveholders.[56] The venerable Cape Cod sea captain added his thoughts too. "The Fugitive-Slave Law," remarked Bearse, "was brought nearer home with its affront to every Northern conscience, and sat before each in clearer light the duty to resist its impious demands." Sims's case proved to Northerners that slavery contaminated the sacred soil of Paul Revere, John Adams and their compatriots. On April 16, 1851, before Sims even landed on Georgia's shores, the *Boston Investigator* invoked the city's Revolutionary heritage. "Boston is peculiarly hallowed in the annals of the Revolution for its love of liberty and hatred of oppression," discerned the paper's editor. With great emotion, he predicted that "the same spirit still survives and burns; and the fact that here, under the shadow of Faneuil Hall and [the] Bunker Hill Monument, a man has been torn from her soil and carried into slavery, will create an excitement throughout the State and the entire North that will never subside until the Fugitive Slave Law is repealed." Sims's fate scarred the Revolutionary record, aroused passions, and, as Bearse recalled, ignited "Theodore Parker in the pulpit, Mr. Garrison in the press, Wendell Phillips on the platform, Charles Sumner in the Senate, Henry Wilson in the Free Soil party, Gerrett [sic] Smith in his unceasing philanthropy, Whittier in song, [and] Mrs. Stowe in 'Uncle Tom's Cabin.'" Through Sims's misfortune, these heirs to the Revolutionary generation popularized the antislavery cause, framing it in terms of Boston's heritage and calling on antebellum Americans to complete the Revolution to ensure American liberties for all—especially on the hallowed ground of their Revolutionary fathers. Sims's fate rallied antislavery forces and inspired hearts.[57]

THOMAS SIMS. The Thomas Sims case heightened the militancy of black Bostonians. Austin Bearse said it also ignited "Theodore Parker in the pulpit, Mr. Garrison in the press, Wendell Phillips on the platform, Charles Sumner in the Senate, Henry Wilson in the Free Soil party, Gerrett [sic] Smith in his unceasing philanthropy, Whittier in song, [and] Mrs. Stowe in 'Uncle Tom's Cabin'" (Boston Athenæum).

Perhaps nobody was more instrumental in popularizing the antislavery cause during and after the drama than Theodore Parker; the crisis catalyzed his radical abolitionism and he took it to antebellum Americans like never before. Perhaps he saw himself as a Thomas Paine taking a message to the people, awakening them to oppression and need for continuing revolution for American liberties. Bowditch now referred to him as "that Martin Luther of our times." Parker demanded more than reform; from the pulpit, from the platform, and in print, the radical preacher called for Americans to carry on the legacy of their Revolutionary forefathers. He inspired Emerson. Writing from Concord on April 18, 1851, Emerson informed Parker that his Fast-Day Sermon on Sims provided "the foremost consolation to me in bad times." Emerson acknowledged having "read every word of Mann, Dana, Loring, Rantoul & Sumner" but he claimed that nothing matched Parker's "brave harangue" and he ranked Parker with America's Revolutionary heroes. "We all love & honour you here & have come to think every drop of your blood & every moment of your life of national value."[58] As Michael Fellman has noted, Parker literally called "white northerners to a new revolutionary battle, a battle which would reinvigorate northern blood, re-steel the backbone of New England and the North, and reclaim the power of ideas with the power of action."[59] He stood at the very center of the Boston abolitionist community, inspiring blacks and whites, in the city and in the country-side, informing them of the "terrible contest between Liberty and Slavery." Reminding Bostonians of the "sad days" of the Stamp Act, the tea in the harbor, and even Lexington and Concord, Parker said that the Sims affair represented the "saddest day of all." It was the day "when a man was kidnapped in Boston, and your court-house hung with chains."[60]

Also significant was that after the Sims drama Parker took his message to a growing number of middle and lower class whites who worked as artisans, wage workers, journeymen, and domestics in Boston and the surrounding area. Wherever and whenever he spoke, Parker emphasized the Sims affair proved that Garrison's doctrine of non-resistance had become increasingly anachronistic. Touching thousands, "his popularity and influence were immense" and remained so through the late antebellum period. He felt close to ordinary folk and he transmitted his passion to them. "In Boston, he preached each Sunday to a basically working-class and lower-middle class congregation of 7,000." After Sims's return, he increased the number of his speaking engagements and his "deep *revolutionary* voice" — as Bowditch described it — promoted a new radicalism.

With the likes of Higginson, he popularized steadfast resistance to the Fugitive Slave Law and ordinary folk swelled antislavery ranks, injecting new radicalism into the movement as few of these recruits had ever embraced Garrisonian pacifism. The Sims crisis marked the new rank and file. For example, John Cluer, a workingman who had been a Chartist in England, and William Kemp, a chair painter, both rose "at three in the morning" to see Sims marched from Massachusetts free soil. Cluer had "tired of speeches" as he huddled with better-known vigilance committee members in the early hours; he wanted action. He was one of a new breed of abolitionists that would not shrink from forcible rescues. Militants like him stood ready to enforce the resolutions published at the Twentieth Massachusetts Anti-Slavery Society Meeting following the Sims drama. Unlike the law-abiding old guard of the Boston Vigilance Committee, these new "revolutionists" were ready to do something about "their deepest disapprobation and indignant protest against the surrender of Thomas Sims by this city, its sanction of the cowardly and lying policy of the police, its servile and volunteer zeal in behalf of the manhunters, and its deliberate, wanton and avowed violation of the laws of the Commonwealth for the basest of all purposes, slave-trading, selling a free man into bondage, that State street and Milk street might make money."[61] They imbibed such words and Theodore Parker's Revolutionary message. They would watch closely as militants just north of the Mason Dixon line in Pennsylvania put their lives on the line resisting the Fugitive Slave Law; a slaveholder would soon die seeking to reclaim his human property.

CHAPTER 4

William Parker and Revolutionary Heroes at Christiana

I look upon the great Anti-Slavery platform as one upon which those who stand, occupy the same position, — I would say, a higher position, than those who put forth the Declaration in 1776, in behalf of American liberty.... They do not want that [a] husband should be any longer sold from his wife. They want that the husband should have a right to protect his wife; that the brother should have a right to protect his sister. They are tired and sick at heart in seeing human beings placed upon the auction block and sold to the highest bidder. They want that man should be protected. They want that a stop should be put to this system of iniquity and bloodshed; and they are laboring for its overthrow. — William W. Brown

Every man must actualize his resistance and rebellion — his treason — by such means as he thinks right and most efficient. Would you deem it right — a duty — to kill the man who would enslave you? Then, you being judge, it is your right and duty to kill the man who would enslave your brother. — Henry C. Wright

As the autumn equinox announced the changing seasons in 1851, William Parker, standing on the deck of a ferry about to leave from the Rochester wharf for Kingston, Ontario, turned to his friend Frederick Douglass, whom he had known in slavery in Maryland and, for the remainder of his life, would know in freedom. With the sun setting on the waters, the ship's bell ringing as the crew released the heavy ropes tied to the dock, and slave hunters still mingling around the wharf looking for the Christiana murderers, Parker bid farewell to Douglass and gave him the revolver that fell from the hand of Edward Gorsuch, the Maryland planter slain ten days earlier attempting to reclaim his slaves at Parker's house. Douglass took the handgun and stepped toward the plank to go ashore. For Parker, the revolver served as "a token of gratitude" for the great black abolitionist's assistance to Abraham Johnson, Alexander Pinckney, and himself on the last leg of their perilous journey to freedom in Canada. For Douglass, the gift was a "memento of the battle for Liberty at Christiana," a great struggle for freedom in the early

morning hours of September 11, 1851 in a quiet Lancaster County hamlet in the gentle, rolling hills of southern Pennsylvania. For some, that frightful struggle represented the first battle of the American Civil War, spilling the war's first blood long before other events that have been typically regarded as initiating that conflict — three years before James Batchelder died in the Boston Courthouse during the Anthony Burns drama, five years before congressman Preston Brooks left Charles Sumner unconscious on the floor of the Senate during the Bleeding Kansas crisis, six years prior to John Brown's raid at Harper's Ferry, and a decade before the early morning shots at Fort Sumter. A Pennsylvanian paper reported on the Christiana affray with the headline, "Civil War — The First Blow Struck."[1]

For black freedom fighters

FREDERICK DOUGLASS. Frederick Douglass considered fugitive slaves "heroic defenders of the just rights of man." He believed that William Parker and his compatriots in the Christiana fugitive slave riot "should be placed side by side with Lafayette." After the Anthony Burns drama, he declared, "slavery has a right to go any where in this Republic and Liberty no where, except where Slavery will let it" (Library of Congress).

such as Douglass, the revolver also symbolized the continuing American Revolution for their natural rights, their God-given liberties. After Parker arrived in Canada the next morning, Henry Bibb, the editor of the black newspaper *Voice of the Fugitive*, said Parker was a man deserving of "the admiration of a Hannibal, a Toussaint L'Ouverture, or a George Washington." Douglass certainly thought so. He considered Parker and his compatriots "heroic defenders of the just rights of man," and he "fed them, and sheltered them." He published a letter suggesting that Parker and his companions "should be placed side by side with Lafayette."[2]

When Douglass said good-bye to Parker that evening, "both men knew that the war against slavery had taken a new and deadly turn, and that more, perhaps much more, violence lay ahead." Coming on the heels of Thomas Sims's return to slavery in Georgia, the battle at Parker's house, quickly dubbed the "Christiana Riot," the "Christiana Outrage," or the "Tragedy at Christiana," ushered in a new era of militancy on the part of blacks and their white allies.[3] Wendell Phillips lauded Parker's defense of the fugitive slaves. He observed that "twenty-five years of antislavery agitation had failed to confine slavery," and he contended before a New York audience that abolitionists needed to "adopt more aggressive measures." The battle in Lancaster County signaled to slaveholders that Northern blacks and their white allies stood ready to forcibly resist attempts to return any fleeing bondspersons to the South. No longer would they permit Southern planters to trample on the freedom of their brothers or sisters once they had made it north

HENRY BIBB. Welcoming William Parker to Canada after the Christiana fugitive slave riot, Henry Bibb, the editor of the black newspaper Voice of the Fugitive, said Parker was a man deserving of "the admiration of a Hannibal, a Toussaint L'Ouverture, or a George Washington" (courtesy Bentley Historical Library).

79

of the Mason Dixon line. They had, said a subscriber to *Frederick Douglass' Paper*, "heard the shrill cry of our own Patrick Henry 'Give me Liberty, or give me death.'" William Parker certainly embraced that message with a "cool determination" that had been hardened by a youth in bondage and his abhorrence of the kidnapping of blacks in the North.[4]

Similar to Frederick Douglass, who had "no accurate knowledge" of his age, Parker never knew his birthday, guessing only that it was probably in 1822, the same year that the Denmark Vesey conspiracy shocked white South Carolinians. His mother Louisa, the slave of William Brogdon, the owner of a plantation with some seventy slaves in Anne Arundel County, Maryland, died very young and Parker's grandmother, "the cook at the great house," raised him. His master died shortly after and Brogdon's two sons, William and David, divided the land and slaves between them; the latter, also known as Master Mack, inherited Parker as human property. The young masters punished their bondspersons from time to time but what their slaves came to fear and resent the most was the young planters' engagement in slave trading. In his autobiography, Parker remembered how every now and then, Master Mack called his slaves from the quarters to the big-house where invariably they would find some greedy "[N]egro-traders" ready to speculate in human flesh even if it meant separating families and leaving "men, women, and children" in tears never "to meet no more on earth." As a child, Parker learned to hate the South's Peculiar Institution — its whips, its scars, its blood, but most of all the auction block, the scene of tearful, emotional devastation. Before he had reached his teens, Parker heard of a place called Canada, a "land far away in the North, where the runaway was safe from pursuit." By the time he was about seventeen, Parker "longed to cast off the chains of servitude" that he now said fettered his "free spirit" and his youthful manliness. Convinced that his bondage "was founded in injustice" and determined that Master Mack was "done whipping" him, Parker fled the same day that he fought off his master when the latter sought to punish him for refusing to work. With his brother, Parker escaped to Baltimore. They avoided the slave patrols as they entered the city by covering their clothes with dust to disguise themselves as local brick-yard workers. After about a week in Maryland's bustling metropolis, the Parker brothers, "with the brightest visions of future independence" fixed in their minds, headed toward York, Pennsylvania, touching free soil for the first time in their lives. Parker recalled that he "felt as light as a feather, and seemed to be helped onward by an irresistible force."

But in York, Parker soon learned of the "imminent danger" of recapture under the detested Fugitive Slave Law, especially in a town that was rife with slave catchers. As such, he and his brother traveled to Columbia and Wrightsville, before finding work in Lancaster County, where on a "pleasant May morning," Parker said, "instead of the darkness of slavery, my eyes were almost blinded by the light of freedom."[5] But there too, Parker found that for African Americans, fugitive slaves or free blacks, freedom could be fleeting. Tranquil, nicely wooded, and blanketed with fertile fields and farms, Lancaster County, home to some 3,500 African Americans at mid-century, was also the hunting ground of such unscrupulous Philadelphia businessmen as George Alberti, famous for kidnapping "easy a hundred" blacks and making huge profits selling them to the South. It was also home to "a band of men known throughout the county as the 'Gap Gang,'" unruly kidnappers who typically worked as laborers, small farmers, or artisans during the day and supplemented their incomes by kidnapping black neighbors at night and selling them to the South. These slave hunters rendezvoused at the Gap Tavern to organize their forays. Sometimes they furnished descriptions of blacks, often free blacks living on adjacent farms, to Southern associates who used them to obtain fraudulent ownership certificates from Southern courts precisely describing the Gap Gang's next prey. Such schemes flourished after 1850 when the Fugitive Slave Law established federal tribunals that prohibited fugitive slaves from testifying in their own defense and paid commissioners higher fees when they ruled in favor of the slaveholder.[6]

When Parker settled in Lancaster County, he found himself in a land of freedom that was, however, scarred by virulent racism and full of danger for blacks. It was a world of contradictions and, though he breathed the air of liberty, he quickly learned to be on the alert for Negro-hating white neighbors ready to do business with the "insolent and overbearing" slavocracy from which he had just fled. Shortly after settling in Lancaster County, Parker resolved to free every slave or fugitive slave "at the risk of my life, and ... devise some plan for their entire liberation."

Attending antislavery meetings, listening to Frederick Douglass and William Lloyd Garrison, and marrying a determined, freedom-fighting fugitive slave named Eliza Ann Elizabeth Howard in 1846 fueled his commitment to black freedom. The Parkers' home became the heart of black militancy in Lancaster County. Although prior to Parker's arrival, some blacks had organized "a league for mutual protection," the increasing kidnapping threats after the enactment of the Fugitive Slave Law of 1850 encouraged Parker to transform the loose-knit group into a "secret black militia ... which mobilized on short notice to fend off slave hunters and recovered kidnapping victims, by force if necessary." Parker made them *minutemen*, ready to fight for freedom at a moment's notice, and he stood as "their leader, their Moses, and their lawgiver," a defender of liberty in the tradition of a Warren or a Washington. Lindley Coates, a white abolitionist in Lancaster County, described Parker as "bold as a lion, the kindest of men, and the most steadfast of friends." As a black American, however, he also became a fighter in the tradition of a Gabriel, a Denmark Vesey, or a Nat Turner, "although unlike them he operated in a free state and was supported by an interracial underground that recognized both his personal courage and his strategic skill."[7] As the mist lifted in the early dawn hours of September 11, 1851, Parker's resilience and leadership was tested by an aging Southern patriarch whose family had long-established roots in Maryland's Baltimore County.

Edward Gorsuch, a fifty-seven-year-old self-righteous slaveholder, a practicing Methodist and Sunday school teacher, lived proudly as one of Baltimore County's "most estimable citizens." He considered himself a benevolent master of his plantation, Retreat Farm, and its twelve slaves; he carried himself as a "man of honor and liberality in his own eyes and in the eyes of his neighbors, of his church, and of his sons." Although his reputation had been somewhat tainted by several runaways, he took much satisfaction from his white neighbors' noticing that some of them had returned "because they lived better with him than they were able to do in the places where they had gone."[8] In the scorching late-summer days of 1851, Gorsuch stood ready to uphold his reputation as an honorable master and a defender of slavery, even if his father had limited the number of years that he could hold the family's slaves. In his last will and testament, Gorsuch's father left him the slaves with a provision that they be freed at the age of 28. Respecting that condition, Gorsuch had already freed one slave named Jarrett Wallace but he had hired him back as "his 'market man' to sell his products in Baltimore."

Such were the circumstances when four of Gorsuch's remaining slaves disappeared suddenly in late 1849. On November 6, three "prime field hands" and Gorsuch's teamster fled from Retreat Farm and headed toward Pennsylvania along the York turnpike to avoid a whipping or worse after they found out that their master had discovered they had been swindling him out of a portion of his wheat. Though the men, "between 19 and 22 years of age," had at most a few years to serve him as property, Gorsuch became so obsessed with retrieving them that he put time, money, and eventually his life on the line to get them back.

When two years later Gorsuch received a note from William Padgett, a devious Pennsylvanian who worked as an informer for slave hunters, telling him that his four slaves—Noah Buley, Nelson Ford, and George and Joshua Hammond—were in Lancaster County, he immediately assembled a posse to go after them. By this time, the slaves had at most another seven years of enslavement and Gorsuch knew that slave catching was expensive and dangerous, but he had become a staunch Southern Nationalist and wanted to defend his honor as a slaveholder. He may also have been encouraged by Thomas Sims's rendition and sought to test the enforcement of the Fugitive Slave Law in Pennsylvania, the home of antislavery Quakers and a large number of free blacks.[9]

Gorsuch's posse gathered at the roadhouse tavern of his cousin Captain Joshua Gorsuch. In addition to the latter and himself, it included his son Dickinson, his nephew Dr. Thomas Pearce, and two Baltimore County neighbors, Nicholas Hutchins and Nathan Nelson. The men traveled to Philadelphia where Gorsuch obtained a warrant from United States Commissioner Edward Ingraham on September 9, 1851. The city's infamous slave catcher Deputy Marshal Henry H. Kline met them at Ingraham's office and joined the expedition. So did two slave-hunting Philadelphia policemen, John Agan and Thomson Tully—but not for long. As the posse headed toward Lancaster County, the two officers began to fear being outnumbered by militant blacks. They decided to sneak back to Philadelphia, leaving Gorsuch with only six men.

Kline spread the word that he was pursuing horse thieves and Gorsuch arranged for the members of the posse to travel separately to Lancaster County to avoid detection by antislavery activists who might inform his fugitive slaves that he was on their trail. A wily Philadelphia black named Samuel Williams, a deeply committed antislavery man, guessed Kline's "real errand" and encouraged by William Still, the legendary Underground Railroad conductor in Philadelphia, set about putting "all persons supposed to be in danger on their guard." Williams shadowed Kline, actually gained his confidence, and then "conveyed the intelligence" of the posse's "imminent arrival" to the Lancaster County blacks.[10] When an unknown local white, most likely William Padgett, guided the Gorsuch posse to Parker's house on the slope of a Lancaster hill, Parker, his wife Eliza, Eliza's sister Hannah and her husband Alexander Pinckney, Abraham Johnson, Nelson Ford (also known as Joshua Kite) and Joshua Hammond (also known as Samuel Thompson) waited in readiness.[11]

When Nelson Ford ran into the house from the laneway where he had been keeping watch and yelled "O William! kidnappers! kidnappers!," Parker moved everyone to the house's second story, putting the slave catchers at the disadvantage of having to mount a narrow staircase in full view of the defenders if they were to get their hands on Gorsuch's fugitive slaves. Gorsuch and Kline reacted by ordering their men to stake out the corners of the house while they sought to parley with the occupants through the front door, which a nervous Ford had left open. Kline announced his purpose, declaring that he had arrest warrants for Nelson Ford and Joshua Hammond, but Parker responded saying that "there were no such men in the house." When Kline advanced through the doorway, Parker warned him that if he took "another step," he would "break [his] neck." Claiming he had taken bold blacks before, Kline threatened Parker who responded, "You have not taken me yet, and if you undertake it, you will have your name recorded in history for this day's work," letting the slave hunters know that he was prepared to fight to the bitter end.[12]

Eliza Parker was just as determined and revealed that she too believed freedom was worth dying for. Brandishing a corn cutter, she announced "she would chop off the head" of any attacker who dared to ascend the stairs, causing Kline to recommend to Gorsuch that they retreat and read the warrants aloud to the black defenders. But the aging planter's stubbornness began to take over and he urged Kline to "go up stairs and take them." The slaveholder moved toward the stairs saying,

"We *can* take them ... I'll go up and get my property" but Parker promised him that if he started up, he would never go down.[13] Kline restrained him and read the warrants, finishing with the words, "We are commanded to take you, dead or alive." Those lines re-ignited Gorsuch's desire to attack and he shouted, "Go up, Mr. Kline ... you are the Marshal." Fearing the black defenders, the timid marshal hesitated and tried to buy some time from the increasingly impatient Gorsuch by threatening to burn the house down. "Burn us up," answered Parker. "None but a coward would say the like. You can burn us, but you can't take us." When Parker coolly added, "before I give up, you will see my ashes scattered on the earth," Gorsuch went into a frenzy and became unstoppable. He started toward the stairs shouting at Ford that he had seen him in the laneway and "if he would come down peaceably and return to Maryland, he would be treated just as well as before." The defenders responded by suddenly throwing a "five-pronged fish 'gig'" down the stairs, narrowly missing both Gorsuch and Kline at the doorway. "A flying axe" followed and it too narrowly missed its mark, but forced the slave hunters to retreat outside.[14] Kline, almost panicking, again counseled retreat as did Dickinson Gorsuch. He recalled later that "I told my father we had better go, for they intended to murder the whole of us," but the planter had decided he would not "give up." Eliza further escalated tensions as she sounded an alarm by blowing a horn "from the garret window," which made the attackers "visibly nervous" and they began shooting at her, forcing her to bend down below the window sill as she "blew blast after blast, while the shots poured thick and fast around her." Almost instantaneously Parker's neighbors began to converge on the scene. The miller Castner Hanway on horseback and the shopkeeper Elijah Lewis on foot arrived along with several blacks, including another former Gorsuch slave Noah Buley who entered Parker's yard with the Indian Negro Zeke Thompson, "a scythe in one hand and a revolver in the other."[15] The Quaker Joseph Scarlett, sometimes portrayed as "a local Paul Revere," spread the news throughout the countryside, galloping on horseback from farm to farm.[16] Just how many blacks "armed with firearms, clubs and corn-cutters" arrived at Parker's place is almost "impossible to determine" given the confusion and chaos that ensued. Initial estimates ranged from a low of about twelve to some "80 armed Negroes." Within days, reports of "two hundred" and "two or three hundred persons" spread across the country, catching especially the attention of increasingly distraught Southern slaveholders. *The Raleigh Register* and the *Mississippian and State Gazette* published the largest numbers that were almost certainly exaggerations as there were not two hundred blacks living close enough to Parker to get to his house by the time the shooting started. But historian Thomas Slaughter estimates that "in the space of half an hour" some 75 to 150 blacks, women and men, arrived and a significant number of them were armed.[17] With the Lancaster blacks outnumbering the posse, everyone in the slave-hunting party except for Edward Gorsuch, who kept on saying "I want my property and I will have it," wanted to retreat. When Hanway and Lewis refused Kline's request to join in the assault, the marshal did not like the odds and "leaped the fence, passed through the standing grain in the field, and ... [soon] was out of sight." Nathan Nelson and Nicolas Hutchins also sought safety in the nearby woods. Before taking what would be his last stand, Edward Gorsuch ordered Captain Joshua to "bring a hundred men from Lancaster" but the tavern-keeper, injured in the fray, stumbled down the lane "wounded and delirious." Hoping that his uncle would follow him, Pearce also retreated but when he glanced back, he saw Joshua Hammond clubbing Edward Gorsuch just before the planter was shot. It is unclear who put the fatal bullet in the slaveholder but likely it was one of his former slaves—Joshua Hammond or Noah Buley. Parker said it was Hammond, but Dickinson Gorsuch blamed Buley. Later the Lancaster black George Washington Harvey Scott testified that one "Henry Sims shot" the planter, although he subsequently changed his testimony. In his autobiography, Parker mentioned that Gorsuch suffered a clubbing after he was shot and said, "*The women put an end to him.*" In any event, as the quiet returned to the Lancaster valley, Edward Gorsuch lay dead in a large pool of blood, and Dickinson, shot twice by Pinckney, was also down. Although most witnesses expected him to die, he survived.[18]

Casualties would undoubtedly have been greater had Parker's white neighbors not intervened. Hanway encouraged the Gorsuch party to withdraw and sought to stop the black defenders from shooting. Hanway also likely saved Pearce by positioning his horse between Gorsuch's nephew and the black defenders as the doctor fled. The miller's refusal to support Gorsuch's posse, however, set the stage for proslavery and law-and-order whites seeking revenge to blame him and Elijah Lewis for the slaveholder's death. When the shooting stopped, Hanway and Lewis returned to their homes, where they soon received news that authorities had issued warrants for their arrest.

Anticipating the official reaction, Parker and his compatriots quickly dispersed and avoided the posses that arrested so many of their fellow blacks and white allies. Parker and Alexander Pinckney hid all day before meeting the wife of Parker's neighbor Levi Pownall that evening. She gave them a "pillow case with food" and advised them to flee. "Determined not to be taken alive," Parker immediately decided to seek safe haven in Canada and Pinckney agreed to follow as authorities posted a one thousand dollar reward for the "arrest and conviction of the person or persons guilty of the murder and violation of the public peace" at Christiana. Abraham Johnson joined them while Eliza Parker went temporarily into hiding "leaving the children with her mother." She would later meet up with William in Canada. Parker, Johnson, and Pinckney embarked on a harrowing five-hundred-mile escape and arrived two days later in Rochester where they met Frederick Douglass. Traveling mostly by "public and private conveyances, including train and horse-drawn carriage," they avoided being identified, even as they conversed with fellow travelers who showed them newspaper reports and advertisements of the reward for their capture. Commenting on the affair, one white traveler told them "I believe he [Parker] did right, and, had I been in his place, I would have done the same as he did." Stressing Parker's courage, the man advised them saying, "all you colored people should look at it as we white people look at our brave men, and do as we do. You see Parker was not fighting for a country, nor for praise. He was fighting for freedom: he only wanted liberty, as other men do."[19]

If antebellum America experienced what Albert Von Frank has called a "pocket revolution," the Christiana riot was such an event, and it made headlines across a dividing nation. By noon on September 11, telegraph operators in Philadelphia sent reports to newspapers everywhere describing some 80 blacks "armed with guns, &c" attacking a Maryland slaveholder, his companions, and a United States marshal, "killing Mr. Gorsuch, [apparently] *mortally* wounding one of his sons, and badly wounding an officer from Baltimore." Twenty-four hours later Americans learned that "the U.S. Marshal [Anthony E. Roberts], the U.S.

District Attorney [John Ashmead], a special Commissioner from Washington City, a company of U.S. Marines and fifty of the Marshal's police" had been ordered to the area to suppress the insurrection. Lancaster County authorities organized their own local posse, which not surprisingly consisted of many whites Parker labeled "Negro-haters," and the latter unleashed a veritable "reign of terror" or, as the *National Era* dubbed it, a "reign of blood" on the black population, sparing no colored household. "Gangs of armed riflemen from Maryland, assisted by the lowest ruffians this region can furnish, are prowling round the country, over a district of ten or twelve miles square, arresting indiscriminately all colored persons whom they meet, gallantly including women," reported the *Anti-Slavery Standard* in Lancaster. "A colored woman, who had been employed by Mr. [Levi] Pownall to wash the clothing ... was seized at the wash-tub, and dragged away."[20] The Reverend Samuel Ringgold Ward summed up the terror inflicted on the valley by saying that the authorities were "determined to have their [black] blood."[21]

Telegraph reports would soon announce that after the forces of law and order "scour[ed] the neighborhood," Justices Robert C. Grier and John K. Kane would probably try the insurrectionists on "charges of treason against the U.S."—a gesture that most antislavery folk interpreted as a means of appeasing unhappy slaveholders. After Governor E. Louis Lowe of Maryland suggested that the affair had "penetrate[d] the soul of the South," Acting United States Secretary of State W.S. Derrick sent him a letter stressing that "the President regards the violation of the rights of the peaceful citizens of Maryland with deep abhorrence." The administration, vowed Derrick, would take all the necessary measures to ensure that justice would be done and the president had already dispatched orders "to the proper officers of the United States in Pennsylvania, requiring them to proceed immediately to arrest all persons criminally concerned." Lancaster County became "a seat of war"; forces of law and order terrorized the once tranquil countryside and "ransacked" homes and farms as they made arrests.[22] "Whites and blacks, bond and free, were roughly handled," said one observer, and the blacks in particular "suffered terrifying scenes." Some thought Lancaster County was "in a state worse than martial law" as overzealous officers under the local, state, and federal governments vied for opportunities to grab prisoners. When deputies returned from the valley with captives in tow, "a controversy arose between the local Pennsylvania District Attorney John L. Thompson and United States Attorney John Ashmead as to whether the prisoners should be held for murder in Lancaster County, or for treason against the United States."[23]

Many Americans believed the official response to be justified; some wanted even stronger measures. Indeed, Pennsylvania's Governor William F. Johnson came under attack for not having been enthusiastic enough in quashing the alleged threat from Lancaster blacks. He received a letter from concerned Pennsylvanians contending that "this insurrectionary movement, in one of the most populous parts of the State, has been so far successful as to overawe the local ministers of justice, and paralyze the powers of law." They demanded stronger measures to deal with a "momentous crisis" and to ensure the "dignity of the Commonwealth." The Reverend J. S. Gorsuch of Washington, a son of the slain planter, fanned these fires as he publicly "assailed the Governor in the most vindictive terms, and imputed to him ... inactivity and gross dereliction of duty in regard to the murder of his father near Christiana," and most white Southerners agreed with him. In Baltimore, the mayor convened an "immense meeting in Monmouth Square" four days after the riot. Emotions rose as some six thousand persons listened to fiery speeches from state leaders, passed resolutions "condemning the outrage," and demanded that the Fugitive Slave Law be faithfully executed in the North. Several participants proceeded directly from Monmouth Square to Pennsylvania to assist in ferreting out anyone who had been involved in the affray; some also addressed a memorial to President Fillmore.

The *Fayetteville Observer* applauded the dispatch of some "eighty U.S. Marines" and praised the Baltimore County citizens who "were currently seconding the authorities." The editor insisted that all the insurrectionists should be brought to justice. Slaveholding Missourians were just as concerned and they reminded Northerners of the Georgia Platform. In an article entitled "The Faithful Execution of the Law," one Missouri newspaper editor lashed out at the violation of Southern rights, affirming that "the laws of this State were recklessly violated — the Constitution and laws of the United States were trampled under foot, and a citizen of another State ruthlessly assassinated by a band of desperate fanatics." He thought it was time for Northerners to stand behind the

Compromise of 1850 and teach those who failed to do so a lesson. Denouncing the Christiana rioters, a Florida journalist asked his readers, "Are such assassinations to be repeated?" He said, "the sword of Civil War is already unsheathed." The *Fayetteville Observer* wanted indictments for treason against Castner Hanway, Elijah Lewis, and even others who had not been at the scene. To ensure that the charges stuck, the paper called for a broad interpretation of treason, arguing that anyone who obstructed the law or participated in "a conspiracy which ripens into treason, whether present or absent from the scene of actual violence," should be charged along with the main actors. Targeting abolitionists who advocated resistance to the Fugitive Slave Law, the editor of the *Fayetteville Observer* wrote that "it would be very much to the advantage of society, if an example [was made] of some of these pestilent agitators, who excite the ignorant and reckless to treasonable violence." He demanded "sleepless justice."[24] Like the late senator Daniel Webster, he claimed that resistance to the Fugitive Slave Law represented treason, the "levying of war" against the United States. The *Washington Republic* used "similar language"; the *Journal of Commerce* wanted the Christiana rioters to suffer "the penalty of Treason —*hanging by the neck.*"[25] The administration listened and on Friday, October 13, 1851, Ashmead announced that four white men, Castner Hanway, Elijah Lewis, Joseph Scarlett, and James Jackson, along with twenty-eight blacks including Samuel Williams, were charged with treason. More indictments followed and the Christiana affair became the largest collective indictment for treason in American history.[26]

If Southerners approved such a hard line, so also did some Northern whites who had been shocked by what some called "a most horrible outrage," especially as several Northern newspapers sensationalized the affair. The *Pennsylvanian*, emphasizing that "Abolitionists are implicated in the Christiana murder," heralded Ashmead's decision to charge Hanway with "High Treason." *The Boston Atlas* portrayed a "general uprising" and described the Lancaster County blacks as savages, "a dangerous enemy" who killed a "respectable old gentleman" and clubbed his son while he was "writhing in agony." *The Cleveland Herald* referred to the riot as a "melancholy and deplorable catastrophe" and thought the administration should "vindicate the honor of the country." Antislavery militants, however, deplored such knee-jerk reactions and the indictment of Samuel Williams particularly irked Frederick Douglass. "[T]he public sentiment is so overawed and the public Press so tamed," lamented the radical black abolitionist, "that scarcely a voice of remonstrance or reproof is heard!" He denounced the administration's policy, arguing that when Williams alerted the fugitive slaves, he only "obeyed an impulse for which he can and if needs be will, go to the Dungeon or the Gallows rejoicing." Praising Williams for having been instrumental in saving his brethren from bondage by warning them of the slave hunters, Douglass reasoned that "to withhold that information from those who were 'flesh of his flesh and bone of his bone,' would have been an offense against the laws of nature and humanity."[27]

From October 13 until November 24th when Hanway's trial began as a test case for the others, Americans, black and white in the North and South, debated the definition of treason, sometimes returning to landmark decisions rendered years earlier by John Marshall and Joseph Story. As he criticized Ashmead's treason charges, Frederick Douglass seethed. "There is no warrant for that proceeding," declared Douglass, "either in the Constitution or in any Law of Congress; nor is there any Judicial precedent for this strained construction." As the seriousness of the charge, the lack of the evidence against Hanway, and the obvious over-zealousness of federal officials loomed large, Northern sentiment began to swing heavily against the administration's policy. The shift also reflected relentless efforts of Northern blacks, their white abolitionist allies, and especially antislavery editors across the North. Even relatively moderate papers contributed to the shift. The *Albany Journal* educated its readers on the definition of treason, noting that "Treason against the United States shall consist in levying war against them or adhering to their enemies, giving them aid and comfort." *The Vermont Chronicle* suggested that the treason charges against Hanway and others could not be "sustained by the Constitution of the United States" and warned that if Ashmead's doctrine became "the law of the land, it is hardly too much to say that there is an end of political liberty." The charges against the miller, who by most accounts had exercised a restraining influence, began to appear ridiculous if not dangerous— and of that William Lloyd Garrison made sure.[28]

As the trial got underway, the outspoken editor rose to the occasion and he fulfilled his promise to be heard. He raised the specter of the slavocracy exercising "a powerful sway" over the new nation, its politicians, its businessmen, and the people. "The perilous times, so often predicted, are upon us. The accursed slave power was once insidious and gradual in its successive encroachments, lest the people of the free States should take the alarm," exclaimed Garrison. He believed the Christiana treason charges now proved that the South had thrown all caution to the wind as it pursued its goal of expanding slavery. "It insolently proclaims its purpose to subject the entire North to its despotic way, and to trend out the lifeblood of all who refuse to bow their necks to its yoke." He said that slaveholders now controlled the national government — "the Executive, the Judiciary, and the Legislature, are alike its own," vowed Garrison after the treason charges. On the eve of the trial, as Pennsylvania authorities finished renovating Independence Hall for the pending spectacle, Garrison hit full stride; he cautioned Northerners that "the whole South are awaiting ... 'WITH ANXIETY' fifty-seven American citizens dangling in the air with broken necks." He also unleashed some of his vintage sarcasm. "Down with the Traitors, Mr. President," Garrison proclaimed invoking the highest ideals of the Revolutionary fathers. "Drag the editor from his desk, the preacher from his pulpit, the merchant from his counting-house. Giving information is treason; denunciation is treason; refusing to aid kidnappers is treason," he wrote and he told President Fillmore "the harvest is ripe, 'thrust thy sickle'; gather the offenders, cast them into the wine-press." The only fault of the Quakers, preachers, and other Americans charged, said Garrison, was that they loved freedom — they were not "bastard sons of 1776." Indeed, declared Garrison, "Rebellion against the enforcement" of Ashmead's treason policy was "necessary to prevent the Revolution of '76 from becoming a failure." It was, he said, the administration that undermined America's founding vision — "the villains who would subvert Liberty in this country in the name of Law, are themselves the Traitors." Remarkably he went a step further and dismissed his traditional pacifism, contending that the black defense at Christiana — even if it included violence — was "*legally* justified and generally honored American tradition." The Declaration of Independence sanctioned it.[29]

As the treason-trial spectacle unraveled on a truly national stage, other leading journalists soon joined Garrison. In the *New York Tribune*, Horace Greeley commented that the Christiana "blacks had opposed civil law, it was true, but a 'divine law of Nature' was on their side." He stressed that they had taken a stand for their "inalienable right ... to their own persons.... No act of Congress can make it *right* for one man to convert another into his personal property, or *wrong* for that other to refuse to be so treated." Gerrit Smith argued this as well and he forwarded a letter to Frederick Douglass for publication. Invoking the memory of the "revolutionary fathers," the letter concluded that "the treason of Benedict Arnold was a small affair in comparison" to the treason policy of the administration that "degrade[d] a nation" and made "war against God and humanity."[30] The Massachusetts Anti-Slavery Society also weighed in assailing the indictments of Hanway and Lewis, who were "truly

MILLARD FILLMORE. When Fillmore's administration charged alleged Christiana rioters with treason, William Lloyd Garrison proclaimed, "Drag the editor from his desk, the preacher from his pulpit, the merchant from his counting-house. Giving information is treason; denunciation is treason; refusing to aid kidnappers is treason." The only fault of the Quakers, preachers, and other Americans charged, said Garrison, was that they loved freedom — they were not "bastard sons of 1776" (Library of Congress).

brave men" and had not levied war against the United States but sought to "save the lives of others." The society lauded the "successful resistance to Gorsuch and his bloodhounds" and praised the "love of Liberty" that still beat in American hearts.[31]

The *Pennsylvania Freeman*, of course, joined other newspapers that considered the Christiana blacks' stand justified. It believed their only crime had been embracing the American motto, "Liberty or Death."

Most blacks agreed, especially in the wake of Thomas Sims's return to bondage. Referring to America's Revolutionary heritage, William Shattuck wrote to Douglass saying that the Fugitive Slave Law exceeded imperial tyranny in 1776. He thought that it trampled "every sacred right a *Warren*, an *Adams*, and a *Franklin* stood for." Henry C. Wright believed it proved that "moral suasion, reason, argument are no longer any avail" and, thus, forcible resistance was the only resort when "Law and Justice have been trampled under foot."[32]

When Hanway's jurors deliberated for only *"ten minutes"* and returned a not guilty verdict forcing Ashmead to plea *nolle prosequi* and drop the treason charges on all the others who had been indicted, antislavery militants lauded the Christiana patriots. At an antislavery meeting held in West Chester, Pennsylvania, one member summed it up saying, "Those colored men were only following the example of Washington and the American heroes of '76." Julia Griffiths, an English reformer working as an assistant editor for Frederick Douglass, thought likewise. She wrote, "I regard William Parker and his accomplices as true heroes ... having for their watchword, 'Liberty or Death.'"[33] Douglass also advanced such views and published several letters heralding the black defenders' actions and asserting that "the right of Revolution belongs to every man, *to black as well as white*, that these men had as perfect a right to fight for their liberty as our revolutionary fathers did for theirs." Douglass also encouraged Northern

WILLIAM LLOYD GARRISON. Attacking the Fugitive Slave Law during the Christiana fugitive slave drama, William Lloyd Garrison declared that the slaveholding South "insolently proclaims its purpose to subject the entire North to its despotic way." Resistance to the law's enforcement was "necessary to prevent the Revolution of '76 from becoming a failure" (Library of Congress).

blacks to meet in support of "the Christiana Patriots" and reported on their proceedings. When Louis Kossuth, the Hungarian freedom fighter visited Washington, Douglass printed the resolutions of a boisterous meeting of black Americans presided over by William P. Powell. The participants resolved, "That it is the duty of every man who thinks his house and his person worth defending to contribute his mite to defend these Christiana patriots against the lawless expression of a cruel, besotted, and self-condemned Executive, which, with one and the same breath, orders American freemen to be incarcerated for striking for liberty, and orders a public salute to welcome those who fought for no more in a foreign land." Garrison was just as quick off the mark; he spoke of William Parker and his compatriots as "our black Kossuths."[34]

Reinforcing Charles Lenox Remond's message to Rhode Island blacks that if they "died in heroic defense of their rights, posterity would reverence and cherish their memories," and Frederick Douglass's advice to black Northerners, "*Count your lives worthless, unless [they are] coupled with the inestimable blessing of liberty,*" two fugitive slaves in England who had been watching developments in America added a few thoughts. Writing to William Lloyd Garrison, William and Ellen Craft said, "We were very sorry that the slaveholders were successful enough to get a slave from Boston, but were much pleased with the difficulty they had in doing so." They believed, however, that William Parker had found the formula to halt slavery's advance. "We think," said William and Ellen Craft, "a few more cases as the Christiana affair will put a damper upon slave-catchers." When they mailed the letter, Syracuse had witnessed another pocket revolution. Blacks and their white friends rejoiced; slaveholders cried foul; and many law-abiding Americans feared for the future of the Union.[35]

95

CHAPTER 5

_____

The Jerry Rescue
Breaking Bondage and
Saving America in Syracuse

[T]he enactment of the "Fugitive Slave Law" and the general acquiescence in it, under the devil-prompted speeches of politicians and devil-prompted sermons of priests, give evidence that this is a doomed and damned nation.— Liberty Party State Convention, October 1851

Though chained, he [Jerry] could not stand still; and in that narrow room, motioning as well as he could with his chained, manacled hands, and pacing up and down as well as his fetters would allow, fevered and almost frenzied with excitement, he implored us who were looking on, in such strains of fervid eloquence as I never heard before nor since from the lips of a man, to break his chains, and give him that liberty which the Declaration of Independence assumed to be the birthright of every man, and which, according to the law of love, was our duty toward a suffering brother.— The Reverend Samuel Ringgold Ward

> Freedom's battle once begun,
> Bequeathed from bleeding sire to son,
> Though baffled, oft is ever won.— William L. Crandall

When the Reverend Samuel Joseph May accepted the ministry of Syracuse's Congregational Church in 1844, the New England minister "made sure the congregation knew he was an ardent foe of slavery." After all, his abolitionism, as well as his support for Prudence Crandall's school for black children in Connecticut, had been the source of tension with previous congregations. Perhaps May, an avid reader, also knew that

96

centuries earlier his adopted home had been the spiritual and political stage for resolution of great conflict. There on the mountain, the Onondaga, the "people of the mountain," embraced the teachings of Deganawidah and spread the Peacemaker's gospel to their neighbors to form the Great League of Peace and Power, creating the *Haudenosaunee*, known to most Americans as the Iroquois or the Five Nations. The teachings of Deganawidah permitted the Mohawks or "the people of the flint," the Oneida or "the people of the standing stone," the Cayuga or the "people at the landing," and the Seneca or "the people of the great hill" to come together at the Onondaga council fire for spiritual ceremonies that mitigated conflict through reciprocal exchange and alleviated suffering through shared condolence rituals. In this way, the *Haudenosaunee* ended incessant warfare with each other and avoided evil that destroyed harmony and inflicted pain. The Onondaga ushered in a new beginning — something May and his antislavery allies sought to do in the 1850s.

Similar to their new Unitarian minister, many Syracuse residents had been raised in New England where they too had been steeped in America's Revolutionary heritage enshrining liberty and God-given inalienable rights. Many also traced their ancestry to the Pilgrims who sought to build a city on a hill, an example for the world. Since Syracuse lay in the heart of the burned-over district, an area especially touched by the evangelical fervor of the Second Great Awakening that peaked in the 1830s, many residents had quite recently come to share May's belief that slavery violated God-given higher law.[1] Some converts were even members of the Democratic Party. At mid-century, the city's unique sense of community and close-knit ties between residents ensured that Syracuse would deal with the issue of slavery in one way or another and that the consequences would be felt by all. Numbering some 21,901 whites and 370 blacks, the city was large enough to have most of the amenities of a major commercial and industrial center at the time yet small enough to have a community identity rooted in the land, in religion, in family values, in a shared Revolutionary heritage and in the New England vision of building a city on a hill.

Beginning as early as 1839, while many Americans still reeled from the Panic of 1837 and debated the annexation of Texas, which some feared might yield two slave states, a fugitive slave crisis foreshadowed how Syracuse would likely deal with slavery. In September of that year, a biracial band of Syracusans, including William M. Clarke and the city's marble dealer John Bowen, decided that J. Davenport, a wealthy Mississippi planter visiting Syracuse, would no longer have a chance to flaunt his human property — at least not in their city. They seized an opportunity to rescue his beautiful twenty-four-year-old slave Harriet Powell, likely an unfortunate victim of the fancy trade that furnished concubines for white Southern men; they grabbed her from his clutches forever as he enjoyed the merriment of a good-bye party given in his honor. Abram Nottingham of nearby Dewitt furnished a carriage and two fleet horses to spirit Harriet from Major W.A. Cook's house, where the reception was held. The rescuers hid her "at the farm of a Mr. Sheperd, near Marcellus," while Gerrit Smith made arrangements to get her safely to

Canada. The rescue sent shock waves through the city; abolitionists rejoiced while Davenport's friends "boiled over." After the incident, the divisions between antislavery and proslavery Syracusans never really healed. National controversies associated with slavery — the annexation of Texas, *Prigg v. Pennsylvania*, President James Polk's Mexican War, David Wilmot's proviso barring slavery in the Mexican cession, the Compromise of 1850, and notorious fugitive slave crises in Boston and Pennsylvania were just some of the events that accentuated differences, even as Syracuse served as an important "conduit for enslaved African-Americans who were escaping to freedom." Although criticized by some of their neighbors, leading abolitionists such as May and the Reverend Jermain W. Loguen,

THE REVEREND SAMUEL JOSEPH MAY. During the "Jerry Rescue" drama, Samuel Joseph May discarded his pacifism, saying, "I have seen that it was necessary to bring the people into direct conflict with the Government" (Library of Congress).

himself a fugitive from bondage, acted as untiring Underground Railroad conductors. Thomas James Mumford recalled that May was often "kept busy until two o'clock in the morning conducting passengers to places where they could stay until the road to Canada should be reported free from all obstructions." Loguen kept an apartment at his house "at the northeast corner of Genesee and Pine Streets" to shelter fleeing bondspersons. By mid-century most Syracusans had taken a stand on America's greatest contradiction, although some had done so more quietly than May or Smith. If they had not, however, the rigid enforcement of the Fugitive Slave Law of 1850 under President Millard Fillmore, a native of the neighboring Finger Lakes region, was about to ensure they would; most would go "on record as opposed to the law."[2]

May did not wait for the controversial bill to be enacted. As senators debated the legislation that represented a major concession to the South in the Compromise of 1850, he unleashed his attack. In a rowdy meeting in the Finger Lakes village of Cazenovia, May spoke to antislavery activists from Syracuse and the surrounding areas. Although still embracing pacifism, the Unitarian minister encouraged Americans to resist the bill, which he argued violated basic American liberties and the principles the Revolutionary Fathers had fought for. His enthusiastic audience "pledged" to continue assisting fugitive slaves even if Congress passed legislation imposing heavy penalties on persons aiding or abetting runaways. Following the meeting, May underscored his opposition to the bill as he announced "the presence of fugitive slaves in the city" and asked for donations to help them in their flight. Although May was said to be "genial and gentle," many Syracuse antislavery people regarded him as "morally heroic," particularly as he openly resisted the pending legislation. Indeed, he set the stage for civil disobedience — if not nullification — in Syracuse and many people leaned his way. The city hosted twelve major antislavery meetings in the five-year period 1845–50 and "twice as many smaller gatherings." Some of the latter were "donation parties" to raise money to help fugitive slaves.[3]

Passage of the Fugitive Slave Bill on September 18, 1850, fueled resentment throughout much of the North but in Onondaga it precipitated a veritable a torrent of protest. "Only eight days" after Fillmore signed the bill into law, May and his abolitionist allies convened a public meeting at Syracuse City Hall. Alfred H. Hovey chaired the assembly.

"The Colored man must be protected — he must be secure among us," declared the city's Democratic mayor as he opened the meeting at "early candle light." Evincing morality and religiosity, he stated, "We are right — this is a righteous and holy cause." Leading black abolitionists also spoke and they stirred the hearts and minds of the biracial audience. "It throws us back upon the natural and inalienable right of self-defence — self protection," asserted the Reverend Samuel Ringgold Ward, a man whom Frederick Douglass regarded as the leading black orator of the time. "Let the men who would execute this bill beware," warned Ward. Likewise, Loguen announced boldly that henceforth he would use force to protect himself and others. "I don't respect this law — I don't fear it — I won't obey it!" declared the fugitive slave preacher. "It outlaws me, and I outlaw it, and the men who attempt to enforce it on me. I will not live a slave, and if force is employed to re-enslave me, I shall make preparations to meet the crisis as becomes a man."[4] Such sentiments sealed the resolve of many Syracusans against the Fugitive Slave Law and they vowed to make it a "dead letter." As they branded it "an outrage upon the inalienable rights of man and a daring assault upon the palladium of American liberties," they formed a biracial vigilance committee to help prevent fugitive slaves from being captured and returned to bondage. They also arranged appropriate funding for the vigilance committee. Like Revolutionary minutemen, these antislavery militants established the tolling of the bells of the First Presbyterian Church as an alarm. "On hearing that signal," recalled May, "we would all repair at once to the [agreed upon] spot, ready to do and to dare whatever might seem to be necessary." If such measures did not test the patience of Fillmore and Secretary of State Daniel Webster who had been championing the new bill in the North, the "spirited meetings" of William Lloyd Garrison's American Antislavery Society, which were held in Syracuse in early May 1851, certainly did. Delegates promised to "trample" on the Fugitive Slave Law.[5]

Later that month, Webster embarked on a whirlwind tour through New England and Upstate New York. "There is but one all-absorbing question and that is the preservation of the Union," declared Webster, and he emphasized that the faithful execution of the new Fugitive Slave Law was the means to that end. He reasoned that resistance to the law was treason. From the balcony of Syracuse's Frazee Hall on May 26, the veteran Massachusetts politician threw down the gauntlet before abolitionists, saying "Depend upon it, the Law will be executed in its spirit and to its letter. It will be executed in all the great cities—here in Syracuse, in the midst of the next Anti-Slavery convention, if the occasion shall arise." He received applause from law-abiding listeners but a "murmur of disapproval" resonated from antislavery militants who sought to make the city Upstate New York's cradle of liberty.

Webster's challenge, followed closely by two fugitive slave renditions in the State of New York, readied Syracuse abolitionists for action. In August 1851, the slave hunter Benjamin S. Rust seized a black cook named Daniel aboard the steamer *Buckeye State* anchored in Buffalo harbor. Brandishing an arrest warrant issued by United States Commissioner H.K. Smith, Rust subdued Daniel with "a heavy blow, upon the head, with a large billet of wood, which knocked him back into the cook room, where he fell upon the stove and was badly burned." Rust took Daniel before the commissioner who remanded him, "with blood oozing out of his mouth and nostrils," to his former owner's agent. Fortunately, some antislavery activists saved Daniel by bringing him before Judge Alfred Conkling on a writ of habeas corpus. Conkling freed Daniel and the fugitive slave's supporters had Rust convicted for assault; he paid a "paltry fine of fifty dollars." The second disturbing case was that of a "recently married" black tailor named John Bolding living in Poughkeepsie, New York, who was remanded to a South Carolina slaveholder. Fortunately, several New Yorkers banded together to raise $2,000 to purchase his liberty, saving him from bondage and separation from his new wife.[6]

In the fall of 1851, Syracusans—unlike residents of the Mid-Atlantic States or the Upper South—generally agreed that the weather had been "delightful." October brought cooler nights and the mornings were fresh with mist hovering over the green valleys and meadows surrounding the growing city. At this time of the year, Syracuse seemed "more pleasant" than any other place in the Republic, the ideal setting for the two major events scheduled for the first day of the month. On the knoll where the campus of Syracuse University is now situated, "an immense crowd" gathered in the morning to enjoy the exhibits and refreshments of the Fair and Cattle Show of the Onondaga County Agricultural Society. The fair's organizing committee had also scheduled sports and recreational activities for the festive occasion; everything seemed to be going as planned on a "beautiful day." In the center of the city, the Congregational Church hosted the state convention of the Liberty Party and a "feisty" audience listened to rousing speeches.[7]

At noon, William Henry, best known as Jerry, was still at work at his bench at Frederic Morell's cooperage shop in Syracuse's First Ward, earning good wages and enjoying his freedom. Having been born in Buncombe County, North Carolina, around 1812, he was about 39 years old. His mother, Celia or Ceil, was a mulatto slave of a planter named McReynolds, originally from Tennessee. Although the identity of Jerry's father remains uncertain, rumors at the time of his rescue suggested that his master had fathered him. If that was so, Jerry was three-quarters white. When McReynolds died, his widow married William Henry and Jerry became his property. Henry apparently took a liking to the young slave and gave him his name. Around 1818, after a roundabout trip through Georgia, Tennessee, Kentucky, and Illinois, Henry settled near the town of Hannibal in Marion County, Missouri. He brought with him much of his moveable property, including his slaves. Jerry learned carpentry, became literate, and eventually assisted his master in his business affairs. Henry had confidence in Jerry and assigned him "clerical matters." During Jerry's youth, the Second Great Awakening swept Missouri and he embraced evangelical Christianity, married, and fathered children. The exact date and circumstances of his flight from Missouri remain uncertain but, although some evidence suggests that he may have escaped as early as 1843, most scholars believe that he fled in 1844.[8] His flight deeply affected Henry and, thinking Jerry had fled to Wisconsin or Illinois, the slaveholder had his son-in-law Joshua Gentry travel to Milwaukee and Chicago to try to locate the runaway. A few days before he died, Henry sold his missing slave to a man named Miller who in turn sold him to William Henry's stepson John McReynolds on July 8, 1851. By this time, Jerry was in Syracuse.

Evidence suggests that toward the end of 1849 or at the beginning of 1850, Jerry decided to head for Canada. On his way, he stopped in Syracuse, found the city agreeable, landed a job, and decided to stay. Syracuse's former mayor Charles F. Williston, Jerry's first employer in the city, praised him, saying that he was a diligent worker. Jerry worked for him for about a year. Williston also noted that he had been "carefully educated" and spent much of his time reading newspapers, notably the *New York Evening Post* and *New York Tribune*.[9] The former mayor liked his employee so much that he began purchasing newspapers "mainly" for Jerry to read until the latter left to earn "better wages" in Syracuse's flourishing barrel-making business.[10] A skilled cooper, Jerry was still "quietly at work" finishing a barrel for Syracuse's salt works when United States Marshal Henry W. Allen, assisted by deputy marshals from Canandaigua, Rochester, and Auburn, as well as a special police force, arrested him for a misdemeanor. Allen actually waited outside Jerry's place of work while Deputy Marshal Bemis executed the warrant. Believing the charge to be a mistake, Jerry allowed himself to be handcuffed and taken to the office of United States Commissioner Joseph F. Sabine, paradoxically a man who "favored abolition" and had refused a request for an arrest warrant from McReynolds's agent James Lear three weeks earlier. When the marshals escorted Jerry into Sabine's office, they informed him of the true nature of his arrest — McReynolds claimed him as a slave and sought to return him to Missouri.[11]

News of Jerry's arrest spread rapidly throughout the city as Marshal Allen's carriage descended North Salina and crossed the Salina Street Bridge into the city center. An alarmed Charles Wheaton rushed from his hardware store to the Congregational Church on East Genesee to inform the antislavery convention; they adjourned the meeting and led by Gerrit Smith repaired immediately to Sabine's office to find the manacled Jerry already before the commissioner. Abner Bates rang the Congregational Church's bell and William L. Crandall, a writer for the *Syracuse Standard*, chimed "three strokes" on the First Presbyterian Church bell signaling the emergency. "Revolutionary Syracuse," said one journalist "sounded the tocsin." During the rest of the day, vigilance committee members ensured "considerable excitement" by intermittently ringing the bells. Bates's pealing of the Old Congregational Church bell gave rise to the myth that it "cracked that day in the cause of liberty."[12] Crowds swarmed to the city center from the fair grounds and other activities.

When May arrived, people were already crammed into the commissioner's office. Sheriff Samuel Smith had come from Marion County to present the deed of sale from Miller to McReynolds, which proved the latter's ownership of Jerry. Joseph Loomis and James R. Lawrence, two well-known attorneys, represented McReynolds. The hearing got underway about one o'clock with the slaveholder's agent James Lear identifying Jerry and testifying that he had known him and his mother in Marion County from 1820 "till 1845." Leonard Gibbs and Gerrit Smith, who had volunteered to defend an increasingly nervous Jerry, resented Sabine's quick start to the hearing. Gibbs sought to delay proceedings by raising objections, including a demand that Jerry's shackles be removed. Sabine indicated that he did not have the authority to order them taken off and "waived all objections aside." Gibbs followed up by demanding an adjournment, which the commissioner also declined. Had Sabine's office not started to overflow, Jerry probably would have been remanded to McReynolds early that afternoon. As people pushed and shoved to get in, however, and then began "spilling down the stairs" and refused to disperse, Sabine became visibly anxious. By half past two, the rowdiness of the ever-growing crowd had become so dangerous and threatening that it disrupted proceedings and the commissioner adjourned the hearing "for the purpose of obtaining a larger room."[13]

As May suggested that Sabine move proceedings to either the Congregational Church or to Syracuse City Hall, somebody shouted, "The shackles must be taken off." Standing on a box or a safe, William L. Salmon, a tanner from Oswego attending the antislavery convention, ignited antislavery folk in the room as he yelled, "We stand no chance before this Commissioner."[14] He shouted, "I move we don't go without the fugitive," which further aroused the gathering. Jerry too was moved. Sensing support, he seized the opportunity to escape. "After a hard scuffle" with one of his guards and helped by a "sympathetic" spectator named Charles Merrick, he bolted through the doorway. Before the guards had a chance to react, "a strong and powerful man, slammed the door after him and held it fast" to prevent the deputies from laying their hands on him. When Marshal Allen's men forced open the door, Jerry had begun to descend the stairs and the crowd had closed in after him. A bystander grabbed Marshall Allen around the waist, stopping him in his tracks. "Hampered by the manacles," Jerry tumbled head-over-heels down the stairs, injuring himself as he fell. Struggling for freedom, he got up immediately and made for the street, sending the crowd into an uproar. The deputies, pushing aside the spectators, endeavored to scurry after him but several blacks, including Prince Jackson, moved "to obstruct" them. Jerry raced along "Water and Genesee Streets, through Market Square, to Lock Street, and over the Lock Street bridge." There, officers Peter Way and Russell Lowell overtook him and a furious fight ensued. Much of Jerry's clothing was torn off. Witnesses stressed that Jerry fought "like a tiger," even though he was manacled and repeatedly clubbed. They recounted him screaming, "For God's sake, kill me, but don't take me back."[15] One man later penned a note to the *Syracuse Journal*, writing that "Jerry's appeals to his captors when taken would have melted any but hearts of flint." Had Jerry been a wild beast, he could scarcely have been treated with less humanity."[16]

Aided by fellow officers, Way and Lowell fettered Jerry and commandeered a local truckman's wagon. They threw Jerry on it and "two policemen sat on him" to keep him still. Spectators continued to gather and were horrified by the sight of the bruised, bleeding, and shackled man some of them knew and liked. "The passions of the multitudes," said Loguen," rose to a "blood heat." May reported that "the people, citizens and strangers, were alike indignant." So was Jerry; he remained in a "perfect rage, a fury of passion" having been stripped of his liberty and suffering the embarrassment of being conveyed to the police office before thousands of onlookers. Marshal Allen had him secured in a back room guarded by deputies Woodruff, Green, Morrow, Welch, Forman, Lowell, and Way. Vigilance committee members gathered at Abner Bates's office on Fulton Street and agreed to reconvene later in the afternoon to devise a "plan of action" to prevent Jerry's return to bondage.[17]

Fearing another rescue attempt, Marshall Allen met with Onondaga County Sheriff William C. Gardiner and he commanded him to order out the militia. When Gardiner called out the Syracuse Citizens Corps, the National Guard, and the Washington Artillery, Wheaton objected, arguing that "keeping the peace was a different thing from hunting slaves—that the sheriff was an officer of the State, and the State knew nobody as a slave." He arranged for Colonel Origen Vanderburgh of the 51st Regiment to countermand the sheriff's order on the basis that the latter did not have the legal authority to call the militia. Vanderburgh sent written notice to Lieutenant Prendergast at the armory, ordering him to disband the assembled units. Meanwhile Jerry, constantly ranting and raving at the police office, remained in such a frightful state that the Syracuse police chief asked May and Ward to come to calm him down. May arrived first. When alone with the prisoner, he whispered, "Jerry, we are going to rescue you; do be more quiet."[18]

Moments afterward, Ward joined them and he later described Jerry's state. "Though chained, he could not stand still; and in that narrow room, motioning as well as he could with his chained manacled hands, and pacing up and down as well as his fetters would allow, fevered and almost frenzied with excitement," remembered the black preacher, Jerry asked us "in such strains of fervid eloquence as I never heard before nor since from the lips of man, to break his chains, and give him that liberty which the Declaration of Independence assumed to be the birthright of every man." The captured fugitive told them that he had been tricked into surrendering by Deputy Marshal Bemis. "If I had known what they were about," said Jerry, "do you think I should have *let that little ordinary man put irons on me?*" He ended his tirade, invoking what he considered to be the Revolutionary legacy. "Gentlemen, is this a free country? Why did my fathers fight the British," he asked, "if one of their poor sons is to be treated this way?" Citing the Declaration of Independence once again, he requested that his chains be broken.[19]

When Ward left Jerry, he joined Charles C. Foote of Michigan to speak to a "large and excited crowd gathered around the building." Inspired by his visit with Jerry, Ward gave "a heart-stirring speech" stating that the detestable Fugitive Slave Law contradicted "the first principles of the Declaration of Independence." Afterward, urging "all friends of Liberty [to] stand by and see the affair through," Foote provoked "frenzy." When Ward left the square with Gerrit Smith, the two men walked arm-in-arm, "defying racial proscriptions" of the day as they made their way to the vigilance committee meeting at Dr. Hiram Hoyt's office. They joined with twenty-five others to plot the rescue that Gerrit Smith wanted and demanded. "It is not unlikely the Commissioner will release Jerry if the examination is suffered to proceed," asserted Smith, "but the moral effect of such an acquittal will be as nothing to a bold and forcible rescue." He argued that "a forcible rescue will demonstrate the strength of public opinion against the possible legality of slavery and this Fugitive Slave Law." Smith also thought that a rescue would "honor Syracuse and be a powerful example everywhere." After the sight of a bruised, bleeding, and battered Jerry, May too was ready to discard his pacifism. "I have seen that it was necessary to bring the people into direct conflict with the Government," concluded May. In so doing, he thought that the administration might "understand that it has transcended its limits—and must recede."[20] May was adamant, however, that rescuers avoid injuring marshals and policemen. "If any one is to be hurt in this fray," he said, "I hope it may be one of our own party."[21]

When Sabine resumed the hearing at 5:30 that afternoon, attorneys D.D. Hillis, Leroy Morgan, and Henry Sheldon defended Jerry, replacing Gibbs and Smith who attended the meeting in Hoyt's office, which Loguen dubbed the "Congress of Freedom." Smith and his co-conspirators

GERRIT SMITH. When deputy marshals held Jerry in a city jail, Gerrit Smith told the Syracuse Vigilance Committee that a forcible rescue would "honor Syracuse and be a powerful example everywhere" (Library of Congress).

agreed to engage "a skillful and bold driver, in a strong buggy with the fleetest horse" to carry Jerry about the city until the driver was sure that he had shaken any pursuers. He was then to leave Jerry with two men "waiting to receive his charge" at an agreed upon place in the city center. Wheaton, whose store was located close to the police office, told the vigilance committee that he would make clubs, axes, and crowbars available for rescuers to use in their assault on the building. When they ended the meeting, the unruly crowd in the square had begun to throw stones, rocks, and other objects through the windows of the police office. With persons inside fearing for their safety and the uproarious mob "drowning out testimony," Sabine proposed adjournment. Wanting to expedite

Jerry's return to Missouri, Marshal Allen insisted on continuing. However, when a rock "barely missed" Sabine's head around seven o'clock, the commissioner postponed the hearing. Proceedings would never resume.[22]

When Allen left the building, he ordered his deputies to keep Jerry locked in the backroom until the crowd had dispersed. They were then to take him to the penitentiary. But the multitudes refused to leave; their numbers and their excitement "continued to increase." Loguen said that more than 2,500 persons—perhaps even 8,000—swarmed into the square. Many were women as "hats and bonnets" were everywhere. The mayor called for dispersal but, knowing that the militia had been disbanded and they outnumbered the police, the people stayed on the square and "cheered the speeches." When the vigilance committee members arrived, the clamor mounted and, hearing it in the backroom, Jerry went into a rant, screaming "he would rather die than go back to slavery." As his guards sought to quiet him, Ira Cobb, later accused of turning out the lights in the police office so the marshals could not identify rescuers, said, "Let him talk. His words will be sought after as much as the words of Washington." At about "half past 8 o'clock" the rescuers initiated a full-scale assault. Men with "clubs, axes, and crobars [sic]" broke down doors, smashed windows, and entered the building. Moses Sumner, John Hornbeck, and William L. Salmon, accompanied by militant blacks— Enoch Reed, Peter Hallenbeck, William Gray, and Loguen—led the attack. Somebody, likely Cobb, shut off the gas, thus shrouding the building in darkness. To reach Jerry in the back room, the attackers used a ten-foot hemlock beam as a "battering ram" to break down the interior wall, which sent Jerry's guards into a panic. Marshal Fitch fired two shots, slightly injuring one of the attackers and then, fearing for his life, he jumped from a window on the canal side of the building, "breaking his arm as he fell upon the stone coping below." The other guards hid in a closet and fearfully listened to Salmon urge on the attackers. "Go ahead; Oswego is here to stand by you," he yelled. Warning the deputies inside and encouraging Jerry, he also shouted, "Open the way old Oswego is coming." Before the battering ram crushed the partition, a guard opened the door and ordered Jerry out saying, "Go out there among those folks!—you can quell this riot—go right off!" The rescuers grabbed Jerry, hoisted him up as his fetters prevented him from walking, and he was "borne away" in triumph to a carriage waiting by Brintnall's Hotel.[23]

When the buggy pulled away, an observer said "a universal feeling of satisfaction" prevailed. In addition to the multitudes in the streets, "spectators of both sexes" peered from neighboring buildings. Loguen claimed that "few families in the city were unrepresented among the thousands"; he said that it became a grand movement to spread "liberty to the continent." Martin Stowell, a Massachusetts artisan who later participated in the Anthony Burns drama, was in Syracuse; he said people cheered "for nearly half an hour" after Jerry was out of sight. Few knew that the black man driving the buggy carrying Jerry was Samuel Thompson; only five persons knew that he would first be taken to a house in the city center where a tinsmith named Peter Lily and a black teenager Susan Watkins, later known as Auntie Watson, hacked off Jerry's shackles and dressed him in women's clothing. On a "beautiful star-lit evening," they then snuck him into the house of Caleb Davis, a butcher and a "staunch Democrat" who lived at the corner of East Genesee and Orange Streets. Davis was not a man whom authorities would have suspected of sheltering a fugitive slave. The day ended with "feelings roused" in Syracuse and telegraphs transmitting news of the excitement "over the whole Union." The *Syracuse Journal* reported that "the persons in this city who do not rejoice in the deliverance of this poor captive ... are few indeed."[24]

Jerry remained hidden at Davis's house from Wednesday night until Sunday while Marshal Allen and his deputies searched and began to suspect that Jerry had already made it to Canada. On Sunday evening, however, when the butcher left for his usual rounds to buy beef from farmers north of the city, he had a pair of swift horses loaned to him by Jason Woodruff, another Democrat and a former mayor. Jerry, armed with a handgun, lay concealed under sacking and straw in the wagon. Caleb Davis managed to get out of the city unnoticed before Marshal Allen got wind of the scheme. Luckily for Jerry, James Davis had ridden north earlier on Sunday to check the escape route and bribed the tollgate keeper at the town of Cicero. When Allen's deputies followed Caleb Davis in hot pursuit, the keeper stalled them by pretending to be asleep. At Brewerton Bridge, Caleb Davis rendezvoused with Jason Hoyt, who drove Jerry to the town of Mexico. There, Orson Ames, an antislavery man who sheltered many fugitive slaves on their way to Canada on the Underground Railroad, hid him.[25] Worrying that the marshals might discover Jerry, Ames took him to Deacon Asa Beebe's farm on Mexico Point the very next day. The Beebes "secreted him in the barn" for about two weeks while they made arrangements with Sidney and Olive Clarke in Oswego County to get Jerry to Canada. The Clarkes were also active on the Underground Railroad and Jerry was just one of "an estimated 125 runaway slaves" they helped escape to Canada. Clarke found a Great Lakes skipper willing to carry Jerry across the lake and four days later he gave Jerry "a small sum of money" and put him on a schooner destined for Kingston, Ontario, where he found work with a chair-maker named Chester Harris. Jerry lived as a freeman until October 1853 when he died of tuberculosis.[26]

While most Syracuse blacks and whites rejoiced when they heard that Jerry had made it safely to Canada, Southerners—and some Northerners—did not celebrate. Coming on the heels of the Christiana riot, the rescue seemed to confirm slaveholders' fears that their ability to reclaim runaway slaves was increasingly at risk in a North infected by abolitionism. The *Daily Morning News* in Savannah, Georgia, printed an antislavery newspaper's account of the Jerry rescue criticizing its writer for saying "everything was all right, it was not even a mob." Like most white Southerners, the paper's editor blamed such abolitionists as William Lloyd Garrison, Wendell Phillips, and Charles Sumner for the affair. He said their fanatical "higher-law" doctrines particularly affected free blacks.[27] He contended that the free black population in the North had become "a festering sore upon the body politic"—one that contributed to the lawlessness evident in the "Christiana and Syracuse outrages." Some Southerners demanded that free states pass more stringent Black Laws to prevent slaves from escaping north of the Mason Dixon line. The *Raleigh Register*, for example, called for Northern states to pass exclusion laws prohibiting blacks from settling within their borders. Southerners also renewed demands that Northerners stand by the Compromise of 1850 and faithfully execute the Fugitive Slave Law. Insisting that the "extreme penalty of the law" be brought to bear on those involved in rescuing Jerry, many Southerners wanted the administration to charge the main actors with treason, the policy adopted in the case of the Christiana rioters. Southerners also re-affirmed their embrace of the Georgia Platform. "The body of the southern people are loyal to the Union — they deprecate any and every circumstance or occurrence by which the bonds which hold it together may be relaxed," stated the *Richmond Dispatch*. "But they will not consent to live under it, if its laws may be set at defiance with impunity."[28] For white Southerners, respect of the Fugitive Slave Law was a must.

A significant number of white Northerners who worried about law and order as a result of growing crime rates and urban riots during the antebellum period shared the white Southerners' concerns. Many had supported Daniel Webster and believed in respecting the compromises of the Constitution and preserving the Union as it was. Several Northern newspapers adopted this stance. In a hard-hitting article entitled "The Syracuse Outrage," the *New York Courier and Enquirer* compared Jerry's rescue to earlier events in Boston and criticized white abolitionists. "The law was violently trampled upon in this [Jerry's] case, in much the same way as in that of Shadrach," said the paper, adding that in the latter "the offense was committed almost exclusively by black persons, and was but the thought and act of the moment." The editor contended that the well-planned Jerry rescue, "strikes at the essential principle of all law and goes to destroy every element that make[s] human legislation authoritative and effectual." Some Syracusans agreed with him and did not like what had gone on in their city; the *Syracuse Star* voiced their concerns. Shortly after the rescue, the paper sardonically noted "it appears that mob law, violence, and outrage are triumphant in Syracuse for the time." Reprinting an article from the *Newark Daily Advertiser*, the *Star*'s editor suggested that he too was not "much surprised to see the brethren of the black" rescue Jerry but he considered it "melancholy to see the white man" destroy order that is "sometimes impossible to restore." A few days later, he pointed the finger at May, asking him whether he had reflected on how such a rescue might affect law and order as well as the nation's ability to survive. Referring to the Georgia Platform, he inquired "If such resistance were not overpowered by the Federal Government would it not be virtually, dissolution of the Union?"[29]

Law-and-order sentiments also underpinned attacks on Colonel Vanderburgh for having countermanded Sheriff Gardiner's ordering out of the militia. Seeking to make Vanderburgh a scapegoat, the *Albany Register* exclaimed, "The military authorities refused to act when legally called upon." Other New York papers joined this chorus. The *Journal of Commerce* viewed the Jerry rescue as a test for state authorities, noting that "the open resistance to a law of the United States at Syracuse will afford opportunity to Gov[ernor Washington] Hunt and his advisers to show how far they were honest in declaring that while the Fugitive Slave Law remained a law of the land, it must be obeyed." Some New Yorkers thought Syracuse should be taught a lesson and they recommended federal authorities remove the import duties on salt that protected the city's salt works from foreign competition. Responding, the antislavery *Syracuse Journal* complained that "the *N.Y. Express* is determined to plug up our Salt Springs unless we repent and join the Castle Garden lovers of law and order." The latter comprised a group of businessmen who wanted authorities to check the spread of what they viewed as disorder, anarchy, or even a "pocket revolution" aimed at nullifying federal legislation. "The assumption that the Fugitive Slave Law is 'no law,' is utterly false," asserted the conservative *Religious Recorder*, voicing the same concern. "It is an enactment of the national legislature.... It is just as fully a law as are the Post Office and the Revenue laws, and so far it claims respect from every citizen."[30]

In light of these sentiments, some antebellum Americans expected federal authorities to follow the heavy-handed policy adopted to deal with the Christiana rioters. A letter to the *Syracuse Standard* from a writer using the pseudonym Coke speculated that "nothing but the death of some of our citizens at the end of a halter will satisfy a northern President and some of his functionaries in this city." Referring to the treason trials in Pennsylvania, Coke wondered "whether the new fangled doctrine of Treason will find tools abject enough to dig graves for innocent men in the city." Another writer warned Syracusans to "*look out for your necks*" and sarcastically suggested that "we are progressing rapidly to the principles of freedom and if we keep on as fast as we are going, we shall soon put *Austria* and *Russia* to shame.[31] Two weeks after the rescue, a suspicious journalist wrote, "It was rumored about town yesterday that a number of arrests for Treason were to be made in the city today." He, along with other antislavery folk, believed the Fillmore administration would attempt to strike "wholesome terror" into the hearts and minds of any Northerner contemplating resistance to the law. May told his sister-in-law Charlotte G. Coffin that the administration was about to bring "charges of treason against himself and other conspirators." Commenting on the government's tardiness in charging Jerry's rescuers, Charles Wheaton wrote to Gerrit Smith, saying, "I am told the officials delayed their proceedings some time, with the hope that they might reach *you, Mr. May and me*; as the ring leaders. They will do it if they can." May and Smith actually viewed indictment as a chance to popularize their views and thus hoped to be arrested — something that did not happen after the Pennsylvania jurors in Castner Hanway's case failed to deliver the guilty verdict that the administration wanted. Smith, in particular, would have welcomed a national stage to argue the unconstitutionality of the Fugitive Slave Law on "seventeen different grounds." When the United States District Attorney indicted thirteen men under the Fugitive Slave Law and excluded the two of them, May also "seemed disappointed that the government had 'ignored' [them]." The administration would actually have indicted several more rescuers but some blacks, including Loguen, fled to Canada. When the preacher departed, the *Syracuse Standard* remarked that "the cheeks of every American should burn with shame that such a man is compelled to fly to a monarchical government to preserve his liberty." The flight of blacks precipitated rumors that Fillmore might request an extradition treaty from Canadian authorities. Such a request was not made and, if it had been, it probably would have been refused as British officials had consistently turned down demands for the extradition of fugitive slaves since the late 1830s.[32]

Deprived of an opportunity to popularize their views in treason trials, May, Smith, and their allies moved quickly to exploit the administration's decision to convene a grand jury at Auburn to charge the rescuers under the Fugitive Slave Law and, later on, to hear their cases at Buffalo and Albany. The abolitionists arranged for reduced-price train tickets to be sold to antislavery activists who wished to attend Judge Alfred Conkling's hearings at Auburn. They publicized their offer, emphasizing that support for the accused would be "strengthened by the countenance and advice of their numerous friends in the city." And they had many friends — including May, Hoyt, Bates, Crandall, and Wheaton to mention only a few who made the trip to Auburn. Senator William Seward, "in fine health and spirits" after providing bail for the accused, attended as well. Equally striking was the presence of Syracuse women, especially given continuing rumors of possible further indictments for treason. On October 21, 1851, some 38 Syracuse women —17 of them single or widowed— had their names recorded in the *Syracuse Journal* as having made the journey to Auburn. Most of them had probably been on the square during Jerry's rescue three weeks earlier.[33] In the end, the only defendant convicted under the Fugitive Slave Law was the Syracuse black Enoch Reed, who died before his appeal was heard. A jury acquitted the militant Oswego tanner Crandall; the juries in two other cases were deadlocked; the remaining cases, initially postponed until 1852, were dropped, underscoring the failure of the Fillmore administration's stringent enforcement.

Other events in Syracuse also indicated strong popular support of Jerry, much of it founded upon the city's Revolutionary legacy. In the *Syracuse Journal* of October 9, 1851, May and his compatriots announced a mass rally "for the friends of Human Freedom — opponents of the so-called Fugitive Slave Law," to be held five days later at the Syracuse City Hall. Their invitation, which also said "Let the Women of Onondaga be there too," was signed by some 150 persons, many of them women. This assembly, which some Syracusans also called the Congress of Freedom, built on a Liberty Party meeting the day after the rescue. It resolved that "the enactment of the 'Fugitive Slave Law,' and the general acquiescence in it, under the influence of the devil-prompted speeches of politicians and devil prompted sermons of priests, give evidence that this is a doomed and damned nation, we, nevertheless, cannot forbear to derive some little hope from the recent resistance to kidnappers in Pennsylvania and from the resistance to them yesterday in Syracuse that a patient and long suffering God has not left this superlatively wicked nation to perish."[34]

Attended by some 500 persons, the Syracuse City Hall meeting proved to be a resounding success, even as rumors about impending treason indictments ran rampant. May rose to the occasion as he implored the audience to be the "conscience of the nation." He argued that "the only claim which a law can have to our respect and obedience *is its justice*." That alone, he reasoned, justified the actions of the rescuers two weeks before. "The citizens of Syracuse and of Onondaga County did not, on the 1st of October, violate the *law*," proclaimed May, "they set at naught an unrighteous, cruel edict; they trampled tyranny."[35] The assembled claimed to be fighting for the "great principles of legal right and justice which our [Revolutionary] fathers supposed to have been settled." May and his compatriots stated that a new tyranny of "Slave power" stretched across the land and now threatened Central New York. They approved a series of resolutions entitled "Address from the Freemen of Onondaga" and harshly criticized the Fillmore administration for considering to "stretch the Law of Treason over men who have done for the colored American" what it applauded Louis Kossuth for doing in Europe. Denouncing again the Fugitive Slave Law for denying the accused a trial by jury and suspending the writ of habeas corpus, the convention declared "so we now reaffirm — that we dare not, we will not, obey this thrice accursed statute, be the consequences to our persons and property be what they may." The convention participants also made sure they transmitted their challenge to the proper authorities: they ordered their resolutions on "domestic tyranny" to be delivered to the President of the United States and the governors of every state in the Union. Finally, they sought to extend their "pocket revolution" saying, "We counsel that there be immediate and thorough correspondence held, and other suitable efforts made, to gather meetings in different parts of the State, and secure a universal uprising of the people, in order to re-establish constitutional right and justice."[36]

Unrelenting in their claim that "their sole object was to strike the chains from the limbs of a man entitled to liberty," Smith, May, Ward, Loguen, and others rejected being labeled as lawless, reckless, or fanatics. They saw themselves as much more than that. They were Americans who had learned from their Revolutionary fathers that "RESISTANCE TO TYRANTS IS OBEDIENCE TO GOD." They believed that Americans who espoused this motto yet enslaved — or even countenanced the enslavement of — fellow human beings were "liars and hypocrites." They also underscored the duplicity of American newspapers that denounced the freeing of Jerry, saying "had a man been rescued from Slavery in any part of Europe, in the manner of the Syracuse rescue, the act would have been applauded from one end of the country to the other." The Syracuse abolitionists saw their mission as that of the Revolutionary fathers — ensuring American liberties. At a meeting convened in late November 1851, they again honored their Revolutionary legacy and they resolved that slavery was "antagonistic to God's eternal law and the Declaration of Independence." The men who rescued Jerry acted with the same "impulse of the spirit that made Bunker Hill, Lexington, Concord, Saratoga and Yorktown holy ground."[37]

Just like their forefathers or the men and women who landed on the shores of Massachusetts Bay more than two hundred years earlier, these Syracusans and many of their antebellum compatriots saw themselves as "revolutionists and rebels," arrayed against tyranny and setting an example for America and for the world. Simply put, they were saving America and they were proud of it. Gerrit Smith stressed this in the second annual Jerry Rescue Celebration. "We admit, that we are rescuers of JERRY.... If we did not all use our hands in rescuing him: if we did not all participate in the counsels, which resulted in his rescue: if we did all make ourselves legally liable for it," proclaimed Smith, "the fact, that we all approve of it, makes us all his morally responsible rescuers: — that is to be his rescuers in the highest sense." In concluding, Smith vowed to continue the fight, saying "We must rescue every other [slave].... We cannot recede." For many antebellum blacks and whites, men or women, renowned or ordinary, perhaps Henry C. Wright summed things up best when he said that "the work of the Revolution is going on." In 1852, members of the Jerry Rescue Celebration Committee obviously shared his view when they corresponded with William Lloyd Garrison about the challenge of sheltering the 5,000 persons expected to arrive in the city. "The best possible preparations will be made," it said, "well knowing, that if need be, the descendants of the men who marked their pathway over the frozen earth of Valley Forge with their blood, for Independence, can for one day suffer the inconvenience

JERRY RESCUE STATUE. In rescuing Jerry, many Syracusans turned to the example of their Revolutionary fathers as they resisted the enforcement of the Fugitive Slave Law and declared, "RESISTANCE TO TYRANTS IS OBEDIENCE TO GOD."

of an 'October sun,' in commemorating a practical illustration of the immortal Principles of the Declaration of Independence." Crandall, that ordinary yet most remarkable Oswego man, penned a few lines: "Freedom's battle once begun, Bequeathed from bleeding sire to son, Though baffled oft, is ever won." But the cases of Joshua Glover, Anthony Burns, and Margaret Garner were about to prove that the Revolutionary struggle was not won quite yet.[38]

CHAPTER 6

Rescuing Joshua Glover and Guarding American Liberties

Though few in number, let us be faithful to ourselves, to our trembling fugitive brothers, and to our God. Let your resolves be bold, let them come from the heart, speaking the voice of men who are determined upon the resolution of Patrick Henry— "Liberty or death."— Lewis Johnson

Citizens of Milwaukee! Shall we have Star Chamber proceedings here? and shall a Man be dragged back to Slavery from our Free Soil, *without an open trial of his right to Liberty?*— Sherman Booth

...[T]he fugitive slave law is not the law of Wisconsin.... The fugitive slave law cannot be enforced in Wisconsin.... The people will not suffer it; they understand too well that great charter of rights which is the birthright of every man, whatever be the color of his skin....—*Racine Advocate*

Arriving at his cabin on the night of Friday, March 10, 1854, after a busy week at Duncan Sinclair's sawmill some four miles from the town of Racine, Joshua Glover must have been glad to stir the coals in the stove and shake off the cold. The winter, his second in Wisconsin after escaping from slavery in Missouri, had been difficult and lately a heavy snow storm followed by "alternating freezing and thawing" had made it tougher. For Glover, it must have seemed that this Wisconsin winter did not to want to end. He also was probably exhausted from sleeping poorly the night before after hearing from the black woman who had been living with him that two white men had come around the day before. Fugitive slaves did not like strangers knocking at the door, especially unannounced or at odd times. Glover's friend, suspecting they were slave catchers and after her, fled earlier in the day. Entering an empty cabin that evening, the skilled carpenter would have had to light the candles himself. The arrival of William Alby and Nelson Turner, two black friends, must have lifted his spirits—particularly when he saw that the latter, a freed slave from Natchez, Mississippi, had a deck of cards and a bottle of whiskey. Glover was reputed to be a hard worker, but the good-looking, five-foot ten-inch mulatto was also a man who enjoyed life's pleasures. Most accounts suggest that he liked drinking, playing cards, and courting women. In early March 1854, rumors surfaced that he had taken to "romancing Turner's wife." Perhaps that explains why the Natchez mulatto "betrayed" Glover and made a couple of trips to St. Louis, where he met with Benammi Stone Garland, Glover's former master.[1]

Garland, a wealthy planter who had moved to Missouri from Lynchburg, Virginia, purchased the thirty-six-year-old Glover at a New Year's Day auction held in front of the St. Louis courthouse. The slaveholder was surely impressed with Glover's "strength," "stamina," and many skills. Garland must have been convinced that Glover had what it took to be a real asset on his Prairie House farm some "four miles west of the city by way of the St. Charles Plank Road." By the standards of the day, Garland's 300-acre farm with a growing herd of dairy and beef cattle, swine, horses, and some 200 acres of cultivated fields was a significant Midwestern operation. Glover joined five other bondspersons, including two female slaves who attended to the needs of Garland's wife Isabelle, the mistress of the big-house, and their three young sons. Apparently, Garland guessed correctly about Glover; it was not long before he came to regard his powerful new slave as the "foreman" of his Prairie House operation. What he did not know was that Glover would not assume that role for long. In the spring of 1852, reportedly after a night of heavy drinking, Joshua Glover decided that he would not be a slave any longer; he stole across the Mississippi and headed north, arriving in Racine "six to seven weeks" later. On May 17, 1852, a disappointed Garland published an advertisement offering a two-hundred-dollar reward for his "ashy black" runaway slave probably wearing "a pair of black satinet pantaloons, [a] pair of heavy kip boots, an old-fashioned black dress coat, and an osnaburg shirt." His advertisement proved worthless; he received no news until Turner arrived in St. Louis during the winter of 1853–54.[2]

When Garland learned of the whereabouts of Glover, he meticulously planned how he would reclaim him. Indeed, the cagey Missourian even "supplied" the bottle of whiskey that the occupants of the cabin enjoyed that Friday night to ensure that he would not have to seize his former slave in a public place where antislavery Wisconsinites might interfere. In addition, not wanting legal technicalities to foil his reclamation, Garland carried a certificate of ownership of Glover, duly stamped by the Court of Common Pleas in St. Louis. When he arrived in Milwaukee, he also sought the counsel of the well-known proslavery attorney Jonathan E. Arnold, a partner in the Milwaukee firm of Arnold & Hamilton. Afterward, Garland and Arnold requested and received a warrant for Glover's arrest from Justice Andrew Galbraith Miller, a Pennsylvania-born judge who had moved to Wisconsin. Miller had been appointed to the bench by President James Polk and remained well-connected to leading proslavery Democrats. With his certificate of ownership and warrant in hand, Garland put together a posse capable of seizing a fugitive, even in the backwoods of antislavery Wisconsin. Deputy United States Marshal Charles G. Cotton and police officer Melvin accompanied the slave owner on the way to Racine, where they met up with another U.S. deputy marshal named John Kearney, a brash, enforcer type of lawman, and Daniel F. Houghton, a native of New York who had settled in Dover, Wisconsin, where he earned the unflattering title "the Slave Catcher of Dover." Joined by two other men and packing extra guns furnished by Captain Gardiner of the Racine militia, a friend of Arnold's law partner, Garland and his associates "hire[d] two wagons at the Armour Livery Stable" and headed out of town, deeming themselves prepared to take Glover. A "fierce struggle" was about to ensue — one that would leave Glover bloodied, battered, bruised, temporarily unconscious, and in a Milwaukee jail.[3]

Under the cover of darkness, the posse rode toward Glover's cabin, stopping about one hundred yards from it. With the occupants focused on their card game and savoring Garland's whiskey, the posse advanced furtively with "the crunching sounds of their footsteps in the hard snow somewhat muffled by the nearby rapids of the Root River." When they reached the door and rapped loudly, Garland brandished a revolver, Cotton clutched a pair of handcuffs, and Kearney wielded a whip. Their knocking surprised Glover and Alby. When Turner immediately arose "to draw the bolt," a very "suspicious" Glover told him not to unlock the door until they knew who was there. Turner ignored Glover's instructions and swung open the door, letting the attackers rush in. Glover instantly realized the assailants' purpose and resisted, shoving away one of the slave catchers who "pressed a pistol" to his head. In a split second, however, Kearney bludgeoned him with the butt of the whip and he fell to the floor, where his assailants attempted, unsuccessfully, to handcuff him as he continued to struggle. Alby leaped through a window, leaving Glover even more badly outnumbered, but the latter fought on until Cotton, from behind, struck him on the head with his irons, "causing a severe scalp wound." As Glover lay dazed, the posse manacled him, threw him in one of the wagons, and covered him with a buffalo robe. He had "nothing on but his pantaloons and a shirt," which were both bloodied and torn. Fearing a strong reaction from antislavery sympathizers and friends of Glover, the slave catchers decided to split up; Kearney and Houghton took one wagon and returned to Racine. When they arrived, they met a group of angry townspeople, led by Sheriff Timothy D. Morris, whom Alby had already alerted. Morris arrested the men immediately "on suspicion of kidnapping and assault and battery."[4]

JOSHUA GLOVER, THE FUGITIVE SLAVE. Supporting Joshua Glover, *The Racine Advocate* said, "The fugitive slave law cannot be enforced in Wisconsin.... The people will not suffer it" (Wisconsin Historical Society, WHi 6270).

Meanwhile Garland and his remaining associates set out for Milwaukee, some thirty miles away, with the manacled Glover lying semiconscious in the back of the wagon. Garland expected a friendlier reception there. With Judge Miller, United States Commissioner Winfield Smith, and Arnold to orchestrate things, he felt sure there would be much less resistance in Milwaukee than in Racine. But getting there on dark, snow-covered trails was another story — especially for men not used to traveling in the wooded country around Racine. The slave catchers took a wrong fork and spent most of the night lost, reaching Milwaukee only around daybreak. Cotton later testified that he "lodged the fugitive, Glover, in jail on the morning of the 11th about 8 o'clock." He probably did not know that when he left the jail to get some rest, the Milwaukee jailor, moved by "commendable feelings of humanity," took the irons from Glover's wrists and attended to the battered fugitive with "care and kindness."[5]

News of Glover's arrest quickly fanned antislavery fires in Racine and on Saturday citizens convened the "largest meeting" ever held in the town. Reports of the enforcement of the Fugitive Slave Law on Wisconsin free soil and revelation that Glover had been "cut in two places on the head" and his clothes were "soaking and stiff in his own blood" fueled emotions, particularly among those who knew him.[6] Charles Clement, the editor of Racine's weekly newspaper published an article with an attention-grabbing headline, "High-Handed Outrage. Attempt to Kidnap a Citizen of Racine by Slave-Catchers!" He adopted an antislavery stance similar to that of Samuel Joseph May and his compatriots after Marshal Allen seized Jerry in Syracuse. But the reaction of Wisconsinites also reflected their disdain for Stephen A. Douglas's Kansas-Nebraska Bill "abolishing the Missouri Compromise." That compromise, brokered by Henry Clay of Kentucky, had allowed Missouri to enter the Union as a slave state at the same time that Maine joined as a free state so as to maintain the balance between free and slave states, but it also outlawed slavery north of Missouri's southern boundary latitude 36° 30' with the exception of the State of Missouri. In the new legislation, Douglas effectively removed this limit on slavery's expansion by advancing the principle of popular sovereignty whereby the people of a given territory would decide for themselves whether or not to allow slavery. The threat that slavery might extend to areas that had previously been designated free soil fell like a heavy stone in Wisconsin.[7]

The arrest of Joshua Glover ensured that henceforth the townsfolk in Racine would fiercely resist the Fugitive Slave Law and also be among Douglas's most vocal opponents. "[W]e as citizens are justified in declaring and do hereby declare the slave-catching law of 1850 disgraceful, *and also repealed*," wrote Clement in the *Advocate* of Saturday, March 11,

1854. Directly challenging President Franklin Pierce who, since his election in 1852, had confirmed the federal government's commitment to enforce the legislation that enabled slaveholders to recover runaway slaves in the free states, he boldly stated that "the fugitive slave law is not the law of Wisconsin." Clement ended his tirade by declaring that "the fugitive slave law cannot be enforced in Wisconsin." He obviously believed Wisconsinites were too committed to man's inalienable right to liberty, a right that the Declaration of Independence endowed to everyone "whatever be the color of his skin."[8] Many of Clement's neighbors shared his views. Assembled in earnest Saturday morning after Glover's capture, they wanted their black neighbor to benefit from privileges enjoyed by others. First and foremost, they resolved that Glover "be

CAPTURE OF JOSHUA GLOVER. Joshua Glover resisted the slave catching posse. After striking Glover on the head from behind with a pair of iron handcuffs, the slave hunters manacled him and took him to Milwaukee where his former master thought there would be "less chance of trouble" reclaiming him than in Racine (Wisconsin Historical Society, WHi 40836).

afforded a fair and impartial trial by jury," the constitutional right of every American. The Reverend Zebulon Humphrey, the pastor of Racine's First Presbyterian Church, also informed the gathering that he would give a sermon on "the moral and religious bearing of the Nebraska

Question" the next day. Before the meeting adjourned, at least one hundred impassioned townspeople agreed to travel immediately to Milwaukee "to see that justice should be done." Before they left, Clement wired his fellow abolitionist, Sherman Booth, the editor of the antislavery *Milwaukee Free Democrat*.[9]

If Garland really believed things would go smoothly in Milwaukee, he must have quickly realized just how badly he had underestimated antislavery sentiments in the city and he must have been terribly disheartened at the way events unfolded. From the moment Booth learned of Glover's arrest, he played "a pivotal role" in shaping the city's response. After receiving Clement's telegraph, the Yale-educated editor hurried to verify events with Judge Andrew Miller. Before reaching the latter's office, however, he met Cotton and asked him if he "had kidnapped a negro" the night before. The deputy marshal responded that he "did not know anything about a man being kidnapped" but he acknowledged having "*arrested*" a runaway slave. When Booth saw Miller, the judge conceded that he issued an arrest warrant but he said that he did not know whether it had been executed. Accompanied by attorney James Paine, an abolitionist lawyer who with his son Byron became instrumental in legal proceedings stemming from Glover's arrest, Booth visited the jailed fugitive slave and confirmed the events of the previous evening.[10]

When black Milwaukeeans heard the news, they too rallied quickly. They were, after all, prepared and resolute. Two weeks after the passage of the Fugitive Slave Law of 1850, they had gathered and applauded the black barber Lewis Johnson who declared that the new legislation left antebellum blacks "no other alternative ... but to choose between Liberty or Death." To resounding cheers Johnson had urged his fellow blacks to resist the law using every means possible. "Let your resolves be bold, let them come from the heart, speaking the voice of men who are determined upon the resolution of Patrick Henry—'Liberty or Death,'" asserted Johnson. Antislavery blacks and whites were ready to stir a tempest in Milwaukee — one that would be felt across the nation.[11]

After getting an affidavit from Glover and a copy of the arrest warrant that Miller had issued, Paine proceeded to the house of Judge Charles Jenkins and asked the Milwaukee County Court justice for a writ of habeas corpus on behalf of Glover, which would require a court ruling on the legality of the fugitive slave's detention. Jenkins issued the writ and it was served on Deputy Marshal Cotton. Meanwhile, Booth set about igniting Milwaukeeans. He drew up a handbill stating that "a colored man" had been "knocked down" and "incarcerated in the County Jail." He also reported that Cotton denied having kidnapped Glover. Hoping to inflame antislavery sentiment, Booth claimed that Cotton's denial served as evidence that federal officials intended to arrange a "secret trial, without giving him [Glover] a chance to defend himself by counsel." The handbill asked, "Citizens of Milwaukee! Shall we have Star Chamber proceedings here? and shall a Man be dragged back to Slavery from our Free Soil, *without an open trial of his right to Liberty?*"[12]

While Booth printed the notice, he made sure his friends began to spread the news by word of mouth and the crowd outside the county jail where Glover was confined grew steadily throughout the morning from some one hundred persons "about ten o'clock" to several hundred by noon.

After lunch, Booth huddled with fellow abolitionists at his office and they decided to convene a public rally at two o'clock that afternoon. They announced the gathering as they distributed the handbills. Booth, however, convinced that the urgency of the situation called for more publicity, mounted his horse and rode about town. Cotton later testified that he saw the abolitionist editor "on horseback riding up and down E. Water Street crying out for the people to assemble at

SHERMAN BOOTH. Riding about Milwaukee on his white horse, Booth was alleged to have acted like a "town crier" rallying support for Joshua Glover as he yelled, "Freemen to the rescue; slave catchers are in our midst. Be at the Court House at two o'clock" (Wisconsin Historical Society, WHi 9485).

125

the Court House." He apparently went over the river and rode through the town's business section, "stopping at street corners and shouting 'A man's liberty is at stake.'" Some reports suggested that, mounted on his white horse, Booth acted like a "town crier" as he yelled "Freemen to the rescue; slave catchers are in our midst. Be at the Court House at two o'clock." At that hour, Booth and his fellow abolitionists also arranged for the ringing of the courthouse and church bells, which caused "thousands to flock to the court-house square and around the jail, the excitement being intense."[13]

At about half past the hour, "several thousand" people had responded to Booth's hasty invitation to "all Free Citizens who were not willing to be made slaves or slave catchers." They milled about Milwaukee's courthouse impatiently awaiting speeches. As the square filled, those who had been selected to speak were forced to move from the courthouse steps to the roof of the county clerk's office. Around three o'clock, an ardent Booth proclaimed that he would "execrate and spit on the [Fugitive Slave L]aw," even as he counseled the estimated three to five thousand people assembled not to break the law. Although Booth later clearly condoned the use of force to free slaves, his initial intentions that day seem to have been to rally public sentiment in favor of Glover in a non-violent fashion. Like many antebellum Americans, Booth probably regarded orderly crowd action as an accepted, democratic means of conveying popular will. H. Robert Baker effectively argues that English constitutional traditions, coupled with practices adopted by American Revolutionaries including such groups as the Sons of Liberty, allowed orderly assemblies to be interpreted as expressions of community demands. Against this background, the assembly in Milwaukee's Court Square on March 11, 1854, assumed special meaning. Furthermore, James Paine's calling the meeting to order and the proper election of Dr. Edward B. Wolcott as president and Abram H. Bielfield as secretary followed accepted procedures, which ensured the meeting's legitimacy as a means of expressing the people's wishes. The assembled also carefully elected an organizing committee, making sure that "one [person] from each ward was appointed to draft resolutions, and present them to the meeting." The committee included both Booth and James Paine.[14]

From the outset, the meeting was boisterous and the speeches fanned the antislavery sentiments of the ever-increasing multitudes. The

Milwaukeeans "loudly cheered" as they listened to the speakers denounce slavery and the execution of the Fugitive Slave Law on Wisconsin free soil. Addressing the Kansas-Nebraska question, James Paine declared that the kidnapping of Glover reflected "the larger national drama" caused by the extension of slave power into the free states. Reacting to concerns that authorities planned to carry Glover off without a trial, the crowd called for the organization of a vigilance committee of twenty-five members "to keep watch over the jail." The vigilance committee too seemed to have been selected in a representative fashion; it included a wide range of people from a variety of occupations and walks of life. Booth's oration that afternoon was particularly noteworthy. After describing the events of the night before in lurid detail, he summarized the morning's legal developments and inspired his audience, telling them "if they all felt as he did, he knew what they would do."[15]

The drafting committee presented three resolutions for the mass meeting's consideration. They also prepared a highly charged preamble that helped to ensure the crowd's approval of their recommendations. "[A] man named Joshua Glover, living in the neighborhood of Racine, had his house broken into, a pistol presented at his head, was knocked down and badly cut by Deputy Marshal Charles Cotton, and Benj. S. Garland, his pretended owner, before any legal process was served upon him," declared the preamble, which also noted that "he was fettered, and brought to this city and incarcerated in our county jail." The gathering unanimously approved the resolutions—the first underscoring every citizen's right to "a fair and impartial trial *by jury*," the second enshrining the writ of habeas corpus, and the third committing the crowd to "stand by the prisoner."[16]

Ominously, while the crowd reacted to the inflammatory rhetoric of Booth and others and passed resolutions supporting Glover, Deputy Marshal Cotton, acting on advice from Judge Miller, decided to disregard the writ of habeas corpus issued by Jenkins. By late afternoon, rumors to this effect began to circulate and an increasingly expectant crowd demanded to know what was going on and asked Byron Paine to explain the "legal technicalities" of Glover's case. Responding, Paine told the assembly that as far as he was concerned the fugitive slave legislation under which Glover had been arrested violated the Constitution "inasmuch as it denied the Writ of Habeas Corpus and the right of trial by jury, which were sacredly guarantied to us." This further agitated the gathering and, when Wolcott sought to adjourn the meeting, many people refused to leave Court Square before knowing how federal officials would respond to Jenkins's writ of habeas corpus. Around five o'clock, the delegation from Racine, one hundred strong, marched from the docks "straight to the jail" and announced they were determined to save Glover from being returned to bondage, causing further excitement in the square. About the same time, the county sheriff served another writ on Cotton — and he dismissed that one too.[17]

"About 6 o'clock," with darkness setting in and the crowd boosted by the recent arrivals from Racine, the radical abolitionist attorney Charles Watkins gave a rousing speech suggesting that "there were times when the people must take the law into their own hands or themselves become slaves." His address was followed by another spirited missive from Booth, which heightened emotion. Immediately afterward, the vigilance committee let it be known that Cotton refused to respect the writ of habeas corpus— and a buzz went through the square. Almost instantaneously, the news propelled the crowd into action. Led by a "burly blacksmith" named James Angove, a group of militants grabbed a timber lying in the nearby yard of St. John's Cathedral. Pushing people aside as they headed toward the jail, the men were joined by others "wielding axes." Using the beam as a battering ram, they attacked the building and had "the bolts of the door broken off" in a matter of minutes. Before long the walls of the building were also "giving way" and Glover's guards looked on helplessly as the attackers swarmed inside. The rescuers triumphantly seized Glover, spirited him to Walker's Point Bridge where he jumped into John Messenger's carriage. Apparently, Glover cried "Glory, Hallelujah!" as the people around the wagon yelled and applauded. The driver headed out of Milwaukee and "Booth rode horseback next to the buggy."[18] Someone telegraphed news of Glover's rescue to Racine and that very evening "cannon were fired, bonfires lighted, and bands of music patrolled the streets." Glover's free soil neighbors and friends celebrated "the triumph of humanity over brutality and the slave driver's power."[19]

Spiriting Glover away, Messenger drove earnestly in the darkness to Waukesha. When he reached the village, the anxious Wisconsinite put Glover in the care of the steadfast Underground Railroad agent

Winchel D. Bacon, who in turn took him immediately to Moses Tichenor's farm where he remained hidden while abolitionists planned his escape to Canada from Racine. Glover's rescuers doubted that the marshals would guess their selection of Racine as the fugitive slave's "departure point" for Canada. Affected by melting snow, road conditions, however, remained poor and hampered travel; Glover did not reach Racine until about "sunrise" Sunday morning. Some reports, perhaps exaggerated as the Underground Railroad agents likely kept Glover's trajectory secret, said the rescued fugitive slave entered his adopted town "amid great rejoicing." An abolitionist drove Glover from the village of Rochester, Wisconsin, some twenty miles away, and took him to the house of the Reverend Martin Palmer Kinney. After Kinney's, Glover stayed temporarily at a number of Underground Railroad stations in rural Wisconsin before leaving by ship for Canada, most likely hidden with cargo in a vessel's hold, during the first two weeks of April 1854. Some three days later, Glover, undoubtedly cold and cramped, arrived on Ontario free soil, out of the reach of slave catchers. He disembarked at "one of two Georgian Bay ports, Owen Sound or Collingwood."[20]

In the final analysis, a handful of militants and crowd action "had trenchantly asserted" Glover's inalienable right to liberty and the Wisconsinites involved believed that they acted in ways sanctioned by their Revolutionary forbears. Booth and his abolitionist friends celebrated and, as they did, they declared the fugitive slave legislation a nullity. "We send greetings to the Free states of the Union, that in Wisconsin, the Fugitive Slave Law is repealed!" announced the antislavery editor in his *Milwaukee Free Democrat*. "The first attempt to enforce the law, in this State, has signally, gloriously failed," he declared. He proudly noted that Wisconsinites ensured that the American Revolutionary presumption of freedom and inalienable rights for all would, on Wisconsin soil, trump the Southern presumption of slavery for those allegedly bound to service, effectively nullifying the Fugitive Slave Law. "FREEDOM, IT MUST AND SHALL BE PRESERVED! PERISH ALL ENACTMENTS ESTABLISHING SLAVERY ON FREE SOIL!" proclaimed Booth. The New England–born editor effectively extended liberties his ancestors cherished and fought for across the continent, abrogating at the same time comity with Southern slaveholders, a point emphasized by both Paul Finkelman and Jeffrey Schmitt. The latter also notes that "significantly, the jail was stormed only when it was announced that the state's legal process [requiring respect of the writ of habeas corpus] would be ignored."[21]

Consistent with Glover's rescue and the affirmation of Wisconsin free soil, Sheriff Timothy Morris, who arrived in Milwaukee with the Racine delegation, carried with him a warrant for the arrest of Benammi Garland on charges of kidnapping, assault, and battery committed on Glover. The warrant had been issued as a result of "the information and complaint of one Charles Clement." Not surprisingly, Garland quickly sought the protection and service of his trusted attorney Arnold, who requested a writ of habeas corpus from Judge Miller. On Monday, a hearing took place before the latter and Arnold argued that Garland had merely assisted federal authorities in the execution of the Fugitive Slave Law. Deputy Marshal Cotton testified on behalf of the Missourian and vowed that "no more force than necessary for the execution of the warrant" had been used against Glover. Although James Paine and Charles Watkins objected to the proslavery lawyer's claims, Miller ruled that Garland had acted under the authority of federal law and ordered the release of the slaveholder. He returned to St. Louis as Booth and others denounced the decision, especially as it re-established the presumption of comity with slaveholders and, by sanctioning the Fugitive Slave Law, opened the way for legal action against those who had aided and abetted Joshua Glover's escape.[22] In short, Miller's decision undermined Wisconsinites' attempt to repeal compromises with slavery and Booth was among the first forced to deal with the consequences.

On March 15, 1854, United States Commissioner Winfield Smith signed arrest warrants for several Wisconsinites who had been involved in the Glover rescue. Their "real prize" was, however, the antislavery editor of the *Milwaukee Free Democrat*. When Booth's hearing commenced on March 21, 1854, it became a forum for the abolitionist to popularize his opposition to the Fugitive Slave Law using his most colorful language. He stated that although he had not initially intended to violate the law nor cause the jail to be broken into, "he was not sorry that the alleged fugitive had been rescued." Almost baiting the commissioner, he also stressed that he would prefer to see the federal officials who executed the Fugitive Slave Law "hanged fifty cubits higher than Haman" instead of the "writ of habeas corpus and trial by jury guarantied [*sic*] by the state of Wisconsin trampled under foot." With the assistance of his counsel James Paine, Booth set about proving his innocence by arguing that the Fugitive Slave Law was unconstitutional; not only did it blemish Wisconsin free soil, it violated liberties enshrined in the state constitution. He claimed also that in aiding Glover he had only defended the legal right of a man to his liberty and exercised his rights to free speech and assembly — rights, of course, guaranteed by the Constitution. Seeking to discredit Booth's defense, United States District Attorney Sharpstein argued that Booth had aided and abetted Glover's escape by inciting the mob to riot and break open the jail. Although Paine challenged Sharpstein's contention that Booth had ridden around town shouting "Freemen to the Rescue," Commissioner Smith refused to dismiss the charges against Booth, and Garland seized the opportunity to have Marshal Stephen Ableman serve a civil suit against the abolitionist editor for $4,000, an amount that included $1,800 for the value of Joshua Glover.[23]

Despite this setback, less than one month later antislavery Milwaukeeans moved forcefully to challenge the federalist vision that underpinned Smith's ruling and they convened the Anti-Slave-Catchers' Mass Convention on April 13, 1854. Drawing heavily on James Madison's Virginia Resolutions, and on Thomas Jefferson's Kentucky Resolutions, penned shortly afterward, they met at Young's Hall. Just as the Virginia Founding Fathers' resolutions branded the Alien and Sedition Laws of 1798 tyrannical, the antislavery Wisconsinites gathered in Young's Hall deemed that the Fugitive Slave Law of 1850 violated fundamental American freedoms. Like Madison and Jefferson, they sought to mount opposition at the state level to halt abuses by federal authorities. Arguing that the national government's enactment and enforcement of the Fugitive Slave Law violated the constitutional pact framed at Philadelphia, as well as the first ten Constitutional Amendments enshrining fundamental liberties, the Young's Hall militants appealed to the great Virginians' interpretation of federalism. In the Virginia Resolutions, Madison had advanced the view that a state could interpose laws that state authorities deemed in violation of the constitutional accord; in the Kentucky Resolutions, Jefferson went even further, suggesting that a state could nullify federal laws that it considered repugnant to the Constitution. In the spring of 1854, antislavery Wisconsinites echoed these sentiments saying, "[W]e view the powers of the Federal Government as resulting from the compact to which the states are parties" and, therefore, a state "could not be subordinate" to the national government, which it had helped to create. As such, they contended that Wisconsin had the right to pronounce upon the constitutionality of acts passed by the federal legislative body. If Wisconsinites determined that the Fugitive Slave Law violated rights enshrined by the state constitution, state authorities could justifiably stop execution of the law within state lines. An "Unconstitutional Act of Congress imposes no obligations on a State, or the people of a State," proclaimed Booth from the Young's Hall podium. It could be "resisted by an individual or a community."[24]

In May, Booth took his resistance to the courts. Seeking to rid himself of the criminal charges filed against him under the Fugitive Slave Law of 1850, the abolitionist editor filed for a writ of habeas corpus before the Wisconsin Supreme Court Justice Abram Smith. Booth and his attorneys — James Paine, Byron Paine, and the feisty Charles Watkins — chose "the timing of their application carefully," aware that Abram Smith, known for his antislavery beliefs, would hear the case, as the other court justices were not sitting. For the abolitionists, it was an ideal chance to test the constitutionality of the law they detested. On May 29, 1854, Byron Paine powerfully argued that the Fugitive Slave Law of 1850 was unconstitutional; his arguments were threefold. Following the reasoning of Massachusetts attorney Robert Rantoul in the Thomas Sims case, Paine claimed that the commissioners who rendered decisions in federal fugitive slave tribunals assumed powers that the Constitution gave only to judges. Second, he stated that the Constitution did not give Congress the authority to enact legislation to reclaim fugitive slaves. Although the Constitution's fugitive slave clause "directly" required the states to deliver up runaways, Paine asserted that there was no "enabling clause attached to the fugitive slave provision" nor had such powers been assigned in Article I. Hence, said Booth's attorney, Congress had no authority to legislate on the subject of fugitive slaves. Finally, Paine contended that because the Fugitive Slave Law denied alleged runaways due process, it violated the Constitution — notably the Fifth, Sixth, and Seventh Amendments. Paine concluded his arguments with "a rhetorical plea for liberty that resonated both within the courtroom and beyond its walls." Just as his client popularized the antislavery clause from Young's Hall one month earlier, Paine called for the extension of American liberties and he did so by "inviting the interposition of Justice Smith and the Wisconsin Supreme Court on constitutional grounds."

One week later, on June 7, 1854, Abram Smith "adopted every major position" put forward by Paine. He ruled that the Fugitive Slave Law of 1850 was unconstitutional because it denied alleged fugitives a trial by jury and bestowed judicial powers on commissioners. Strikingly, the justice also declared that Congress did not have the authority to legislate on the subject of fugitive slaves. Rejecting previous rulings by Associate United States Supreme Court Justice Joseph Story, New York Supreme Court Judge Samuel Nelson, and Massachusetts Chief Justice Lemuel Shaw, Smith shocked Southern slaveholders and many law-abiding Northerners. The *Richmond Enquirer* said that his opinion was clear evidence that Northern abolitionism had become so strong that judges had become "infected by its spirit" and they now bowed to "its treasonable purposes." In contrast, antislavery Milwaukeeans rejoiced as Smith clothed the stance they had embraced at Young's Hall with the authority of the law. As they had claimed, Wisconsin was free soil and the tentacles of slavery were not going to be allowed to contaminate it.[25]

Even more remarkable, however, was that when the Wisconsin Supreme Court returned from vacation and ruled on the case, the majority sided with Abram Smith and effectively agreed with the tenets Byron Paine had advanced. The majority rendered an opinion founded on the "doctrine of state sovereignty" and sanctioned the "state's sovereign right of self-defense" to prevent its citizens' rights from being trampled upon. Paine believed that state interposition of federal laws judged to be repugnant to a state's constitution gave citizens a means to check federal power without resort to armed resistance. It was rebellion without violence; as Paine put it, "state interposition sought to preserve rather than rend the peace."[26]

Such successful legal maneuvering in state courts on cases arising from Glover's rescue placed fundamental American liberties in sharp relief and Wisconsinites celebrated the legacy of their Revolutionary forefathers—but not for long. The guilty verdicts rendered against John Ryecraft in November 1854 and Booth in January 1855 in federal tribunals presided over by Judge Miller foreshadowed a continuing rough road for antislavery militants, even as the rulings set the stage for additional resistance through court appeals aimed at limiting the enforcement of the Fugitive Slave Law. In particular, Booth's conviction early in the new year "very naturally excite[d] attention" and accentuated rifts between antebellum Americans supporting compromises with slavery and abolitionists. Law-abiding Northerners who wanted to appease slaveholding Southerners lauded Miller for upholding the "majesty of the laws" and suggested it at last reflected "a proper regard to the laws of the country in the North." In contrast, antislavery militants denounced Miller's decision, again assailing the federal fugitive slave legislation and questioning its constitutionality. Wisconsinites of all stripes anxiously awaited the results of an appeal by Booth and Ryecraft to the Wisconsin Supreme Court.

On February 3, 1855, the state court ruled unanimously that the indictments of Booth and Ryecraft, which did not identify Joshua Glover as a slave, were defective and the defendants should be released. Although the majority opinion of state justices did not specifically revisit the issue of the constitutionality of the Fugitive Slave Law, Justice Abram Smith stressed once again the court's earlier decision, stating, "We have decided that the fugitive act of September 18th, 1850, is unconstitutional." To the satisfaction of abolitionists, however, the majority opinion clearly underscored the centrality of fundamental American liberties, notably the writ of habeas corpus, and the right of the state to interpose federal laws to protect its citizens. It thus drew on Revolutionary traditions of "popular constitutional resistance" founded upon the separation of powers and basic rights enshrined by the Founders at Philadelphia and in the Bill of Rights. It also reflected the Virginia and Kentucky Resolutions' doctrines of state interposition or nullification to protect their citizens' fundamental liberties.[27]

Joshua Glover, living in freedom in Britain's northern dominion, likely did not realize the political, legal, and constitutional resistance to the Fugitive Slave Law that his rescue and fate precipitated. By February 3, 1855, however, such resistance had in many respects reached its high tide. Two days later, Judge Miller reiterated his view that state courts did not have the power to set aside decisions rendered by federal courts, a view that the United States Supreme Court Chief Justice Roger Taney strongly upheld when he pronounced on *Ableman v. Booth* some four years later and "chastised" the Wisconsin Supreme Court justices for having overstepped their authority — especially after their refusal to forward an official transcript of the *Ableman v. Booth* proceedings to the nation's high court for review. Wisconsin's enactment of a new personal liberty law giving fugitive slaves the right to writs of habeas corpus also provoked Taney. In his opinion, the South Carolina–born chief justice considered the Fugitive Slave Law "fully authorized by the Constitution of the United States" and he told law-abiding Wisconsinites that in the future it would not be a "humiliation to the citizen of the republic to yield a ready obedience to the laws as administered by the constituted authorities." Also disconcerting for abolitionists at the time of Taney's ruling was that an impoverished Booth had already lost the civil suit filed against him by Garland. Indeed, on February 2, 1857, authorities seized Booth's printing press to cover the $1,246 that he owed the slave-holder.[28]

For antislavery activists, Taney's opinion suggested that events had taken a very different turn from the triumphant moments in Milwaukee's Court Square on the night of Glover's rescue, during the Young's Hall rally, or upon the Wisconsin Supreme Court's affirming state sovereignty — moments that seemed to resonate with Wisconsinites' Revolutionary heritage, sanction free soil, and ensure the extension American liberties to everyone regardless of his or her color. The stage upon which the Glover rescue drama played out had become truly national and the nation itself had become perilously divided. Antebellum Americans had also witnessed an unprecedented show of force — indeed the largest ever in a time of peace — to return Anthony Burns, another fugitive slave, to bondage. For Anthony Burns — and other black Americans — Patrick Henry's motto of *Liberty or Death* took on special meaning.

CHAPTER 7

Anthony Burns
"Resolution to Strike the Blow, for Freedom or the Grave"

Faneuil Hall is the purlieus of the Court House ... where the children of Adams and Hancock may prove that they are not bastards. Let us prove that we are worthy of our liberty.— Wendell Phillips

The growling of the storm has never ceased since that pregnant cloud of last June lowered on Massachusetts ... the explosion of the tempest seems to be very near, for the revolutionary deed is actually done.— Harriet Martineau

The strokes on the Court House door that night ... went echoing from town to town, from Boston to far New Orleans, like the first drum beats of the Revolution — and each reverberating throb was a blow upon the door of every Slave-prison of this guilty Republic.— Thomas Wentworth Higginson

> I'm on my way to Canada, that cold and dreary land,
> The dire effects of slavery I can no longer stand.
> I'm now resolved to strike the blow,
> For freedom or the grave.— Underground Railroad song

By the winter of 1853–54, twenty-year-old Anthony Burns disdained the startling disparities between slaves and citizens in Richmond. In the bustling Virginia capital, well-dressed planters in elaborate carriages, often accompanied by slaves forced to satisfy their every need, graced the city with their presence and wealth while slave traders and drivers marched new arrivals of African descent from the Manchester Docks to the auction block. In the Virginia legislature, slaveholders denounced Northern abolitionists and spoke of liberty, property, and Southern rights while a stone's throw away, Robert Lumpkin formed the next slave coffle outside his infamous jail to trek black men, women, and children to brutal bondage in the Deep South. In the Richmond hiring-out market, white businessmen and planters from the surrounding area looked over slaves available to ply their trades or offer manual labor to help line their owners' deep pockets or, in some cases, pay their masters' mortgages and receive nothing in return. Southern white ladies enjoyed the city's vibrant social life while attractive young black women, especially lighter-skinned mulattos, experienced the horrors of the fancy trade, which typically put them at the mercy of some ravishing master often twice their age.

Such contradictions deeply disturbed the alert, proud, and determined young Burns. Moreover, like Gabriel Prosser half a century earlier, the literate bondsman had imbibed republican ideology and was aware of the new nation's politics. Unlike Gabriel, however, Burns did not underestimate the strength of slave power and he realized the dangers of challenging it directly. If he wanted to live and breathe as a freeman, he knew that he would have to flee the South; he could not overthrow the Peculiar Institution — its wealth, whips, guns, manacles, chains, and other instruments of power that spread "its blighting influence" across the land. For Burns, freedom would mean leaving behind everything he had ever known, including the Richmond slave woman he loved.

What the thirteenth child of John Suttle's aging female slave wanted to do without was the toil, abuse, and emotional nightmare of Southern slavery. His father had died early, the victim of stone dust inhalation from working long days at Suttle's quarry in Stafford County, which supplied much of the stone for the nation's new capital on the Potomac River. Having watched Suttle's widow sell away his brothers and sisters, having been hired out at the age of seven by Suttle's son Charles, mistreated and disfigured at the age of thirteen by an abusive master, and finally rented to a profiteering Richmond druggist named Millspaugh who received Burns's hard-earned wages from working at the Richmond docks, Burns had experienced the villainy and degradation of slavery. On a cold, dark night in early February 1854, his yearning for liberty trumped everything else. Believing that he had an inalienable right to freedom and "the Bible set forth only one God for the black and white races," the tall, handsome bondsman readied himself to meet a sailor on a ship leaving for New England. The seaman had agreed to help him in his flight to the North and now Burns was determined to be a slave no more. Before dawn, wearing four layers of clothing — his usual dock-worker's outfit on the outside — he left his lodgings with a few belongings and walked to the Richmond docks for the last time.[1]

Three weeks later, having endured a perilous voyage cramped in a "coffinlike space," constantly fearing detection by unfriendly crew, eating only morsels of food that his friend occasionally snuck to him, and "frozen stiff in his boots" as the vessel battled ever-colder Atlantic winds heading north, Burns disembarked in Boston, "pretending to be a seaman going ashore." Mingling with laboring folk and lesser sorts around the harbor, Burns landed a job as a cook on "a mud-scow operating on Boston's noxious tidal flats." Unable "to make the bread rise," he soon, however, found himself back on the streets looking for a job. A black window cleaner named William Jones befriended him, gave him part-time work washing windows at the Mattapan Iron Works, and introduced him to Coffin Pitts, a secondhand clothing dealer and a deacon at the Reverend Leonard A. Grimes's legendary Twelfth Baptist Church, some-times called the fugitive slave chapel. Pitts offered Burns permanent employment. Since the enactment of the Fugitive Slave Law in September 1850, Grimes and Pitts, two respected members of Boston's tightly knit black community, had harbored and helped fugitive slaves, often spir-iting them to Canada when their masters or slave catchers arrived in the city.[2]

Breathing the air of freedom in Massachusetts, Burns wrote a letter to his brother in Virginia telling him of his journey and his exciting new life on free soil. Like many fugitive slaves in Boston, he arranged to have his letter mailed from Canada; envelopes bearing Dominion of Canada postmarks helped to conceal fugitive slaves' whereabouts. Burns, how-ever, made the grave error of addressing the letter inside from Boston. Intent on finding and recovering his runaway slave, Burns's master Charles Suttle intercepted his letter.

At the end of the workday on Wednesday, May 24, 1854, Burns closed the shutters and locked up Pitts's Brattle Street clothing store. He walked toward Court Street as Massachusetts Democrats honored con-gressmen who voted for the Kansas-Nebraska Bill with a "113-gun salute." That legislation sponsored by Senator Stephen Douglas of Illinois embraced popular sovereignty as the means to determine the legality of slavery in the western territories, opening up the possibility of the Peculiar Institution extending its reach north of latitude 36° 30', the limit previously established under the Missouri Compromise. Burns suddenly felt "a hand roughly laid upon his shoulder," and before he had time to react, the slave catcher Asa Butman, helped by several surly accomplices, seized and manacled him. They acted on orders from United States Marshal Watson Freeman, who held a warrant for Burns's arrest under the Fugitive Slave Law of 1850, which Commissioner Edward Greely Loring had signed earlier that day. Fearing resistance from Burns or antislavery Bostonians who might witness the arrest, Butman and his deputies charged Burns with petty theft. They immediately brought him to the Boston courthouse and placed him in an upper-floor jury room, actually the same one in which Thomas Sims had been confined some three years earlier. Surrounded by "a strong guard of officers" and still suffering from brutal handling, Burns knew the score when Marshal Freeman, Charles Suttle, and William Brent, Suttle's agent, walked into the room later that evening.[3]

Early the next morning, news of Burns's arrest spread across Boston Common, along the narrow streets and alleyways of what racist whites called "Nigger Hill," and in the colored boarding houses down near the docks, precipitating a flurry of activity among black Bostonians and their white abolitionist allies. Upon hearing the news, Pitts hastened to the Twelfth Baptist Church to inform Grimes and others in the black congregation. Grimes contacted the members of the Boston Vigilance Committee. The Reverend Samuel Joseph May hurriedly wrote to Thomas Wentworth Higginson, one of the most radical vigilance committee members. Since Thomas Sims's rendition, Higginson's militancy had increased steadily. His Worcester church had become renowned as a veritable antislavery bastion; he also "received" fugitive slaves at his home and drove them to the country under the cover of darkness. "Last night a man was arrested here as a fugitive," said May in his note. "Come strong. In Haste." Higginson received a second message from Wendell Phillips also urging him to hurry to Boston for "another kidnapping case." Wasting no time, Higginson "drummed up" others to go with him, including Martin Stowell, who had participated in the Jerry rescue in Syracuse. The Worcester militants took the next train leaving for Boston and Higginson declared, "a revolution is begun!" In his "Massachusetts in Mourning Sermon," preached a few days later, the radical abolitionist said that after the kidnapping of Anthony Burns, antislavery was no longer "reform, but a Revolution."[4]

Before nine o'clock on Thursday morning, Grimes dashed to the courthouse to see Burns, arriving as attorney Richard Henry Dana Jr., famous for his autobiographical account *Two Years before the Mast*, and the antislavery preacher Theodore Parker entered the courtroom in which Loring prepared to start proceedings. Dana offered to defend Burns, but the latter, appearing despondent, refused help. "[I]t is of no use," Burns told Dana. [T]hey will swear to me & get me back; and if they do, I shall fare worse if I resist."[5]

Seth Thomas, previously branded "the legal pimp of the slave catchers" after Sims's rendition, and his partner, Edward Parker, presented Suttle's claim. They read Burns's arrest warrant and filed a Virginia circuit court transcript certifying Suttle's ownership of Burns, who was described as "a man of dark complexion, about six feet high, with a scar on one of his cheeks, and also a scar on the back of his right hand, and about twenty-three or twenty-four years of age." The court record confirmed that he was "held to service and labor" by Suttle and that he had "escaped from the State." After being asked to take the stand, William Brent testified that Burns "admitted he was Suttle's slave" during the conversation in the upper-floor jury room the night before. Shocked by such testimony, Dana interjected, declaring that the prisoner was in a "state of alarm and stupefaction" and proceedings should be adjourned. He told Loring that Burns was "in no condition" to stand trial or even "to determine" his need for legal counsel. Thomas and Parker protested. Stressing Burns's alleged confession, they demanded that the hearing continue so that he could be remanded to Suttle that very day. When Charles Ellis, an abolitionist attorney who had participated in Sims's defense, also addressed the court "*amicus curiae*" saying the prisoner was in no shape to stand trial, Loring agreed to adjourn the hearing until Saturday, May 27.[6]

Upon leaving the courtroom, Grimes, Theodore Parker, and other members of the Boston Vigilance Committee convened an emergency meeting. Though radicals argued that Boston must not countenance a "repetition of the Sims debacle" and wanted extreme measures, moderate members disagreed. The hastily called meeting proved to be a "fractious" affair and "there was neither plan nor prospect of unified action." The members revealed their "conflicting ideologies" and, as Gary Collison has effectively argued, they were especially divided on the "question of pacifism versus forcible resistance." In fact, when Higginson arrived from Worcester that afternoon, moderates had just rejected a rescue scheme and the meeting had become so deadlocked that the members had been forced to select a smaller committee of seven to try to come up with recommendations that might be accepted by the committee of the whole. The smaller group included Wendell Phillips, Samuel Gridley Howe, Theodore Parker, and Higginson, but they too could not agree on what to do beyond calling a rally in support of Burns to be held at Fanueil Hall the following evening. This frustrated Higginson and Martin Stowell when the two met on Friday afternoon before the rally. They decided the Fanueil Hall meeting was simply not enough and Higginson proposed a forcible rescue after the rally, a strategy that Howe had suggested the day before. Perhaps thinking of the Jerry or Joshua Glover rescues, he also liked the idea of a rescue attempt early Saturday morning, when a large number of people could be expected to have assembled in Court Square. Stowell disagreed; he wanted prompter action. Arguing that marshals would expect a rescue attempt after the rally, he suggested an attack on the courthouse while the meeting was in progress, which he thought would catch authorities off-guard. When Higginson agreed, they embraced the plan and "briefed their followers."[7]

Meanwhile, other antislavery men sought legal means to free Burns from the marshal. Rather than seeking a writ of habeas corpus as Sherman Booth did for Joshua Glover, Seth Webb Jr. opted for a writ of personal replevin that would release Burns from Marshal Freeman's custody and provide him with a trial by jury. When Webb received the state-authorized writ, Marshal Freeman refused "to comply," contending that he held Burns under United States federal law, which he said took precedence. Confronted with this roadblock, Samuel Sewall and Dr. Henry Bowditch approached Massachusetts Governor Emory Washburn and requested that he support a writ of personal replevin on Burns's behalf and order the state militia to take the prisoner from the marshal's custody. Despite his antislavery leanings, Washburn yielded to the counsel of Attorney General John H. Clifford, who supported the Fugitive Slave Law, and deferred to the opinion of Massachusetts Chief Justice Lemuel Shaw, who had upheld the law's constitutionality in the Sims case. The governor informed Sewall that he felt obligated "to defer to the Supreme Court."[8]

On Friday morning, Bostonians and visitors to the city who had arrived for the annual celebration of Anniversary Week found its landscape covered with placards and handbills that vigilance committee members had prepared to publicize their rally. Theodore Parker authored one proclaiming, "KIDNAPPING AGAIN!! A Man was Stolen Last Night by the Fugitive Slave Bill Commissioner. He will have His MOCK TRIAL ... SHALL BOSTON STEAL ANOTHER MAN?" Another poster invoked Boston's Revolutionary legacy and the Fugitive Slave Law's violation of an alleged fugitive's right to a trial by jury, an issue that had ignited antislavery Wisconsinites a few weeks earlier. "THE KIDNAPPERS ARE HERE! MEN OF BOSTON! Sons of Otis, and Hancock, and the 'Brace of Adamses!'" said the broadside. "See to it that Massachusetts Laws are not outraged with your consent. See to it that no Free Citizen of Massachusetts is dragged into Slavery, WITHOUT A TRIAL BY JURY! '76." Antislavery newspapers also reflected such heightened concern. Elizur Wright's *Commonwealth* linked the Burns's drama to Stephen Douglas's Kansas-Nebraska Bill with a headline reading, "ANOTHER MAN SEIZED IN BOSTON BY THE MAN HUNTERS!! THE DEVIL-BILL [IS] RENEWING ITS VIGOR AND GETTING UP A JUBILEE AMONG US, ON THE PASSAGE OF THE NEBRASKA BILL."[9]

Bostonians, visitors, and people from the surrounding areas responded to the alarming publicity. On Friday evening, "an immense concourse of people" packed Fanueil Hall. Before Sewall officially opened the meeting, organizers "turned away" many people as some five thousand persons had converged on Boston's Cradle of Liberty. George R. Russell spoke first and fanned antislavery feelings, stating, "When the foreign slave trade is reestablished, with all the appalling horrors of the Middle Passage, and the Atlantic is again filled with the bodies of dead Africans, then we may think it time to waken our duty." John L. Swift spoke next and challenged the audience: "If we allow Marshal Freeman to carry away [Burns], then the word cowards should be stamped on our foreheads." He referred to the Boston courthouse as "the tomb of liberty."

Howe followed and he venerated the Revolutionary generation as he told an already excited audience that they were "united in the glorious sentiment of our Revolutionary fathers—'Resistance to tyrants is obedience to God.'" For Howe, that was the very meaning of higher law and he believed that Southern slaveholders were tyrants "who den[ied] the natural right of a man to his own body—of a father to his own child—of a husband to his wife."[10] Howe concluded, saying "Nothing so well becomes Fanueil Hall, as the most determined resistance to a bloody and overshadowing despotism."[11]

While Russell, Swift, and Howe had stirred listeners, Wendell Phillips and Theodore Parker ignited them with "powerful rhetorical performances of a revolutionary character." Their speeches "drew heavily upon Boston's proud heritage of resistance to tyranny."[12] Phillips urged the audience to follow in that tradition. He encouraged Bostonians to act as "the children of Adams and Hancock," and "not bastards." He wanted them to be "worthy of liberty"—just as their Revolutionary fathers had been—and declared Burns should be "set free on the streets of Boston." He asked Bostonians whether the precedent of "Shadrach or the case of Sims" would rule the day. With the examples of the Christiana Riot in Pennsylvania, the Jerry rescue in New York, and the Joshua Glover drama in Wisconsin also in mind, Phillips challenged the citizens of Massachusetts, declaring that no other "state in the Union would consent" to have a fugitive slave such as Burns taken from it to be returned to slavery. To resounding cheers, he called for listeners to reassemble in front of the courthouse the next morning to "see to it that Anthony Burns has no master but his God."[13]

Speaking next, Theodore Parker also challenged Fanueil Hall, addressing the assembly as "my fellow subjects of Virginia" and declaring that he would only retract the insult "when they accomplished deeds worthy of freemen." He further goaded them saying that Virginia extended all the way to the Canadian border. As the crowd enthusiastically applauded, he proposed that the meeting adjourn to "Court Square tomorrow morning at 9 o'clock," which elicited cries of "no tonight," and "let us take him out tonight." When Parker asked for a show of hands to see how many were in favor of immediately rescuing Burns, pandemonium ensued and some one hundred people cried out "to the courthouse." Unaware of the plan that Higginson and Stowell had hatched that afternoon, Phillips took the podium once again and desperately sought to re-establish order. He told the crowd that they had to be sure when they assumed the task of vindicating the "fair fame" of Boston. Advising the aroused descendants of the Sons of Liberty to wait until the next morning, he vowed "we'll tar and feather" the slave catchers tomorrow. "If there is a man here who has an arm and a heart ready to sacrifice any thing for the freedom of an oppressed man, let him do it tomorrow," cautioned Phillips. "[T]he zeal that won't keep until tomorrow will never free a slave."[14] But as the antislavery Golden Trumpet spoke these words, a man shouted from the back of the hall, "Mr. Chairman, I am just informed that a mob of Negroes is in Court Square, attempting to rescue Burns. I move we adjourn to Court Square." The Cradle of Liberty erupted — this time with cries of "Rescue him." People started for the doors and began to storm up the hill toward the courthouse just as Higginson and Stowell had hoped they would.[15] They found everything dark as "the lamps that lighted the Square had already been extinguished so that under cover of darkness the assailants might more easily escape detection."[16] Higginson and Stowell had cleverly arranged this.

Everything did not, however, go as planned. Within moments, "confusion reigned" and, as the crowd reached the square, it seemed leaderless and disoriented. Some people headed toward the west side of the courthouse while others gathered at the south side door. When Higginson, Stowell, and a small band of militant blacks led by Lewis Hayden — some crying "Rescue him! Bring him out!" — attacked the west door with a battering ram, most onlookers just mingled about and watched. Hayden's group probably included men who had spirited Shadrach from the building in February 1851. With the exception of Bronson Alcott, none of the Boston Vigilance Committee members rushed up to the courthouse, and Alcott proved to be no help at all. The transcendentalist surveyed the scene and asked Higginson, "Why are we not within?" The latter answered curtly that the crowd did "not stand by us." Alcott did not lend a hand; he just continued to watch, although later he confessed to being "ashamed of the Union, of New England, almost of myself, too" for not having contributed to the rescue attempt.

Higginson's most serious problem was that though he and Stowell had told their small group of militants about the plan, they had not been able to inform everyone, notably the leading speakers. As a consequence, Phillips unknowingly undermined the scheme when he advised the audience against acting that night. The result, as Higginson later despairingly described it, was that only "the froth and scum of the meeting, the fringe of followers" arrived in the square; they threw stones, "brickbats," sticks, and other objects at the courthouse windows but did not help rescue Burns. The Worcester radical yelled at the crowd on the square, "Will you desert us now?" They did.[17]

From Higginson's perspective, most of the Boston Vigilance Committee had deserted them too. Swift remained outside Fanueil Hall, although he directed others up the hill. When Dr. Henry Bowditch eventually arrived on the scene, he regarded Higginson, Stowell, and the band of black rescuers as "too ardent" and did not join them. Phillips, not knowing of the planned rescue, returned home immediately to attend to his wife, who was ill. Sewall too headed home and reported that the boisterous Fanueil Hall crowd had proved they did not want Burns to be returned to bondage.[18] Despite his professed support of forcible rescues of fugitive slaves and his rallying cry of "Resistance to tyrants is obedience to God" less than an hour earlier, Howe failed to engage in the rescue, even though he did show up later on the square. Howe also had a wife at home who was not well; afterward, he "wept for sorrow and shame" and confessed to being part of a "disgraced community."[19]

Higginson was not the only radical to voice frustration. In fact, since the Sims crisis, Theodore Parker had consistently criticized Bostonians for their unwillingness to take a stand, and during the Fanueil Hall rally, he admonished citizens of "the city of John Hancock and the 'brace of Adamses'" for allowing the Fugitive Slave Law to be executed on free soil. He asked, "[A]re we to have deeds as well as words?"[20] He received his answer that night and joined Higginson in again castigating moderates, including Harriet Beecher Stowe, whom he regarded as definitely one of them. Although she attended the Anniversary Week festivities with her husband, she — like many upstanding Boston women — did not show up at the Cradle of Liberty or on Court Square. The Boston ladies did not follow the example of their Syracuse sisters during the Jerry rescue in 1851, and some radical female abolitionists chided them. Sarah Pellett, a steadfast Burns defender, chastised the women of the Old Bay City for their poor showing. With Revolutionary fervor rivaled by few, she reminded them of the city's heritage, calling on them to take a stand and follow in the footsteps of their forbears in 1776 — to act "up to the dignity of true women." When Burns was later returned to Virginia, she declared, "If the women of Boston turned out *en masse*, and placed themselves before the cannon's mouth, would any man have dared to fire?" She, like Abby Kelley Foster, who ran a farm with her husband Stephen to which Higginson often sent fugitive slaves "at midnight," sought to radicalize women against the hated law.[21]

Black Bostonians needed little convincing. Disillusioned with the new fugitive slave legislation and appalled by Sims's return to bondage in Georgia, men like Lewis Hayden and Grimes were poised for action. Indeed, their militancy shocked some of their law-abiding white neighbors and, of course, intimidated Southern slaveholders. An anxious Suttle bunkered himself in Boston's Revere House after the Courthouse Riot and confessed that the militancy of blacks in Boston "excited his fears." He resented "four or five powerful fellows" who kept an "unceasing watch" upon him as they played the part of a Paul Revere who stalked the British so effectively during the imperial crisis.[22]

Higginson, Theodore Parker, and Pellett especially complained about the complacency of most Boston clergymen, noting that they acted the part of "solid middle class citizens" and refused to support a rescue of Burns. The Reverend James Freeman Clarke, an outspoken Unitarian, agreed with them as he upbraided ministers who had not embraced higher law and defended Burns. On June 4, he spoke to a large audience in Williams Hall and lashed out at Bostonians for having failed to live up to the examples of Paul Revere, the Adamses, John Hancock, and their compatriots. He felt ashamed that when "the eyes of the whole North" had looked toward Boston, the city had abandoned Anthony Burns. Clarke wondered if "the tocsin of liberty" would ever again "sound out from Fanueil Hall and State Street." He confessed to suspecting that economic concerns had made Bostonians too focused on their own material wealth to care about the fate of an oppressed fugitive slave. Referring to the city's Revolutionary heritage, the Unitarian minister declared "The rich Boston of 1854 ... [have] not the same energy and patriotism as the poor Boston of 1776."[23]

But many Bostonians, whom radicals regarded as too moderate, ambivalent, or complacent, also drew on their Revolutionary heritage, believing they honored the wisdom of the Founders who had made compromises that still needed to be respected. These antebellum Americans thought they had a responsibility to conserve the fruits of the Revolution, even if that involved respecting the Fugitive Slave Law, which obviously compromised the liberty of enslaved blacks. They pointed out that the administration of George Washington, America's Revolutionary hero, enacted the initial legislation allowing slaveholders to reclaim their human property in the North and argued that the fugitive slave clause of the Constitution revealed the Founders' belief in the need for sectional compromise. Many believed the republican experiment still had to be secured and those who failed to respect the Fugitive Slave Law "commit[ted] treason against their country." They supported the late Daniel Webster's advice to "let patriotism, loyalty to law, the recollections of the past, regard for the present, the good name and fame of this place" guide their actions and reject what Southerners called "mad abolitionism."[24]

When Hayden's battering ram wrenched the courthouse door from its hinges, Higginson and an unidentified man rushed inside. The Worcester minister received "a saber cut across the chin." Sidestepping debris and the broken door, the band of rescuers followed, but a guard quickly sounded an alarm summoning reinforcements. When Marshal Freeman and a handful of deputies rushed to the west side door, they came face-to-face with the rescuers in the dark passageway. A shot was fired just as a "large deputation of police" charged into the square and began to make arrests.[25] Stowell was among the nine persons taken into custody, four of whom were "colored." As the crowd became "quiet," few knew that a guard named James Batchelder, blood gushing from his groin, lay dying and soon "expired" in the courthouse basement. Most onlookers watched the Boston Artillery, led by Major Evans, march smartly along the west side of the building. When the city's mayor, Jerome V.C. Smith, called out a second company of militia, the crowd had begun to disperse. Around two o'clock in the morning, 80 marines paraded into the square; on Saturday morning, the Boston Light Infantry and a detachment of the Boston Light Dragoons also arrived, making the courthouse a "veritable fortress."[26]

That morning, President Franklin Pierce set the stage for the Anthony Burns drama to become the largest American military show of force ever seen in peace-time. When he received a telegraph from Marshal Freeman stating, "I have availed myself of the resources of the United States.... Everything is now quiet," Pierce responded saying "Your conduct is approved." He also authorized the marshal to "incur any expense" that he believed necessary "to ensure the execution of the law." By the time Dana and his law partner Charles Ellis arrived for the resumption of Burns's hearing, they had to make their way through "2 or 3 companies of volunteer militia" and "a company of U.S. marines from Charlestown & a company of Artillery fr[om] Fort Independence."[27] The lawyers requested another adjournment until Monday morning, arguing that they had not had sufficient time

FRANKLIN PIERCE. President Franklin Pierce set the stage for the Anthony Burns drama to become the largest American military show of force ever seen in peacetime when he told officials in Boston to "incur any expense" that were necessary to enforce the Fugitive Slave Law (courtesy Library of Congress).

to prepare Burns's defense. Despite protest from Suttle's attorneys who feared "a renewal of the sad scene of the night previous," Loring agreed. Mayor Smith issued a law-and-order message to Bostonians. "Under the excitement that now pervades the city," proclaimed Smith, "you are respectfully requested to cooperate with the Municipal Authorities in the maintenance of peace and good order. The laws must be obeyed, let the consequences be what they may." He received applause and reports indicated many law-abiding citizens "retired" from the square.[28]

Smith, however, could not quiet the radicals. If anything, he set them more on fire. On Sunday morning in Boston's Music Hall, Theodore Parker was unrelenting in his criticism of Loring for having issued Burns's arrest warrant and he blamed him for Batchelder's death. That day, some congregations, notably those of black churches, took collections for the bondsman and prayed "for the escape of Burns." Grimes preached in earnest to the members of the Twelfth Baptist Church, especially those who had subscribed to the purchase attempt that U.S. District Attorney Benjamin Hallett had foiled the day before.[29] On Saturday, Grimes had jumped on a chance to purchase Burns's liberty when Edward Parker, arguing for continuing the hearings, said that if the tribunal surrendered Burns to Suttle that day, the latter would offer him for sale. When Loring adjourned proceedings, Grimes met with the slaveholder and convinced him to sell Burns for $1,200, conditional on the transaction being completed by midnight. After Hamilton B. Willis, a wealthy Bostonian merchant, agreed to fund the purchase if Grimes obtained sufficient pledges, the pastor spent all day Saturday trying to come up with donors. Despite the city's wealth, Grimes, having exhausted all his sources and still missing $400 when darkness set in, even turned to U.S. District Attorney Hallett and Suttle's counsel Edward Parker for pledges. When the latter agreed to cover the outstanding balance, however, the clock had struck midnight. With much satisfaction, Hallett blocked the sale, informing Grimes that even if Suttle extended his deadline, the deal could not be completed as Massachusetts law prohibited such transactions on the Sabbath.[30]

When Loring commenced proceedings on Monday morning, it was standing room only in the courtroom. Journalists, Bostonians, visitors to the city, proslavery Southerners, and such out-of-state antislavery politicians as Joshua R. Giddings crammed inside. Thomas and Parker opened for the claimant, presenting copies of the Virginia slave code and the court transcript identifying Burns and confirming Suttle's ownership of him. Strengthening what many thought was already an "iron clad" case, the claimant's lawyers had Brent confirm that the prisoner was the "same Anthony Burns whom he had so well known" and the Virginian also testified that he hired Burns to work on his Falmouth plantation during "the years 1846, 1847, and 1848." Suttle's agent added that Burns had been rented to Millspaugh and that he had escaped from his service. He indicated that the last time he saw the prisoner in Virginia was on March 20 — a date when some Bostonians knew Burns was in Massachusetts. Thomas asked Brent about the conversation between Suttle and Burns in the courthouse on the evening of the arrest; the Virginian answered, saying that the prisoner had admitted he was Suttle's slave.[31] Burns's attorneys objected, arguing that the Fugitive Slave Law prohibited an alleged fugitive's testimony and, hence, whatever Brent had reported Burns as having said should be struck from the record. The commissioner, however, accepted Burns's alleged remarks, saying "the word testimony in the law must be regarded as referring only to evidence given by a witness, and not, to confessions or admissions." Simply put, Loring allowed Burns's words to be used against him. Dana and Ellis also questioned the use of a transcript from a Virginia court to certify Suttle's ownership of Burns as evidence before a tribunal in Massachusetts.

That afternoon, Burns's lawyers sought to strengthen their defense by contesting the Fugitive Slave Law, putting forth arguments similar to those of Byron Paine in Sherman Booth's trial. Challenging the law's constitutionality, Ellis singled out its abridgment of fundamental common-law writs, including the writ of habeas corpus. Noting that the Fugitive Slave Law deprived the accused of liberty "without the due process of law," he also said that the Constitution did not empower Congress to legislate on the subject of fugitive slaves. Additionally, consistent with Robert Rantoul's arguments in the Thomas Sims case, Ellis questioned the constitutionality of the law on the grounds that it "conferred judicial power on a commissioner 'who is not a judge.'" Loring listened to these arguments and the testimony of several witnesses, including the window cleaner William Jones and the Mattapan Iron Works accountant George Drew, who said that the Anthony Burns whom Brent saw in Virginia on March 20 could not have been the prisoner because he had worked in Boston on that day. Concluding for the defense, Dana stressed the question of identity, arguing that Burns should be regarded as a freeman until the claimant had conclusively proved him to be his slave, which he said the Virginia court record and Brent's testimony had not accomplished.[32]

At dawn on Friday, June 2, Boston's Court Square was already a scene of great activity as "a company of United States Infantry and a detachment of Artillery" mounted a cannon in front of the courthouse and pointed it "towards Court Street." The forces of law and order were soon joined by a throng of Bostonians and visitors to the city. "As early as six o'clock," people filed into the square, seeking to secure good positions in front of the courthouse — three hours before the time that Loring had scheduled to announce his ruling.[33] Many people had come from quite far away; some "six or seven hundred" persons had followed Higginson and Stowell from Worcester. The biracial crowd included men and women from all walks of life and Charles Emery Stevens claimed "an overwhelming number" opposed the execution of the Fugitive Slave Law on Massachusetts free soil. By seven o'clock in the morning, "streets resounded with the strains of martial music" as United States troops, state militia, police, and a detachment of marines marched into the square. Before nine o'clock, when thousands milled "about the square," city officials distributed copies of Mayor Smith's proclamation. "To secure order throughout the city this day, Major-General Edmands and the Chief of Police ... are clothed with full discretionary power to sustain the laws of the land," declared the mayor. "All well-disposed citizens and other persons are urgently requested to leave those streets which it may be found necessary to clear temporarily, and under no circumstances to obstruct or molest any officer, civil or military, in the lawful discharge of his duty."[34]

Mingling about the square, Bostonians and other spectators engaged in speculation about the likely outcome of the Burns drama. Many believed that the arguments of Dana and Ellis on the issues of identity and the constitutionality of the Fugitive Slave Law would sway Loring. A journalist for the *Evening Transcript* noted that Dana had demonstrated that "any dark complexioned man, having a scar and a cut like those mentioned, was liable for arrest as Col. Suttle's slave." Dana himself was happy with his defense, although in his diary he noted that Loring listened to what he had said on identity but had taken "no notes" regarding his arguments on the conclusiveness of the Virginia court record, proof of Burns's escape, and Suttle's title to Burns as a slave. Speculative sentiment shifted, however, when news surfaced that Asa Butman and some guards gave Burns "a complete new set of clothes" — coattails and a top hat similar to those slaves were often forced to wear at auctions in Southern slave pens. People guessed that the guards had "foreknowledge" of Loring's decision and their gesture "betrayed" it.[35] Butman paid $40 for Burns's outfit, a significant sum at the time.[36]

Their reading proved to be correct. Looking "haggard and jaded," Loring had difficulty facing his audience and the Harvard law lecturer read his decision like a nervous schoolboy. "Soldiers with fixed bayonets filled all the avenues" around the courthouse and inside the courtroom Mayor Smith's volunteer guards, many of them recent immigrants from Ireland "armed with bludgeons and pistols," surrounded a discouraged Burns wearing his new suit of clothes.[37] As Theodore Parker put it, Loring confirmed "the subserviency of Boston to the slave oligarchy of the South" at the expense of Burns, who sat manacled before him.[38]

Loring began his ruling by addressing the issue of Burns's right to a jury trial. He stated that the purpose of the Fugitive Slave Law was the extradition of the alleged fugitive, which he considered to be a "ministerial, not a judicial act" that could be carried out by an official exercising executive rather than judicial authority. Dismissing the argument that commissioners assumed powers that the Constitution granted only to judges, Loring stated the tribunal's task was to verify the identity of the individual arrested and he reasoned that "there is no provision in the Constitution requiring the identity of a person to be arrested to be determined by a jury."[39] He also overruled Burns's lawyers' questioning of the Virginia transcript as evidence in a court of law in Massachusetts and upheld the constitutionality of the Fugitive Slave Law, citing the opinion of Massachusetts chief justice Lemuel Shaw in the Sims case. Loring declared that he had only two issues to rule on — whether Burns owed Suttle service and the identity of the prisoner before him. On the former, he stated that Thomas and Parker had given the court "conclusive evidence" that Burns owed service to Suttle. On the question of identity, he ruled on the basis of the prisoner's statements on the night of his arrest, thus disregarding Burns's attorneys' arguments that the law specifically prohibited an alleged fugitive slave's testimony.[40] Loring concluded that the slaveholder was "entitled to the certificate" authorizing him to take "the said Burns, from the State of Massachusetts back to the State of Virginia."[41] Burns's departure from the courthouse was set for two o'clock that afternoon. The *John Taylor*, already waiting at Boston's Long Wharf, had been consigned to carry Burns to the *Morris*, a federal revenue cutter anchored in the bay ready to take him back to bondage in the Old Dominion.

Moments after Loring rendered his decision, the military began to clear the multitudes from in front of the courthouse and officers were "stationed at every avenue leading to the Square." Marshal Freeman's guards and some 120 volunteers armed with revolvers and sabers formed a hollow square into which they led Burns. Before the procession began to move shortly after two o'clock, the artillery regiment placed the cannon behind Burns's escort to protect it from the rear. As people lined the streets between the courthouse and the harbor, a group of antislavery militants arrived carrying a coffin with the word LIBERTY inscribed upon it. Encountering opposition from some bystanders, they entered the building on the corner of State and Washington Streets and suspended the coffin from an upper window. Nearby, three American flags were "draped" in mourning. The offices of the antislavery newspaper *The Commonwealth* and other businesses owned by abolitionists were closed; some establishments were "festooned in black" to mourn the death of liberty. People crammed into offices, rooms, and passageways that had good views of the Burns procession's route. In John Andrew's law office at the corner of State and Washington Streets, the Reverend James Freeman Clarke joined the future governor of Massachusetts and several other people. It was "time for this community to put on mourning — to wear black crepe on the arm," lamented Clarke, "because Honor is dead, because Humanity is dead, because Massachusetts has been placed by her own acts beneath the feet of Virginia."[42]

Not all the "thousands upon thousands of people" who took in the spectacle mourned for Burns. Like the ruffians who attempted to seize the LIBERTY coffin, some spectators supported the execution of the Fugitive Slave Law. With cheers, they sought to drown out hisses, cries of "Shame! Shame!" and shouts of "kidnappers, kidnappers" that resonated throughout the narrow streets of the Old Bay City. Some even joined troops singing "Carry Me Back to Old Virginny," a gesture that shocked Burns supporters, notably the young free black Charlotte Forten, who thought the soldiers were "without mercy." Still others showed themselves to be "indifferent spectators" who gathered for "no other motive than curiosity" and they too did not "clamor for his [Burns's] release." As the procession headed toward the harbor, many of the estimated 50,000 persons who caught "a parting glimpse" of Virginia's most famous fugitive slave moved down to the docks, where authorities had stationed troops from Fort Independence and U.S. marines patrolled the waterfront. The unprecedented show of military force prevented anyone from attempting a rescue and three weeks later Suttle lodged Burns in Robert Lumpkin's slave trading jail in Richmond.[43]

Reactions to Burns's departure underscored antebellum Americans' different "commitments to law and order," diverse political ideologies, and competing views of the republican experiment. For some, the challenge was to conserve the order the Revolution had produced. For others, notably Northern blacks and their white abolitionist allies, the Revolution continued. Militants, especially blacks like Frederick Douglass and Lewis Hayden, advocated force as "a means to achieve emancipation" but so also did a growing number of whites who, invoking the Revolutionary legacy and heroism of their forebears, called on Americans to "complete the revolution" and extend American liberties to blacks. Parker Pillsbury, for example, now advocated that the enslaved "should be encouraged to rise up and assert their liberty in the spirit of 1776." He said that "the time for bullets had come." The English abolitionist Harriet Martineau wrote that after Burns's return to bondage a "pregnant cloud ... lowered on Massachusetts." "The tempest," she thought, "seems to be very near." She believed that the clash involved ancient English liberties—the very liberties that antebellum Americans' forefathers had fought and died for, "privileges which had been transplanted from the field of Runnymede into the valleys of Massachusetts." Martineau saw it as "the battle of Independence over again." The Revolution continued.[44]

Blacks shared her view. Speaking to the New England Antislavery Society while Burns languished in Boston's courthouse, Charles Lenox Remond railed against the South's Peculiar Institution as well as the Fugitive Slave Law. He also defended African Americans' rights to share in the "glory of Bunker Hill" and the "noble deeds" of Lexington and Concord. When blacks witnessed many of their white neighbors acquiescing to Burns's return to the "iron house of bondage," an increasing number of them began to believe that they had to take the lead in the antislavery fight. "We have, as a people, depended upon the [white] abolitionists to do that for us, which we *must* do for ourselves," declared James Watkins speaking in Columbus, Ohio. Frederick Douglass declared that blacks had "a special mission to perform in the United States—a mission which none but themselves could perform." As far as he was concerned, the Burns rendition demonstrated that "slavery has a right to go any where in this Republic and Liberty [for African Americans] no where, except where Slavery will let it."[45]

Burns, humiliatingly escorted back to slavery before thousands of spectators, imprisoned at Lumpkin's jail, and finally sold at auction to a North Carolina slave-trader from whom the Reverend Grimes purchased his liberty a few months later, took a similar message. Studying at Oberlin College after he became free, Burns heard that some proslavery whites wanted to re-enslave him. He reacted by drawing on what he considered the Revolution's legacy. "[S]hould [someone] attempt to deprive me of my liberty," proclaimed Burns, "then I would enforce the motto of Patrick Henry, 'Liberty or Death.'" And he continued, claiming his natural right to liberty. "God made me a man — not a slave," declared the black Virginian. "I utterly deny that those things which outrage all right are laws. To be real laws they must be founded in equity."[46] Burns strived for the ideals enshrined by the greatest patriots of 1776. After his studies at Oberlin, Burns continued to do so as he lectured against slavery and preached at the Zion Baptist Church in St. Catharines, Ontario. Many in his congregation were fugitives who, like him, bore the scars of slavery. He died from tuberculosis at the age of only 28.

CHARLES LENOX REMOND. As Charles Lenox Remond attacked slavery in the American South and the federal government's enforcement of the Fugitive Slave Law on free soil, he claimed American liberties for his enslaved brothers and sisters, saying African Americans had just as much right as whites to share in the "glory of Bunker Hill" and the "noble deeds" of Lexington and Concord (courtesy Trustees of the Boston Public Library).

Remarkably, just as blacks and white abolitionists turned to the example of their heroic forebears during the Burns drama, so did slaveholding Southerners. In

ANTHONY BURNS. If anyone sought to re-enslave him, Anthony Burns said that he "would enforce the motto of Patrick Henry, 'Liberty or Death'" (Library of Congress).

their view, their rights to human property were rooted in the compromise agreed to by the Founders. Abolitionist agitation and the inflammatory rhetoric heard during the Fanueil Hall rally fueled secessionist sentiment as Southerners firmly embraced the Georgia Platform demanding "a faithful execution of the *Fugitive Slave Law*" as a condition for remaining in the Union. For many white Southerners, the display of military might required for Suttle to reclaim his property in Boston proved that abolitionism ran rampant in the free states and that Northerners were unwilling to respect Southern rights and the compromises of the Constitution. "No man of sound mind can read the Debates of the Convention that framed the Constitution and not be convinced that without the clause for the rendition of fugitive slaves, no compact could have been formed between our ancestors," said John Reuben Thompson, the outspoken editor of the *Southern Literary Messenger*. Thompson reasoned that "when that compact is set at naught — when we can no longer safely repose under its over-arching canopy ... it will be time to dissever the bonds that unite us as the fetters of an ignominious thralldom."[47] Embracing such messages and reading antislavery newspaper reports applauding the "riotous and disgraceful proceedings of the Boston Abolitionists," slaveholding Southerners concluded that Southern Nationalists such as the late John C. Calhoun had been right all along. The "equilibrium between the two sections" was very much "endangered" and Southern interests were increasingly at risk. As a *Richmond Enquirer* editorial said, it was now time for them to "sever a connexion ... maintained only for their oppression."[48]

Taking their cue from their Revolutionary forefathers, white Southerners reacted to the Burns drama in two ways. First, they sought to construct a socio-political order led by virtuous elites — benevolent planters who stood at the apex of a republican order that ensured their natural rights to property as they cared for their extended families, which included their bonded laborers. A new generation of proslavery advocates, men like George Fitzhugh, James Hammond, and Edmund Ruffin, helped to construct a vision that evolved into a powerful Confederate ideology based on slavery as a positive good. Slavery was no longer a necessary evil; rather, it "made the South a better society" and promoted "human happiness" as it helped lend stability through "a hierarchical, almost organic, order that assigned everyone an appropriate station in life but ensured that even the weakest members of society — slaves and poor whites — would be cared for." Second, calling for boycotts against Northern manufactures — similar to those their Revolutionary forefathers had implemented against British goods — Southern whites sought to distance themselves from the North to avoid exposure "to the evil influence of Northern fanaticism and vice" as they also strengthened Southern manufacturing.[49]

Paradoxically, however, it was the Pierce administration's rigid enforcement of the Fugitive Slave Law to protect a slaveholder's right to his human property with an unprecedented display of military force that convinced many white Southerners, "steeped in the doctrines of liberty and limited government," that they alone were the true heirs to the Revolutionary legacy. For them, secession became the means to ensure what they saw as their Revolutionary heritage. Commenting on events in Massachusetts, the editor of the *Richmond Enquirer* remarked, "Such instances of the violent repression of the popular passions by military force as we have just seen in Boston, are terrible necessities in a republican Government." But he did not stop there. Reflecting fear and hatred of standing armies, born under Stuart kings in Early Modern England and re-ignited on American soil during the imperial crisis, the editor reasoned that "despotism executes its purpose with the bayonet, but in free Governments the supremacy of law is dependent on the voluntary submission of public opinion." He contended that "institutions of liberty cannot co-exist with military violence, and when a free Government is driven to invoke the aid of the soldiery to carry out its laws, the day of its overthrow" is close at hand. Juxtaposing this reasoning on the implementation of martial law in Boston, from the night of the Courthouse Riot until Burns's departure from the city, he concluded that the "decay has already begun, the contagion of insubordination will rapidly spread, and the exercise of military power in repression of popular outbreaks will be no longer a remedy in great emergencies but an expedient of every day and [a] familiar resort." For many white Southerners, secession became a duty to conserve their Revolutionary heritage, to protect *their* ancient liberties, and to preserve their honor as virtuous slaveholding elites.[50]

During the Anthony Burns drama, antebellum Americans claimed their Revolutionary heritage and the liberties they believed it bestowed upon them or should bestow upon them. Blacks and whites, men and women, Northerners and Southerners exercised agency as they invoked their heroic forbears as examples. They transformed themselves into American Revolutionaries and Anthony Burns was certainly one of them. The drama marked one of nineteenth-century America's great poets:

> ... And, as I thought of Liberty
> Marched handcuffed down that sworded street,
> The solid earth beneath my feet
> Reeled fluid as the sea.
> I felt a sense of bitter loss, —
> Shame, tearless grief, and stifling wrath,
> And loathing fear, as if my path
> A serpent stretched across.[51]

CHAPTER 8

Margaret Garner
Tragedy and Revolutionary Resistance in Cincinnati

Patrick Henry spoke the words—"Give me liberty or give me death!" Margaret [Garner] did the deed, and with her own hand took the life of her child, dearer to her own heart than her own life, and would have done the same to her other three children, and then to herself, had there been time, to save herself, and them from the cruelties and sufferings of [slavery].—*Liberator*

...[S]he appealed to the Government in vain, and then she heroically gave her child to the pale messenger, and bade him carry her little one back to the bosom of its Maker.— Parker Pillsbury

...[I]f ever there was a time when it was a good deed to give a weapon to those who fought the battle of liberty on Bunker's Hill—if those patriots had the right to use the arms supplied to them—she who said, "Let us go to God rather than go back to slavery," had the same right ... the same right that those had who seized their weapons to fight about a paltry tax on tea.— Lucy Stone

On the evening of January 27, 1856, President Franklin Pierce, a native son of New Hampshire, had begun his final year at the White House. Having filed suit for his freedom in Missouri courts in 1846, Dred Scott had been engaged in a legal fight for his liberty for a decade. In Kansas, the Wakarusa War pitted proslavery ruffians against Free Soilers and the death toll continued to rise. The great Massachusetts Free Soil senator Charles Sumner relentlessly attacked slavery. In less than five months, he would give his "Bleeding Kansas" speech, insulting Senator Andrew Pickens Butler of South Carolina, for which congressman

Preston Brooks caned him nearly to death in the Senate chamber. During the fall elections that year, antebellum Americans would talk about Bleeding Sumner–Bleeding Kansas, the Sack of Lawrence, the Pottawatomie Massacre, and John Brown. But at dusk that evening, most Northerners just hoped to survive probably the worst winter any of them had ever experienced. Biting winds and freezing temperatures transformed a "sleet-tempest" in Kansas into an artic blizzard that swept across Northern Kentucky, Ohio, Pennsylvania, New York, and New England, covering the landscape with a record snowfall, making travel virtually impossible, and freezing anyone who ventured outdoors. In Binghamton, New York, the editor of the *Daily Republican* reported that a snow plow pushed by four train engines had not been able to clear the drifts that "accumulated on the track during the previous forty-eight hours." In "the Queen City of the West," the storm hit on Sunday afternoon as temperatures dropped and heavy snow began to fall. By Sunday night, Cincinnatians complained of "snow-clogged" streets and police chased mischievous youths who caused pandemonium by throwing snowballs that "frightened horses into bolting with the sleighs they pulled."[1] In Boone and Kenton Counties on the Kentucky side of the Ohio River, two separate groups of slaves watched the snow accumulate as they waited for their owners to fall asleep. Late that night, under the cover of darkness and blinding snow, they made their bid for freedom. In the months ahead, antebellum Americans would be talking about some of them as well.

Eight members of the Garner family comprised one of the groups of fleeing bondspersons. Robert Garner, a twenty-two-year-old, six-foot-tall slave of James Marshall, borrowed his master's horse-drawn sleigh to make the fifteen-mile trip to Covington, the Kentucky town situated just across the river from Cincinnati. After embarking his parents Simon and Mary, who were also owned by Marshall, Robert drove to Archibald Kinkhead Gaines's neighboring Maplewood Plantation where he picked up his pregnant, mulatto wife Margaret, known also as Peggy, and their four children — six-year-old Thomas, four-year-old Samuel, the almost-white two-year-old Mary, and the infant Priscilla, usually called Cilla. Born on June 4, 1833, at Richwood Station, the attractive Margaret, a year older than her husband, was initially the property of Archibald's older brother John P. Gaines, the former congressman and Mexican war hero whom President Zachary Taylor appointed Governor of the Oregon Territory when Margaret was about sixteen. Before moving west, the older Gaines sold Maplewood and some ten to twelve slaves "including Margaret" to his younger brother. Unlike John, who acted as a benevolent patriarch, the new owner ruled the plantation with an iron hand. He had a violent temper and few qualms about using the cowhide or putting his slaves in irons. The Garners sought to escape "cruel treatment on the part of their master," which, in the case of the attractive Margaret, almost certainly included sexual abuse. She also had been beaten and had a scar on her face that she claimed was the result of "being struck by a 'white man'" — most likely Archibald Gaines, the only adult white male at Maplewood after he acquired the plantation. Margaret was a member of the Richwood Presbyterian Church and perhaps her Christian faith helped her through her suffering. That Sunday night Garner drove the sleigh "through the snowswept hills," arriving on the banks of the Ohio at the "twilight of the morning."[2]

Garner left Marshall's horses and sleigh "standing" beside a livery stable in front of Covington's Washington Hotel. He led his parents and young family through the snowdrifts on the banks of the Ohio and then across the frozen river, hoping that the blowing snow would hide their tracks from slave catchers. After making "several inquiries" on the Ohio side of the river, the Garners reached the house of Joe and Sarah Kite just "below Mill Creek" in lower Cincinnati some time around daybreak. A former slave in Kentucky, Joe Kite had purchased his freedom, as well as that of his wife Sarah, from their master William Harper. In the mid–1840s, the Kites had moved to Cincinnati and Joe, Margaret Garner's uncle, had become well-known in Bucktown, the city's black community. The Kites' son Elijah, Margaret's cousin, lived with his parents. He too had been manumitted by Harper and worked in one of Cincinnati's slaughterhouses. Elijah "had been advised" of the Garners' planned arrival and he welcomed them at the house. The Kites gave the family breakfast by the hot stove, which they undoubtedly appreciated after a fifteen-mile sleigh ride followed by a two-mile walk in wintry conditions. Shortly afterward, Elijah left to see Levi Coffin, then living at the corner of Sixth and Broadway Streets, to arrange for the family to get out of the city unnoticed. Coffin, Cincinnati's most active Underground Railroad conductor, helped some 3,000 runaways escape to Canada. That morning he and his associates had been busy guiding the other group of runaway Kentucky slaves who reached Ohio free soil before the Garners. Six of that group of nine belonged to a wealthy Covington merchant named Levi F. Daughtery; three other Kenton County slaves had joined them in their flight. After their escape had been discovered, Covington Deputy Marshal Clinton Butts led a posse across the river, only to find that the fugitive slaves had headed uptown and by daybreak Coffin had already managed to get them out of the city and on their way to freedom in Canada. In contrast, the Garners' tragedy was about to begin. Before the family stepped on free soil at Western Row on the Cincinnati side of the river, Archibald Gaines had discovered their flight. He and James Marshall's son Thomas, joined by their neighbor Major William B. Murphy, saddled their horses and were in "hot pursuit" before sunrise.[3]

Entering the city "about 7 o'clock" that morning, the Kentuckians hastened to the Cincinnati police station and then to the office of Commissioner John L. Pendery where they "swore out" an affidavit confirming James Marshall's ownership of Robert and his parents and Gaines's title to Margaret and the children. Meanwhile at the Kite house, the Garners finished breakfast and waited impatiently for Elijah to return from meeting Coffin. Under the authority of Fugitive Slave Law of 1850, Pendery prepared an arrest warrant and, since the city's Marshal Hiram Robinson, also the publisher of the *Cincinnati Enquirer*, was in Columbus, the commissioner summoned Deputy Marshal George Bennet to organize another slave-catching posse. By about half past nine, warrant in hand, Bennet left the commissioner's office accompanied by Kentuckians Gaines, Marshall, and Murphy, Clinton Butts and his Covington deputies, and some well-armed Cincinnati recruits who had been quickly deputized. They headed directly to the Kites' house as the Covington slave catchers had received "intelligence" confirming that the Garners were there. As the slave-hunting procession made its way along the snow-covered streets of the nation's sixth largest city of some 110,000 people, including about 3,500 African Americans, Cincinnatians, black and white, swarmed in behind them. When the slave catchers reached Kite's place around 10 o'clock, not long after Elijah had returned with Coffin's instructions to move the Garners to a safer hiding place on the outskirts of town, a large biracial crowd had gathered. Within the hour, it reached "several hundred" people and many appeared indignant, which caused

Bennet to worry about a rescue attempt. Some onlookers surely wondered how the deputies had known where to find the Garners.[4] Robert Garner did, and he later concluded that Elijah had betrayed the family for a payoff from slave hunters.[5]

With Gaines, Marshall, and Murphy looking on, the drama dubbed "The Dreadful Slave Tragedy" or "A Tale of Horror" quickly unfolded. Within days thousands, perhaps millions, of Americans would know about what the American Antislavery Society said was "the most touching and the most terrible" fugitive slave story. For the next several weeks, many Americans shifted their gaze from the troubled soil of Kansas to Cincinnati and the city suddenly found itself at the center of the national debate over slavery. With his men stationed around the Kite house, Bennet approached the front door, read the arrest warrant, and ordered the occupants "to surrender." When he received no response, Murphy joined him and also called upon those inside to give themselves up. Murphy knew the Kites from their days in Kentucky and he convinced Joe and Elijah Kite to submit. But Robert Garner, revolver in hand, overruled them; nobody surrendered, so the officers decided to storm the door.[6] Two Kentuckians, the deputy marshals Butts and Robertson, led the charge and, with chunks of wood, attempted to batter down the door. Determined to resist the assault, Garner threw open a window and leveled his gun to fire at the attackers. The deputy marshal John Patterson, standing directly in front of him, "threw up his hand" to protect his face just as Garner pulled the trigger. The bullet severed one of the deputy's fingers and lodged just above his mouth, "inflicting a severe flesh wound," fracturing his jaw, and breaking several teeth. Just then, however, the front door broke from its hinges and the Covington deputies burst into the house. Garner fired three more times "without effect" before the officers overpowered him and "wrenched the pistol from his hand."[7]

Having eliminated the threat from Garner and hearing "agonized" cries, the deputies looked into the backroom of the small Kite house. In one corner lay two-year-old Mary, bleeding to death with her throat cut "from ear to ear" and blood "sprouting out profusely" with every beat of her heart. The deputies described the head of "the little girl of rare beauty" as having been almost "severed" from her body and she lay "weltering" in a growing pool of her own blood.[8] Some accounts said Margaret still brandished one of Elijah Kite's slaughterhouse butcher knives "literally dripping with gore over the heads" of her two young boys who screamed for help. Although she had not fatally wounded them, she had slashed the youngsters "across the head and shoulders." Some witnesses claimed that when the deputies entered the house, Margaret had a fire-stove shovel in her hands and had just "inflicted a heavy blow" upon her little Cilla's face, causing the infant's nose to bleed profusely. Most accounts suggested that Robert and Margaret Garner resisted the deputies "with the ferocity of tigers" and, when overpowered, Margaret admitted to having slain Mary, declaring also that "she would like to kill the three others rather than see them reduced to slavery." Robert's mother later testified that Margaret, weapon in hand, had asked for her help in slaying the children, shouting "before my children shall be taken back to Kentucky I will kill every one of them."[9] A few days later, when the Reverend P.C. Bassett visited her in the county jail, Margaret explained that she did not want her children "to suffer as she had done" and that she had intended to kill them before taking her own life. Bondage, asserted Margaret, was "a life more bitter than death" and she said her little ones were better "to go home to God than back to slavery." Gazing at the ghastly scene in the back room, Bennet sent for Dr. John Menzies, the Cincinnati coroner; surveying the angry, ever-growing throng outside, he also called for more deputies.[10]

When officers led the manacled Garners and their "little sufferers" to the horse-drawn baggage wagons waiting on the street, a "prodigious" crowd had gathered. News of the arrests had spread with the speed of lightning, especially in black Cincinnati. "Hundreds of blacks" converged on the area and the city that sometimes seemed to straddle the Ohio served again as a stage for the contest between slavery and African American freedom. Though journalists described the melancholy child-murder as "too horrible," undoubtedly Margaret's black sisters understood what she had endured. But the multitudes also reflected the increasing organization of black Cincinnati. In 1849, the black community had mobilized in an attempt, albeit unsuccessful, to save George Washington McQuerry from being returned to bondage. In 1853, a fugitive slave named Louis slipped out of a packed courtroom and black Cincinnatians spirited him out of the city and off to Canada. By the mid–1850s, black Cincinnati boasted several vibrant groups modeled and distinctly named after associations that had been instrumental in the struggle for American Independence. The Cincinnati-based Sons of Liberty, the Daughters of Samaria, the Life Guards, and the Anti-Slavery Sewing Society strived to advance black freedom and help runaways escape to Canada.[11]

It was thus not surprising that the deputies dreaded a rescue attempt, and Bennet pulled a few proslavery men from the crowd and deputized them at the scene. Only then did the officers convey their charges to the wagons before the increasingly rowdy crowd. Bennet's recruitment of special deputies that morning began a process that Marshal Robinson continued until the end of the Garner drama. By then, the special-deputy count totaled more than four hundred and Cincinnati was, for all intents and purposes, under martial law. Although many of Robinson's recruits came from "the Kentucky side" of the Ohio River, many had come recently from Ireland and competed with Cincinnati blacks for manual work. After the officers secured the Garners in the carts, the procession headed to the marshal's office on Fourth Street between Main and Walnut. "A large crowd of excited people" closed in after the wagons and followed them all the way.[12]

The deputies' troubles did not end there. When Pendery opened proceedings around three o'clock, the mob had become quite unruly. Examining the documents before him, Pendery realized that Thomas Marshall did not have a signed power of attorney to act on behalf of his father and the commissioner had to adjourn the hearing. When he ordered the fugitive slaves to be taken to the Hammond Street jail and officers escorted them toward carriages waiting on the street, "a wild and exciting scene" erupted with antislavery bystanders yelling, "Drive on! Don't take them!" Fearing the crowd's intentions, the coachmen "put the whip to their horses" and rode away as fast as they could, leaving the deputies stranded on the sidewalk with the prisoners. The officers had to call for help before making their way on foot to the jail with a "very large crowd of whites and blacks" threatening them all the way. The hearings lasted over two weeks, unprecedented for Fugitive Slave Law proceedings, which typically lasted a day, and "a large and threatening multiracial crowd" constantly intimidated Robinson's force of deputy marshals. When black Cincinnatians and their allies organized a meeting on Wednesday night to support the Garners—and an even larger rally on Thursday—Robinson and Bennet anxiously watched thousands assemble in the heart of the city. The rallies took place at the Smith and Nixon Hall on Fourth Street, "the best public hall in the city at that time" according to Coffin. On Thursday night, organizers charged an admission fee of twenty-five cents "for the benefit of the slaves," arranged for several leading speakers to address the assembly, and asked the renowned Hutchison Family from New England to sing, making the meeting a compelling movement demanding the extension of American liberties to the now famous African American family.[13]

Federal authorities soon confronted challenges in the courts as well; antislavery militants made sure of that. About two hours after deputies secured the Garners in the Hammond Street jail, Judge John Burgoyne, a probate court judge with antislavery leanings, issued a writ of habeas corpus ordering the county sheriff to bring the fugitive slaves before him. Deputy Sheriff Jeffrey Buckingham served the writ and immediately met resistance from the federal marshal who refused to surrender the Garners. Another boisterous throng gathered quickly. After heated debate and the intervention of Cincinnati Mayor James Faran, the parties agreed to lodge the prisoners in the county jail "ready to be taken out at the order of Judge Burgoyne." When Buckingham left for the county jail with the prisoners, however, Bennet and several special deputies hijacked the procession. They took the family back to the courthouse only to have them taken again later that evening by County Sheriff Gazoway Brashears and a larger force of well-armed officers. The Garners finally arrived at the county jail with Margaret and Robert still wearing clothes stained with Mary's blood. But the saga did not end there. The next morning Brashears, having discovered an error in the writ issued by Judge Burgoyne and likely also acting on proslavery legal advice, announced that he had remanded the prisoners once more into the United States marshal's custody. Although they remained in the county jail, he officially informed Burgoyne that the family was "not in his custody." About the same time, Pendery announced he would postpone hearings for a day to allow for the completion of the coroner's inquest on Mary's death. When the six-person coroner's jury convened at Menzie's office that morning, crowds gathered outside, waiting to hear details on the terrible deed and the expected murder charges. When the jurors went to the county jail to interview Margaret, the crowd followed.[14]

The inquest raised the question of whether criminal indictment under state authority took precedence over federal proceedings under the Fugitive Slave Law, an issue that had not arisen since Thomas Sims's case in 1851 when his supporters unsuccessfully sought to delay his return to Georgia by having him charged for stabbing the slave catcher Asa Butman. Garner supporters saw criminal charges as a means of keeping Margaret — and possibly the other adults—from the clutches of their masters. After the jury interviewed the Garners and news circulated that Margaret confessed that she "cut the throat of the child" and would have killed "all the children," and Robert's mother confirmed that her daughter-in-law had "caught a butcher knife" and done the deed, antislavery Cincinnatians waited impatiently for the criminal charges to be announced and the Garners' attorney John Joliffe began preparing his defense, arguing that the criminal indictment under state law "took priority" over the Kentucky slaveholders' claims under federal legislation. Many observers, including Hamilton County prosecutor James Cox, claimed that the "heroic spirit of that mother" would prevent any Cincinnati jury from agreeing on a guilty verdict on first-degree murder charges and speculated that Margaret would be found guilty on a lesser charge and confined to a state penitentiary, which would give her supporters time to arrange the purchase of her liberty. Similarly, if convicted as accessories to murder, the other adult Garners would remain in Ohio out of the reach of their master.[15]

The child-murder quickly grabbed the attention of the nation's antislavery leaders and a number of militants seized on the drama to denounce slavery, arguing that Margaret's deed reflected resistance to the horrific sexual abuse of female slaves by Southern masters. Margaret, they stated, had denied her status as chattel and fought desperately for inalienable rights to her person and her liberty, contesting the Peculiar Institution's socio-political order and the absolute power of her master by destroying his property — even if it was her child. They said that the almost-white Mary was the child of Archibald Gaines. While her body was still warm and the coroner had not yet arrived, Gaines attempted to leave the scene with the dead child in his arms, presumably intent on taking his own offspring "to Covington for internment." A witness recounted that the slaveholder sobbed "uncontrollably over her corpse." Deputies who moved quickly to stop him from leaving the Kite house premises with the corpse had difficulty wresting little Mary's body from him. Other evidence also suggests that Gaines sexually abused Margaret. Her three youngest children had all been conceived after her husband had been hired out at some distance from the Maplewood Plantation; Margaret's youngest were considerably lighter-skinned than her oldest son Tom, and they were all conceived while Archibald's wife was pregnant. Since most Southern white women "avoided sexual relations during pregnancy," the probability that Gaines wandered into the slave quarters to satisfy his desires is very likely, especially as Robert had not visited Maplewood since Margaret became pregnant with the child she carried at the time.[16]

Lucy Stone, Henry C. Wright, and William Lloyd Garrison led the chorus of activists contending that Margaret was not a frenzied murderer but a "loving, heroic mother." They claimed her actions had been motivated by "her maternal heart" and a desire to save her little girl "from the lash and lust" of a Southern master, nightmares that she had endured. Visiting her in jail, Stone comforted and condoned her, saying "Margaret, we are glad that with the Constitution against you, the law against you and the Court against you one of your children has found its freedom with the angels."[17] As Stone defended Margaret, she elevated her to heroic status and cast her deed as a Revolutionary act. Framing the bondswoman's plight as a struggle for American liberties and natural rights, Stone effectively extended the American Revolution and appropriated it on behalf of Margaret. Speaking to a packed courtroom after proceedings adjourned on February 9th and later to the American Antislavery Society, Stone constructed Margaret Garner's narrative "with epic flourish" and placed her alongside America's pantheon of Revolutionary heroes. She spoke of "heroic times" and Margaret's "heroic action" and she predicted that future chroniclers would make Garner a heroine and write Gaines into history as "her oppressor." For Stone, Garner's valor rivaled that of Washington, Warren, Adams, Hancock, Revere, and their compatriots. "I thought ... the spirit she manifested was the same [as] that of our ancestors to whom we had erected the monument at Bunker Hill," declared Stone. Like the heroes of 1775 and 1776, Margaret proved she had "the spirit that would rather let us all go back to God than back to slavery."[18] With her gripping oratory and vivid descriptions, Stone caught the attention of Americans everywhere, especially when a journalist reported her saying that she had just as much right to put a knife in

Margaret's hand to finish her deed as "those who distributed weapons to the combatants on Bunker's Hill."[19]

Wright seconded Stone as he penned an open letter to William Lloyd Garrison entitled "Liberty or Death — Ohio and Kansas — Anthony Burns Excommunicated...." He too contended that Margaret's actions measured up to the achievements of Washington, Jefferson and their compatriots. "Patrick Henry spoke the words—'Give me Liberty or give me death!'" wrote Wright. "Margaret did the deed, and with her own hand took the life of her child, dearer to her heart than her own life, and would have done the same to herself ... to save herself and them from the cruelties and sufferings" of American slavery.[20] Wright asked the likes of Harriet Beecher Stowe, Henry Ward Beecher, and Theodore Parker to publicize Garner's story and enshrine it alongside the legendary tale of "the noble Virginius [who] seized the dagger, and thrust it into the heart of the gentle Virginia, to save her from the hands of Appius Claudius of Rome."[21] They did, and Theodore Parker also harshly criticized the hypocrisy of whites who claimed liberties for themselves while they countenanced continuing oppression of four million enslaved blacks in the American South. The Garners' story made headlines across the nation, particularly after Robert and his parents also confirmed they would "rather die than be taken back to servitude."[22]

On Wednesday, January 30, 1856, Pendery opened

LUCY STONE. During the Margaret Garner crisis, Lucy Stone asserted that Garner's valor rivaled that of Washington, Warren, Adams, Hancock, Revere, and their compatriots. "[T]he spirit she manifested," said Stone, "was the same [as] that of our ancestors to whom we had erected the monument at Bunker Hill" (Library of Congress).

hearings to decide the fate of the seven Garners who appeared before him — the infant Cilla in her mother Margaret's arms. Antislavery attorneys John Joliffe and James Gitchell represented the Garners; Cincinnati lawyer Francis T. Chambers, along with Samuel T. Wall and John W. Finnell of Covington, acted for the slaveholders. The heavily armed deputy marshals who decided a few days later to wear the "badge of the [French] Legion of Honor," a red ribbon in the breast of their jackets presumably signifying the importance of their duty, guarded the courtroom and surrounded the Garners on the prisoner's bench. Considerable excitement erupted outside the courtroom when deputy marshals refused blacks entry and arrested two men who attempted to force their way in. An irate crowd of some three hundred blacks, supported by a large number of antislavery whites, began protesting and throwing snowballs at the officers. Inside the courtroom, Joliffe challenged the discrimination, complaining also that

HENRY C. WRIGHT. Henry C. Wright said Shadrach's rescuers were "Patriots, heroes, friends of God and Humanity!" They evinced "the spirit of Washington, of Warren, of Hancock, of Adams." During the Garner crisis, he reminded Americans that "Patrick Henry spoke the words — 'Give me Liberty or give me death!'" but he said, "Margaret did the deed, and with her own hand took the life of her child, dearer to her heart than her own life, and would have done the same to herself ... to save herself and them from the cruelties and sufferings" of slavery (courtesy Trustees of the Boston Public Library).

black witnesses for the defense had not been allowed in. After debate, Pendery asked Robinson to appoint a mulatto named William Beckley as a "special deputy" to escort black witnesses into the courtroom. As these events played out, state authorities announced the verdict of the coroner's jury — "That said child [Mary] was killed by its mother, Margaret Garner, with a butcher knife with which she cut its throat." The jury named Robert and his father Simon as accessories to the murder. The jurisdictional contest between federal and state authorities began and Joliffe mounted a twofold defense for the Garners.[23]

The prohibition of slavery in Ohio, which dated from the Northwest Ordinance in 1787, served as Joliffe's first argument. Noting that the state constitution of 1802 had also outlawed slavery, he claimed that when Margaret Garner stepped on Ohio free soil, "the slave fell, and the free woman stood." He told Pendery that he would show that Margaret Garner's master had previously brought her to Cincinnati, which he contended made her legally free. He said the same was true in the cases of the other adult Garners. Wanting time to furnish affidavits and produce witnesses, he demanded a continuance until Thursday, January 31, 1856. Establishing a second line of defense rooted in the jurisdictional issue, Joliffe read the Tenth Amendment stating that "powers not delegated to the United States by the Constitution, nor prohibited by it to the States, are reserved to the States respectively, or to the people." He argued the amendment allowed for the State of Ohio to reserve the execution of criminal law within its jurisdiction "to itself, and no act of Congress can interfere with it." As such, Joliffe reasoned that criminal action under state authority had precedence over the Fugitive Slave Law proceedings and the Garners could not be remanded back to their masters in Kentucky. Chambers objected strongly. "The practical effect of all these sorts of motions," complained the proslavery attorney, would be "to abolish the Fugitive Slave Law at once." Even fugitives committing "some trifling offence," proclaimed Chambers, would be put beyond the reach of their masters. According to him, this was contrary to the Constitution, which guaranteed that "property in slaves shall be held sacred."[24] Joliffe, at his best throughout the Garner drama, responded with sophisticated arguments based on his clients' First Amendment rights. "The Constitution," he affirmed, "expressly declared that Congress should pass no law prescribing any form of religion or preventing the free exercise thereof. If Congress could not pass any law requiring you to worship God, still less could they pass one requiring you to carry fuel to hell." Levi Coffin recalled that "these ringing words called forth applause from all parts of the court-room" and Jolliffe, concluding with stunning oratory, declared

MARGARET GARNER. Attorney John Joliffe contended that all the Garners would "go singing to the gallows rather than be returned to slavery" (Library of Congress).

that "it is for the Court to decide whether the Fugitive Slave law overrides the law of Ohio to such an extent that it can not arrest a fugitive slave even for a crime of murder." Just before Pendery granted continuance and separated the cases of the Marshall and Gaines fugitive slaves, Joliffe confirmed that all the adult Garners wanted liberty or death saying, "It might seem strange that as attorney for these people I should demand that they be given up on a charge of murder, but each and all of them has assured me that *they would go singing to the gallows rather than be returned to slavery.*"[25]

On February 26, 1856, Pendery, having obviously listened carefully to Chambers, rendered judgment. He disregarded Joliffe's argument that the Garners be "discharge[d]" from the motion to reclaim them under the Fugitive Slave Law in order for them to stand trial "upon an indictment found by the Grand Jury of Hamilton County, Ohio, charging them with the crime of Murder in the First Degree, and a *capias* issued upon said indictment for their arrest." Pendery proceeded to rule on the claims under the federal fugitive slave legislation. Indicating that the identity of the Garners was not at issue, the commissioner reasoned that the only question to be resolved was whether the Garners' temporary visits to free soil affected their status as slaves. He accepted Joliffe's evidence that the Garners had spent time on free soil, but he cited jurisprudence that undermined the attorney's arguments — the first being United States Supreme Court Chief Justice Roger Taney's decision in *Strader et al. v. Graham*, a case involving three slave musicians from Kentucky who had entertained in the Free states and, after returning home, fled to Canada on the steamboat *Pike* owned by Strader & Gorman. Their master sought damages from the owners of the vessel. The case went to the Supreme Court on a writ of error and Taney ruled "that the condition of the Negroes as to freedom or slavery after their return depended altogether upon the laws of Kentucky." The implication of this ruling was that the Garners were not freed as a result of having spent time on Ohio free soil; they still owed service under the laws of Kentucky. The second precedent Pendery cited was Taney's opinion in *United States v. The Ship Garonne*, a case involving the status of a Louisiana slave taken on a round-trip to France. The chief justice ruled that the key issue was whether or not the slave left free soil willingly. Juxtaposing Taney's judicial reasoning against the facts of the Garner case, Pendery asked, "the slave having been brought to Ohio by the master, returns with him voluntarily to the State of Kentucky, what, then, is the relation between them?" Because the Garners had voluntarily returned to Kentucky with their master when they previously visited Ohio, Pendery ruled that they had "abandoned [their] right to freedom" under the laws of the free State of Ohio. The Garners, concluded Pendery, had waived their rights to liberty by returning voluntarily to Kentucky.[26]

Although the Garners' fates seemed to be sealed, the jurisdictional contest between federal and state authorities remained and antebellum Americans now looked toward the county jail to see whether Brashears would release the prisoners to the claimants who threatened to file for damages if the sheriff refused to deliver up their human property. A heated public debate ensued with antislavery forces repeating arguments that state criminal charges trumped civil suits under federal fugitive slave legislation; proslavery advocates countered saying the principle of comity required "that where a process, civil or criminal, from one court, either State or Federal, has attached [an action], a process from the other must wait until the first has terminated." Observers noted that the federal authorities' return of Thomas Sims to Georgia prior to his trial on charges of having attempted to murder Asa Butman had precluded resolution of this issue in 1851. As expected, Brashears refused to hand over the prisoners and resolution of the question fell to United States District Court Judge Humphrey Leavitt before whom another writ of habeas corpus was filed on February 26, 1856, immediately after Pendery's decision. Although some antislavery observers hoped Leavitt would confirm the priority of the state criminal process, which would have allowed the sheriff to retain the Garners in his custody, they were soon disappointed. On the morning of February 28, 1856, Leavitt declared that the sheriff's detention of the prisoners was "unlawful" and he ordered that the Garners be remanded immediately to the "possession of the Marshal" so that they could be returned to their owners. Robinson took no chances. With more than four hundred special deputies guarding the route from the jail to the docks, Robinson took custody of the fugitive slaves and conveyed them to a ferry waiting at the banks of the no-longer-frozen Ohio. Robinson also had militia standing by ready to be deployed in the event of an attempted rescue. Multitudes watched the procession; the Garners touched slave soil on the Kentucky side of the river about "an hour after the decision."[27]

Meanwhile, Judge Burgoyne ruled on yet another habeas corpus suit ordering Robinson to bring the fugitive slaves before him. Seeking to delay the Garners' return to Kentucky — at least until they appeared before Judge Burgoyne — Joliffe had arranged for Jesse Beckely, a Cincinnati black involved in the Life Guards, to file this action. When Robinson failed to comply with the judicial order, state authorities charged the marshal with contempt of court and quickly jailed him. Not surprisingly, he "extricate[d] himself" from these circumstances by appealing to Judge Leavitt for a writ of habeas corpus under which he was soon released "on the ground that he was only doing his duty as an officer of the United States."[28]

Even as the Garner family returned to bondage, the legal jousting had not yet come to an end. Under substantial pressure from abolitionists, Ohio's governor Salmon P. Chase, a leading antislavery politician, sought the extradition of Margaret and the other adult Garners in order to prosecute them on charges related to Mary's murder. Chase, who had been absent from Cincinnati during the Garner drama and severely criticized by Wendell Phillips and others for not having prevented them from being removed to Kentucky, sent a requisition to Kentucky's governor Charles Morehouse asking for the Garners to be returned to stand trial.[29] When Morehouse sought to comply, Gaines who by this time had purchased Robert and his parents from Marshall revealed just how devious he could be. When Attorney Joseph Cooper, also carrying money to purchase the Garner children's liberty, sought to take possession of the slaves, he found that news of Morehouse's compliance with Chase's requisition had been "leaked" to the Kentucky planter. "To evade" fulfillment of Chase's request, Gaines had quickly sent the Garners south. He had contracted Clinton Butts to escort them to Louisville and lodge them in the city jail until they could be shipped downriver to one of his two brothers in the Deep South — Benjamin in Gainesville, Arkansas, or Abner Legrand, a cotton broker from New Orleans.[30]

On March 7, 1856, Butts led the Garners to the Louisville docks and placed them on the *Henry Lewis*, a multi-decked, side-wheeler riverboat about two hundred feet in length. The Covington deputy marshal secured the slaves in the hold on the main deck behind the paddle wheels, shackling them two-by-two alongside other bondspersons being sold downriver. The *Henry Lewis* pulled away from the shore around ten o'clock that morning, setting the stage for another Garner tragedy — this one again on an icy cold day.[31] About four o'clock the next morning, the riverboat *Edward Howard*, heading upriver to Cincinnati, collided with the *Henry Lewis*, breaking it in two and setting it ablaze. Some passengers and crew were killed instantly; others were severely injured; and still others were thrown into the icy river. Although the crew quickly released the shackled slaves, including the Garners, from their irons, Margaret, her infant Cilla, and a white woman fell into the river as the section of the *Henry Lewis* on which they were standing keeled over. In the ensuing commotion, the *Henry Lewis*'s black cook "sprang into the river and saved Margaret" who, some reports said, "displayed frantic joy when told that her child had drowned." Butts escaped injury and recovered the remaining Garners. The body of the drowned infant body was never found, causing an antislavery reporter in Boston to write that Cilla died with "a gurgle of despair" and her body had been "swept to sea" where she would confront "the respectable signer of the Fugitive Slave Act [Millard Fillmore] before the bar of Eternal Justice." After the accident, Gaines sent the surviving Garners to Benjamin Gaines's plantation but two weeks later, seeking to silence criticism suggesting that he had been dishonorable by not respecting Chase's requisition, he asked Butts to bring Margaret back to Kentucky. She arrived at Covington on April 2, 1856, and Butts lodged her in the town jail where she stayed until Chase issued a second requisition. When officials sought to claim her for the second time, however, they discovered that Gaines had again shipped her south—first to Lexington by train and then downriver on the *Eclipse* to New Orleans. Antislavery reports cast the detestable slaveholder in "a worse light than ever before" and, in his annual message to the Ohio legislature, Chase complained that under the Fugitive Slave Law, federal officials had been disposed "to encroach" on state authority.[32]

Gaines arranged for the other Garners to be sent to New Orleans as well. Abner Legrand Gaines sold the family to his neighbor Judge Dewitt Clinton Bonham, the owner of Willow Grove Plantation where Margaret lived out the last two years of her life in bondage before dying of typhoid fever in 1858. On her death bed, she urged Robert "never to marry again in slavery" and "to live in hope of freedom." He took her advice. Some five years later, just before the Battle of Vicksburg, Garner fled to Union lines and remained in active service until the end of the Civil War. After the war, he remarried as a freedman and lived in Cincinnati where he sometimes spoke of the dark days of 1856.[33]

Long after Margaret Garner left the Queen City of the West, Cincinnatians continued to feel her presence and her past. Although on the eve of the American Civil War, other events—the Sack of Kansas, Bleeding Sumner, the Pottawatomie Massacre, the Dred Scott decision, the Harper's Ferry Raid, and John Brown's execution—captured the attention of a divided nation and seemingly eclipsed Garner's drama, most Cincinnati residents never forgot it. Indeed, for many of the city's blacks and whites, little Mary's blood represented the first blood of the American Civil War. Other Americans too did not forget the Garner drama and it remained firmly imprinted on their hearts and minds. The immediate effect of the melancholy tale was a veritable "outpouring of sympathy" that destroyed the Compromise of 1850 by making federal fugitive slave legislation "a virtual dead letter." The drama also re-ignited Northerners' demands for stronger personal liberty laws to guarantee rights that had been trampled on by slave catchers. Simply put, the Garner tragedy radicalized antebellum Americans. Sarah Ernst, previously an advocate of Garrisonian pacifism, felt "compelled" to take a more militant stand. "We feel we *can not, dare not* relax in our endeavors," wrote the member of the Ohio Ladies Education Society and the founder of the Cincinnati Anti-Slavery Sewing Circle, "when a *mother* kills one child, and rejoices in the death of another."[34] Ernst was not alone.

From Cincinnati's Fairmount Theological Seminary the Reverend Bassett escalated his attack of Southern slaveholders' "exacting and brutal" oppression of their bonded labor. The Reverend H. Bushnell spoke of slavery as "a life more bitter than death" and, like Lucy Stone, glorified Margaret as "the heroic wife" and a "noble, womanly, amiable, *affectionate mother*."[35] Lydia Maria Child ranked Garner's return with the infamous renditions of Thomas Sims and Anthony Burns. She called on Americans to rekindle the revolutionary spirit as she worried that the Garner case served as evidence that "the reverence for Liberty, which we inherited from our fathers, will gradually die out in the souls of our children."[36] Speaking in Dublin, Ireland, the black abolitionist Sarah Remond cast Margaret Garner as a true martyr who along with Anthony Burns, William and Ellen Craft, and William Parker embraced rights enshrined by the Declaration of Independence. She also thought Garner represented "womanhood defenceless [*sic*], exposed to the very wantonness of insult and without protection from the licentiousness of a brutal master." Like Lucy Stone earlier, Remond singled out the special oppression endured by female slaves. William Lloyd Garrison publicized Remond's Dublin speech, printing key extracts alongside the Reverend A.D. Mayo's address to the New York Legislature entitled "No Slave Hunting in the Empire state." In the fall of 1856, such leading abolitionists as Parker Pillsbury, Samuel Joseph May, and the black Bostonian William C. Nell traveled to Ohio for the Annual Meeting of the Western Anti-Slavery Society. They joined Ohioans in declaring Margaret Garner's rendition "an outrage." Later, Pillsbury also spoke to the Vermont State Anti-Slavery Society and he obviously thought Vermonters shared the same view. Condemning the influence of slavery in politics and religion, he said, "Should a slave-hunter be found prowling in this neighborhood, he would probably find that 'General Stark' and 'Molly Stark' did not die without descendants.... Vermont will tolerate no Anthony Burns or Margaret Garner scene within her borders."[37]

In Massachusetts, antislavery folk were not to be outdone. They too took a strong message from the Garner tragedy. Reciting his work in Boston's Tremont Temple on March 18, 1856, William Wallace Hebbard, a Harvard professor and writer, "deeply moved" his audience and became the first person to immortalize Margaret in verse, including the lines:

> *All hope of Liberty on earth has fled —*
> "But shall they not be free in heaven? she plead;
> And from that heart by man's oppression riven,
> Up went the dread appeal of woe to Heaven: —
> "Forgive, O righteous God, if sin it be,
> I give these treasures back, unstained to Thee!"
> The blade flashed in the light! — one babe was free![38]

Margaret Garner's tale inspired others to write novels. In the summer of 1856, Hattia M'Keehan penned "the first full-length novel" based directly on the tragic story. Entitled *Liberty or Death!; or, Heaven's Infraction of the Fugitive Slave Law*, M'Keehan's work focused on key themes, including sexual abuse and miscegenation, that reflected concerns of ordinary folk who developed an obsession with Margaret's tale.

Evidently, large numbers of Americans supported Margaret Garner, often glorifying her as they underscored the plight of enslaved women. Denouncing the Republican Party for not vehemently attacking the proslavery constituency in the Midwest, Lucy N. Colman penned a letter to the Reverend Samuel J. May asking, "I wonder if ... the triumph of the Republican party in the State of Ohio would carry one throb of joy to the heart of poor Margaret Garner! Would she, in view of such a fact, attempt to make her escape from the hands of those who so wickedly enslave her? Would there be any probability that her liberty would be secured?" Writing from Salem, Ohio, Josephine Griffing honored Margaret Garner, describing her as a "heroic woman" whom Cincinnatians "welcomed upon the soil, with the glorious unction of Samuel Adams, of Revolutionary fame." Her actions, thought Griffing, represented a "vindication of Higher Law." Daniel Mann invoked the legend of Virginius slaying his daughter and, writing to Garrison, suggested that Garner had "proved her title to an equal immortality of honor." The editor of a German American paper, Ludvigh, also wrote to Garrison, remarking that Margaret Garner's sacrifice was superior to that of most mothers during the "glorious Revolution of our fathers."[39]

Like the Founders, on her antebellum landscape Margaret Garner assumed a truly "mythic status," one that the accomplished Garner scholar Steven Weisenburger stresses Kentucky artist Thomas Noble embellished with his painting "The Modern Medea" and novelist Toni Morrison would renew with *Beloved* more than one hundred years later. Indeed, Morrison corrected an outrageous century of cultural amnesia about a truly "compelling" Revolutionary figure whom many antebellum Americans recognized as the embodiment of Patrick Henry's American motto "Liberty or Death" and whose inspiration many black soldiers took with them as they transformed the American Civil War into a war of liberation.[40]

Epilogue
An Enduring Revolution

The Abolitionists, though held up as fanatics and madmen by priest and demagogue, have no madness, either as to their object or the spirit which animates them. WE BELIEVE IN THE DECLARATION OF AMERICAN INDEPENDENCE; and all our fanaticism, from the beginning to this hour, has consisted in this—in meaning just what we say of that Declaration.—William Lloyd Garrison

In the name of our common nature—in the name of the Declaration of Independence—in the name of the law in the Bible ... do break these chains, and give me the freedom which is mine because I am a man, and an American.—The Reverend Samuel Ringgold Ward

In America's exciting past, the contribution of great Americans looms large; it was particularly striking during the nation's first two major defining moments—the American Revolution and the American Civil War. The late antebellum fugitive slave dramas of William and Ellen Craft, Shadrach Minkins, Thomas Sims, William Parker, Jerry, Joshua Glover, Anthony Burns, and Margaret Garner also served as defining moments for Americans and their country, and these events placed another set of heroes on the national stage. These determined African Americans and their allies—black or white, men or women— believed the American Revolution was not yet completed and they fought in earnest, emulating the patriotism and commitment of their forebears as they sought the "more perfect union" that would extend American liberties to all. They embraced Patrick Henry's famous words, "Give me Liberty or Give me Death," and the liberty they strived for was that enshrined in the Declaration of Independence. "In the name of our common nature," said the Reverend Samuel Ringgold Ward, all Americans had a right to their liberty.

Recognizing that these striking fugitive slave dramas reflected continuing revolution and changing the periodization of the American Revolution to acknowledge such reality would give twenty-first-century Americans a more inclusive grand narrative. Furthermore, this would permit African Americans to share fully in, and fully identify with, America's first great defining moment, the American Revolution. African Americans would no longer have to search for some 5,000 blacks who joined the patriot forces of '76 to find their Revolutionary heroes; they would have many remarkable heroes, men and women who merit standing with America's most well-known Revolutionary heroes who until now have been mostly white.

THOMAS WENTWORTH HIGGINSON. After the enactment of the Fugitive Slave Law of 1850, Thomas Wentworth Higginson said that he had become a "revolutionist." When Anthony Burns was returned to bondage, he preached his *Massachusetts in Mourning Sermon* and declared antislavery was no longer "reform, but a Revolution" (Library of Congress).

In linking America's two greatest defining moments, these fugitive slave dramas help underscore the nature of the American Civil War as a war of liberation. They also reveal that the war of liberation actually preceded the Emancipation Proclamation and some 180,000 blacks joining the Union forces and putting their lives on the line, a moment that scholars traditionally argue transformed the war into a struggle for liberation. Prior to the Militia Act of July 1862 and President Abraham Lincoln's landmark proclamation, yes, it was a war primarily for the Union—but it was also a war for "a more perfect union," one to extend American liberties to all just as the late antebellum fugitive slave dramas sought to. During the latter crises, mid–nineteenth-century "revolutionists" strove for the liberties their forebears fought for. Indeed, in many ways, they also engaged in the enduring struggle for that "city on a hill" initiated some two centuries earlier. The late antebellum fugitive slave dramas reflected rehearsals for what was to come and replays of what had gone before. Academic historians need to return these dramas — and the remarkable individuals involved in them — to center stage in the grand American narrative.

Chapter Notes

Introduction

1. George Bancroft, *History of the United States from the Discovery of the American Continent* (Boston: Little Brown, 1854).

2. Alfred F. Young, *The Shoemaker and the Tea Party* (Boston: Beacon Press, 1999), 180. For discussion of Americans seeking to appropriate the Revolution, see Young, 180–194.

3. Gary B. Nash, *Race and Revolution* (Madison: Madison House, 1990); Mary Beth Norton, *Liberty's Daughters: The Revolutionary Experience of Women, 1750–1800* (Boston: Little, Brown, 1980); Linda Kerber, *Women in the Republic* (Chapel Hill: University of North Carolina Press, 1980).

4. Gordon S. Wood, *Radicalism of the American Revolution* (New York: Vintage Books, 1993). For a concise discussion of the various scholarly interpretations of the Revolution advanced by academic historians, see Richard Brown, *Major Problems in the Era of the American Revolution, 1760–1791* (Boston: Houghton Mifflin, 2000), especially 1–26. On Wood's critics, see *William and Mary Quarterly* 3:51 no. 4, 677–704.

5. Peter Linebaugh and Marcus Rediker, *"Many Headed Hydra": Sailors, Slaves, Commoners, and the Hidden History of the Revolutionary Atlantic* (Boston: Beacon Press, 2000).

6. Benjamin Quarles, *The Negro in America* (Chapel Hill: University of North Carolina Press, 1996), xiv (Spirit of '76 quotation); George W. Williams, *History of the Negro Race in America 1619–1880* (1885; New York: Arno Press, 1968), 363, 369.

7. In the introduction to the most recent edition of Quarles's *Negro in America*, Gary Nash describes challenges confronting African American writers who sought to raise the image of blacks in times of virulent white racism. Discussing Williams, Nash points out that he "shared Nell and Brown's nearly exclusive focus on the small number of black Americans who fought to break the chains of slavery on the side of the Americans while ignoring the massive number who fought for freedom on the side of the British." The first black scholar to stress the flight of African Americans to the British was Carter G. Woodson in the work *The Negro in Our History* (1922). Quarles, xv, xvii.

8. Ibid., xviii.

9. Duncan J. MacLeod, *Slavery, Race and the American Revolution* (London: Cambridge University Press, 1974), 28.

10. Douglas R. Egerton, *Death or Liberty: African Americans and Revolutionary America* (New York: Oxford University Press, 2009), 12.

11. Frey, Sylvia, *Water from the Rock: Black Resistance in a Revolutionary Age* (Princeton: Princeton University Press, 1991), 108–143; Malcolm, Joyce Lee, *Peter's War: A New England Slave Boy and the American Revolution* (New Haven: Yale University Press, 2009).

12. Albert Reville, *The Life and Writings of Theodore Parker* (London: Simpkin, Marshall, 1865), 116; Williams, 381. Williams wrote, "The thunder of the guns of the Revolution did not drown the voice of the auctioneer. The slave-trade went on. A great war for the emancipation of the colonies from the political bondage into which the British Parliament fain would precipitate them did not depreciate the market value of human flesh," 402.

13. I refer especially to the outpouring of African American literature that began with John W. Blassingame's *The Slave Community: Plantation Life in the Antebellum South*, which challenged Stanley Elkins's Sambo thesis.

14. Adopting this approach, we could go further and argue, from the African American perspective, for the ratification of the Four-

185

teenth or Fifteenth Amendment as the appropriate date for the end of the Revolution. By analogy the appropriate date for women would be the adoption of the Nineteenth Amendment when their full claim to citizenship and realization of their natural rights as persons were achieved. Similarly, we might argue that gay and lesbian Americans are still struggling for full recognition of their liberties and rights.

15. Douglas R. Egerton, "The pervasive language of liberty and equality, which reached its rhetorical peak during the overheated partisan warfare of the late 1790s, could not help but politicize black Virginians.... His [Gabriel's] faith was that white mechanics would see in his own struggle for liberty and economic rights grounds for accepting his support — and that of his soldiers." Egerton, *Gabriel's Rebellion*, x–xi.

16. Daniel Rasmussen, *American Uprising: The Untold Story of America's Largest Slave Revolt* (New York: HarperCollins, 2011), 90–91. Rasmussen stresses "the links to revolutionary Haiti were far closer than the planters would have liked. And there is little doubt that Kook and Quamana [not to mention Deslondes] used the stories of this revolution to inspire and cajole their fellow slaves into joining their planned insurrection."

17. Stephen B. Oates is one of several authors who has underscored the revolutionary visions of both Turner and Vesey. He highlighted Turner's "epochal vision" and the "rage [that] burned in him —fed by the prodigious chasm between what he was and what he aspired to be"; Oates described Vesey as an "appalled" yet "inspired" leader who also "lectured fellow blacks on the Declaration of Independence." Oates, *The Fires of Jubilee: Nat Turner's Fierce Rebellion* (New York: Harper, 1990), 48–49.

18. Theodore Parker, *The Collected Works of Theodore Parker*, ed. Frances Power Cobbe (London: Trübner, 1864), 271.

19. Jane H. Pease and William H. Pease, *They Who Would Be Free: Blacks' Search for Freedom, 1830–1861* (New York: Atheneum, 1974), 299. On Samuel May, see also Donald Yacovone, *Samuel Joseph May and the Dilemmas of the Liberal Persuasion, 1797–1871* (Philadelphia: Temple University Press, 1991). Some Southerners, even slaveholders, believed that the Founders had not intended to enshrine slavery. Edward Coles, who emancipated his slaves going down the Ohio River, was an example of a Southerner who still sought "a more perfect Union." See Kurt E. Leichtle and Bruce G. Carveth, *Crusade Against Slavery: Edward Coles, Pioneer of Freedom* (Carbondale: Southern Illinois Press, 2011). Other emancipators took their cue from natural rights philosophy and believed themselves to be acting as good revolutionaries as they sought the emancipation of their slaves. See Melvin Patrick Ely, *Israel on the Appomattox: A Southern Experiment in Black Freedom* (New York: Alfred A. Knopf, 2004), 5–15.

20. Cassandra Pybus, *Epic Journeys of Freedom: Runaway Slaves of the American Revolution and their Global Quest for Liberty* (Boston: Beacon Press, 2006), 4. Pybus stresses that it is not surprising that African Americans, including George Washington's Harry, imbibed Patrick Henry's ideology. She notes, "Henry's rhetorical flourish gave a heroic gloss to sentiments reverberating through the colony for more than a year. The cries of 'liberty' heard at rowdy gatherings at the county courthouse, and in ardent talk swirling about the streets of every town, were discreetly absorbed by enslaved people who mingled unobtrusively in the excitable crowd. Passionate chatter about liberty and despotism, which animated drawing rooms of Virginian plantations, was not lost on the footmen and cooks, the valets and maids, who were as much a fixture of the plantation house as the furniture." Pybus, 5.

21. Louis Ruchames, ed., *The Letters of William Lloyd Garrison: From Disunion to the Brink of War, 1850–1860* (Cambridge, MA: Belknap Press of Harvard University, 1975), Vol. 1, 87 (Garrison quotation); Anthony Burns, letter published in *Liberator*, August 13, 1858.

22. Yuval Taylor, ed., *I Was Born a Slave: An Anthology of Classic Slave Narratives* (Chicago: Lawrence Hill Books, 1999), Volume 2, 749, 768–69 (Parker quotations); W. Freeman Galpin, *New York History* (1945) Vol. 26, No. 1, 31.

23. Quoted in John White Chadwick, *Theodore Parker: Preacher and Reformer* (Boston: Houghton, Mifflin, 1900), 253.

24. Wendell W. Brown, "A Lecture delivered before the Female Anti-Slavery Society of Salem" in *Four Fugitive Slave Narratives* (Reading, MA: Addison-Wesley, 1969), 84.

25. Quoted in Steven Weisenburger, *Modern Medea: A Family Story of Slavery and Child-Murder in the Old South* (New York: Hill and Wang, 1998), 5.

26. Dorothy Porter Wesley and Constance Porter Uzelac, eds., *William Cooper Nell: Nineteenth-Century Abolitionist, Historian, Integrationist, Selected Writings from 1832–1874* (Baltimore: Black Classic Press, 2002), 270, 271.

After the passage of the new Fugitive Slave Law, the major concession to the South in the Compromise of 1850, even blacks who had supported William Lloyd Garrison's pacifist abolition adopted a more militant stance that reflected their belief that blacks had to look out for themselves. Nell was an example and he endorsed Hayden's resolution, "That while our hearts gratefully acknowledge the noble stand taken by many in this city [Boston] and elsewhere volunteering their positive co-operation in our remaining free in the Old Bay State, we shall tenaciously remember, that eternal vigilance is the price of liberty, and that they who would be free, themselves must strike the blow." *Liberator*, October 4, 1850.

27. Jane H. Pease and William H. Pease, *They Who Would Be Free: Blacks' Search for Freedom, 1830–1861* (New York: Atheneum, 1974), 218.

28. Quoted in Donald Yacovone, *Samuel Joseph May and the Dilemmas of the Liberal Persuasion, 1797–1871* (Philadelphia: Temple University Press, 1991), 146.

29. Ibid., 146

30. Pease and Pease, *They Who Would Be Free*, 218.

31. Frederick Douglass, *Life and Times of Frederick Douglass* (New York: Macmillan, 1962), 281.

32. *Liberator*, June 23, 1854.

33. Quoted in Stacey M. Robertson, *Parker Pillsbury: Radical Abolitionist, Male Feminist* (Ithaca: Cornell University Press, 2000), 129.

34. John W. Blassingame, ed., *The Frederick Douglass Papers* (New Haven, CT: Yale University Press), 3: 123.

35. Ralph Volney Harlow, *Gerrit Smith: Philanthropist and Reformer* (New York: Henry Holt and Company, 1939), 298 (Smith quotation); Jane H. Pease and William H. Pease, *Bound Them in Chains: A Biographical History of the Antislavery Movement* (Westport, CT: Greenwood Press, 1972), 297 (quotation on Syracuse); Jayme A. Sokolow, "The Jerry McHenry Rescue and the Growth of Northern Antislavery Sentiment During the 1850s," *Journal of American Studies* Vol. 16, No. 3 (Dec., 1982), 431.

36. Truman Nelson, ed., *Documents of Upheaval: Selections from William Lloyd Garrison's The Liberator, 1831–1865* (New York: Hill and Wang, 1966), 222.

37. *Pennsylvania Freeman* quoted in Jonathan Katz, *Resistance at Christiana: The Fugitive Slave Rebellion, Christiana, Pennsylvania, September 11, 1851* (New York: Thomas Y. Crowell Company, 1974), 141–2; Arthur S. Bolster Jr., *James Freeman Clarke: Disciple to Ad-*

vancing Truth (Boston: Beacon Press, 1954), 234 (John Andrew quotation).

38. Stephen Hole Fritchman, *Men of Liberty: Ten Unitarian Pioneers* (Port Washington, NY: Kennikat Press, 1944), 146.

39. The radical abolitionists who supported Brown's raid at Harper's Ferry were Theodore Parker, Thomas Wentworth Higginson, Samuel Gridley Howe, Gerrit Smith, Franklin Sanborn, and George Luther Stearns.

40. Tilden G. Edelstein, *Strange Enthusiasm: A Life of Thomas Wentworth Higginson* (New York: Yale University Press, 1968), 104–105 (first quotation); Thomas Wentworth Higginson, *Massachusetts in Mourning: A Sermon Preached in Worcester, on Sunday June 4, 1854* (Boston: James Munroe, 1854), 13, 4–5.

41. *Boston Morning Journal*, May 27, 1854 (Howe quotation); *Boston Slave Riot and the Trial of Anthony Burns Containing the Report...* (Northbrook, IL: Metro Books, 1972), 8–9.

42. Odell Shepard, ed., *The Journals of Bronson Alcott* (Boston: Little, Brown, 1938), 243–244.

43. James Freeman Clarke, *The Rendition of Anthony Burns: Its Cause and Consequences: A Discourse on Christian Politics Delivered in Williams Hall on Whitsunday, June 4, 1854* (Boston: Crosby, Nichols and Prentiss & Sawyer, 1854), 16–17.

44. Quoted in *Liberator*, May 23, 1851.

45. Katz, 147.

46. *Boston Morning Journal*, June 3, 1854 (Pellet quotation); Truman Nelson, ed., *Documents of Upheaval*, 222 (Foster quotation); Ray Allen Billington, ed., *The Journal of Charlotte L. Forten: A Free Negro in the Slave Era* (New York: Collier Books, 1961), 46.

47. Quoted in Stacey M. Robertson, *Hearts Beating for Liberty: Women Abolitionists in the Old Northwest* (Chapel Hill: University of North Carolina Press, 2010), 96, 115. For a discussion of M'Keehan's work, see Steven Weisenburger, *Modern Medea: A Family Story of Slavery and Child-Murder from the Old South* (New York: Hill and Wang, 1998), 271–73.

48. Nelson, ed., *Documents of Upheaval*, 220. Elsewhere, I have underscored the clash between antebellum Americans who sought to conserve what they saw as the fruits of the Revolution — America as it was — and those who sought to extend American liberties to the slaves. See Gordon S. Barker, *The Imperfect Revolution: Anthony Burns and the Landscape of Race in Antebellum America* (Kent: Kent State University Press), 121–122.

49. [E. Wendell Phillips], *No Slave Hunting*

in the Old Bay State: An Appeal to the People and Legislature of Massachusetts in *Anti-Slavery Tracts Series 2: No. 1–14* (Westport, CT: Negro Universities Press, 1970), 3, 4, 10, 11. In referring to "unholy parchments," Phillips is referring to slave commissioners' decisions and certifications of masters' claims to runaways. "*Sub Libertate Quietem*" is taken from the Massachusetts Coat of Arms adopted by the Provincial Congress in 1775 the full English translation of which is "with a sword, she seeks quiet peace under liberty."

50. Oscar Sherwin, *Prophet of Liberty: The Life and Times of Wendell Phillips* (New York: Bookman, 1958), 186; Truman Nelson, *Documents of Upheaval*, 225, 230 (last two quotations).

51. James Oliver Horton and Lois E. Horton, *Slavery and the Making of America* (New York: Oxford University Press, 2005), 110–111.

52. David W. Blight, *Beyond the Battlefield: Race, Memory, and the American Civil War* (Amherst: University of Massachusetts Press, 1997), 37.

53. Wesley and Uzelac, eds., *William Cooper Nell: Nineteenth-Century African American Abolitionist*, 271–274.

54. Valerie Cunningham and Mark Sammons, *Black Portsmouth: Three Centuries of African-American Heritage* (Durham: University of New Hampshire Press, 2004). 63.

55. Yuval Taylor, ed., *I Was Born a Slave*, Vol. 2, 742.

56. Samuel Ringgold Ward, *Autobiography of a Fugitive Negro* (New York: Arno Press, 1969), 118–121. Frederick Douglass regarded Ward as a tremendously powerful and effective abolitionist. He wrote of him: "As an orator and a thinker he was vastly superior, I thought, to any of us, and being perfectly black and of unmixed African descent, the splendours of his intellect went directly to the glory of race. In depth of thought, fluency of speech, readiness of wit, logical exactness, and general intelligence, Samuel R. Ward has left no successor among the colored men amongst us...." Douglass, *Life and Times of Frederick Douglass*, 277.

57. Barker, 63–86; Edward Magol, *The Antislavery Rank and File: A Social Profile of the Abolitionists' Constituency* (Westport, CT: Greenwood Press, 1986), 132.

58. Bruce Laurie, *Beyond Garrison: Antislavery and Social Reform* (New York: Cambridge University Press, 2005).

59. Quoted in Katz, *Resistance at Christiana*, 147. For a concise discussion of Personal Liberty Laws and abolitionism, see Norman Rosenberg, "Personal Liberty Laws and Sectional Crisis: 1850–1860," *Civil War History* Vol. 17, No. 1 (March, 1971), 25–44.

60. Quoted in Harlow, *Gerrit Smith*, 304–5.

61. Truman Nelson, ed., *Documents of Upheaval*, 238.

62. Higginson, 13; see also Edelstein, *Strange Enthusiasm*, 104–5.

63. For an excellent discussion of the Joshua Glover rescue and Sherman Booth, see H. Robert Baker, *The Rescue of Joshua Glover: A Fugitive Slave, the Constitution, and the Coming of the Civil War* (Athens: Ohio University Press, 2006).

64. As Rhys Isaac shows, Patrick Henry, embodying the ordinary and extraordinary, the popular and distinguished, the dissenter and unifier, became symbolic of Revolution and republican virtue. See Isaac, "Preachers and Patriots: Popular Culture and the Revolution in Virginia," in Alfred F. Young, *The American Revolution: Explorations in the History of American Radicalism* (Dekalb: Northern Illinois Press, 1976), 127–155.

65. Ward, *Autobiography*, 115–116.

66. Michael Fellman, "Theodore Parker and the Abolitionist Role in the 1850s," *Journal of American History* Vol. 61, No. 3 (Dec., 1974), 672.

67. Theodore Parker, *Trial of Theodore Parker for the Misdemeanor of a Speech in Faneuil Hall Before the Circuit Court of the United States* (Boston, 1855), vi–viii, 7, 9–11.

68. Edelstein, *Strange Enthusiasm*, 166, 105–6.

69. Quoted in Robertson, *Parker Pillsbury*, 130. Discourse surrounding fugitive slave crises often drew on notions of masculinity. This was true for both blacks and whites. In defiance of the Fugitive Slave Law, Jermain Loguen said, "I will not live like a slave, and if force is employed to re-enslave me, I shall make preparations to meet the crisis as becomes a man." Quoted in Earl Ofari, "*Let Your Motto Be Resistance*": *The Life and Thought of Henry Highland Garnet* (Boston: Beacon Press, 1972), 61. Thomas Wentworth Higginson often spoke of manliness. See Edelstein, *Strange Enthusiasm*.

70. Merton L. Dillon, *The Growth of a Dissenting Minority* (DeKalb: Northern Illinois University Press, 1974), 186; [Mumford ed.], *Memoir of Samuel Joseph May*, 221.

71. *Massachusetts Anti-Slavery Society Annual Report*, January 28, 1852, 18.

72. Ward, *Autobiography*, 108.

73. Edelstein, *Strange Enthusiasm*, 163.

74. Deborah Anna Logan, ed., *Writings on Slavery and the American Civil War: Harriet*

Martineau (DeKalb: Northern Illinois University Press, 2002), 94–97; Higginson, 13.

75. Letter of Anthony Burns to the Baptist Church at Union, Fauquier County, Virginia, in Carter G. Woodson, ed., *The Mind of the Negro as Reflected in Letters Written During the Crisis, 1800–1860* (1926; New York: Russell and Russell, 1969), 661.

76. Taylor, ed., *I Was Born a Slave*, Vol. 2, 482.

Chapter 1

1. For a brief discussion of the national displays, see http://www.bl.uk/learning/histciti zen/victorians/exhibition/greatexhibition.html.

2. Charles Sumner's oft-used expression "lords of the lash" is quoted in Leonard W. Levy, "Sims' Case: The Fugitive Slave Law in Boston in 1851," *Journal of Negro History*, 35:1 (January 1950), 40.

3. Harold Schwartz, "Fugitive Slave Days in Boston," *New England Quarterly*, 27: 2 (June 1954), 193 (first quotation); John White Chadwick, *Theodore Parker: Preacher and Reformer* (Boston: Houghton, Mifflin and Company, 1900), 250 (second quotation); Stephen Hole Fritchman, *Men of Liberty: Ten Unitarian Pioneers* (Port Washington, NY: Kennikat Press, 1944), 146 (third quotation). Benjamin Quarles mentions the cost of the Crafts' crossing. See Quarles, *The Negro in America* (Chapel Hill: University of North Carolina Press, 1996), 204.

4. *Running a Thousand Miles for Freedom or, the Escape of William and Ellen Craft from Slavery* in *I Was Born a Slave*, edited by Yuval Taylor (Chicago: Lawrence Hill Books, 1999), 482; Peter Kolchin, *American Slavery, 1619–1877* (New York: Hill and Wang, 2003), 4.

5. Stephen Knadler emphasizes Henry C. Wright's interest in an antislavery exhibit at the world's fair. "Above all," wrote Wright in the *Liberator* as he discussed the Crystal Palace Exhibition, "an American slave auction must be there, with William and Ellen Craft on the block, Henry Clay as auctioneer, and the American flag floating over it." *Liberator*, 28, 1851. See Stephen Knadler, "At Home in the Crystal Palace: African American Transnationalism and Aesthetics of Representative Democracy," *ESQ: A Journal of the American Renaissance* 56:4 (2010), 328–362.

6. *Liberator*, September 27, 1850 and March 7, 1851 (second quotation). Joining the Crafts on the British antislavery lecture circuit, William W. Brown stressed the same irony, noting "it should be a humiliating thing to the people of the U.S. that the English Government furnishes the only asylum ... for the poor oppressed Negro." *Liberator*, March 7, 1851.

7. *Liberator*, September 27, 1850.

8. Taylor (ed.), 491. Garrison reported on the transatlantic crossing of Remond and Purvis. See *Liberator*, May 16, 1851. He also printed a letter from Henry C. Wright remarking "Would that [Frederick] Douglass could be there [at the Crystal Palace], to aid in the exhibition!" See *Liberator*, February 28, 1851.

9. *Liberator*, January 12, 1849 (first and fourth quotations); *North Star* July 20, 1849 (second and third quotations); *Liberator*, August 9, 1850.

10. Taylor (ed.), 483 (first and second quotations); John White Chadwick, *Theodore Parker: Preacher and Reformer* (Boston: Houghton, Mifflin, 1900), 248.

11. *Liberator*, July 18, 1851. William W. Brown, who joined the Crafts in England and Scotland, told Garrison that "The natural eloquence and simplicity with which Wm. Craft narrated the story ... created a deep feeling of hatred against the 'peculiar institution.' The reception on this evening [in Edinburgh] was very flattering." See *Liberator*, January 24, 1851.

12. *Liberator*, February 28, 1851. William and Ellen Craft contributed to this transatlantic correspondence themselves, which some writers stressed reflected their new-found literacy. See *Liberator*, January 2, and October 22, 1852, and *Frederick Douglass' Paper*, October 29, 1852. Sometimes rumors about the Crafts spread across the Atlantic. During the world's fair, the *Semi-Weekly Raleigh Register* reported that Ellen wanted to return to Southern slavery, something Ellen later vehemently denied in a letter. See *The Semi-Weekly Raleigh Register*, September 4, 1852, and *Frederick Douglass' Paper*, February 4, 1853.

13. Taylor (ed.), 482 (first quotation); Dorothy Porter Wesley and Constance Porter Uzelac, *William Cooper Nell: Nineteenth-Century African American Abolitionist, Historian, Integrationist* (Baltimore: Black Classic Press, 2002), 271.

14. Harold Schwartz, 193 (first quotation); *Frederick Douglass' Paper*, August 26, 1853 (second quotation). Gary Collison notes that, "The 1850 census recorded six unrelated blacks (including William and Ellen Craft, a fugitive slave couple from Georgia) and one white domestic servant living with black leader Lewis Hayden, his wife, and their children at 66 Southac Street." See Gary Collison, *Shadrach Minkins: From Fugitive Slave to Citizen* (Cambridge: Harvard University Press, 1997),

64. On William's Cambridge Street business, see Collison, 91–3.

15. Chadwick, 251.

16. *Liberator*, February 4, 1853.

17. Barbara McCaskill, "'Yours very truly': Ellen Craft — the Fugitive as Text and Artifact" *African American Review* 28 (1994); *The Congregationalist*, January 25, 1867; *St. Louis Globe-Democrat*, December 30, 1881.

18. Taylor (ed.), 482.

19. *Emancipator & Republican*, January 19, 1849 (first quotation); Taylor (ed.), 498 (second quotation); *Liberator*, February 4, 1853. See also *Frederick Douglass' Paper*, February 25, 1853. For a detailed description of the Crafts' flight, see Taylor 487–531. The Crafts' ruse of binding Ellen's arm in a sling was described by newspapers throughout the North. For example, the *Cleveland Herald* emphasized that "Ellen, knowing that she would be called upon to write her name at the hotels ... tied up her right hand, as though it were lame, which proved of some service to her, as she was called upon several times to register her name at hotels." *Cleveland Herald*, January 25, 1849.

20. On Henry Box Brown, see Henry Box Brown, *Narrative of the Life of Henry Box Brown, Written by Himself* (Manchester: Lee & Glynn, 1851).

21. *Liberator*, February 9, 1849. This meeting had been extensively publicized and promoted. It had been announced as follows: "WILLIAM W. BROWN, A fugitive slave will lecture in Abington Town Hall on Sunday Feb. 4th, commencing at 10 o'clock, A.M. William and Ellen Craft, two fugitive slaves from Georgia, who made their escape from slavery by the wife dressing in man's apparel and passing as the master, while the husband passed as the servant, will be present, and tell the story of their escape. Come one, come all!" See *Liberator*, February 2, 1849.

22. *Liberator*, April 27, 1849.

23. *Liberator*, March 9, 1849.

24. Scott Reynolds Nelson and Carol Sheriff, *A People's War: Civilians and Soldiers in America's Civil War, 1854–1877* (New York: Oxford University Press, 2008), 29. It is interesting to note that William and Ellen Craft participated in antislavery meetings in England held to publicize Stowe's *Uncle Tom's Cabin*. See letter from William Wells Brown printed in *Liberator* June 10, 1853 and another report that William Lloyd Garrison reprinted from the *London Daily News*, *Liberator*, March 25, 1853.

25. Taylor (ed.), 492–497.

26. *Emancipator & Republican*, June 2, 1949

(first quotation); *North Star*, July 20, 1849 (third quotation); Taylor (ed.), 490–497 (other quotations); *Liberator* April 2, 1852. William Lloyd Garrison first learned of the Crafts from William W. Brown. The latter wrote to the Boston abolitionist on January 4, 1849, saying that "Ellen is truly a heroine."

27. *The North Star*, July 20, 1849 (first quotation); *Mississippian and State Gazette* (Jackson), February 28, 1851 (second quotation); *Liberator*, November 26, 1852 (last quotation). In the first days after her arrival in England, Ellen's status as a heroine was accentuated by her fatigue and frail health. In letters to friends in America, notably antislavery militants like Samuel Joseph May, William W. Brown conveyed his concerns about Ellen's "feeble state" which served to fuel sentiment against the institution from which she had so courageously run. See *Liberator*, November 4, 1853.

28. *Liberator*, May 30, 1851.

29. *London Morning Advertiser*, May 30, 1855 reprinted in *Liberator*, June 29, 1855.

30. *Liberator*, April 2, 1852.

31. *Liberator*, March 9, 1849.

32. *Liberator*, July 26, 1850.

33. *Weekly Herald* (New York), February 10, 1849.

34. *Liberator*, June 2, and February 2, 1849. In reporting on this convention, the *New York Weekly Herald* emphasized the abolitionists' stance against slavery in the District of Columbia and also support for "the repeal of all laws in this commonwealth in derogation of the rights of our colored citizens." The paper also reported on Parker Pillsbury's rebuke of proslavery churches. *Weekly Herald* (New York), February 10, 1849.

35. *Liberator*, June 8, 1849.

36. *North Star*, February 16, 1849.

37. In addition to his plantation, the prosperous Collins had interests in railroad and telegraph businesses. See Collison 91–2.

38. Chadwick, 248 (first quotation); Schwartz, 193.

39. Odell Shepard, *The Journals of Bronson Alcott* (Boston: Little, Brown, 1938) 246; Schwartz, 193 (second quotation); *Liberator*, December 6, 1850.

40. *Liberator*, December 6, 1850; *Boston Daily Atlas*, December 2, 1850.

41. *The Cleveland Herald*, October 30, 1850 (first quotation); *North American and United States Gazette*, October 31, 1850.

42. *Liberator*, October 4, 1850. The Crafts proved unrelenting in their attack against the Fugitive Slave Law and in their demands for increased militancy. For them, forcible resist-

ance was not just needed but it was also effective. For example, after the couple had settled in England, they commented on both the Thomas Sims and William Parker dramas, clearly endorsing all means of resistance. William wrote an open letter to the *Liberator* on the Christiana affair, saying "We think a few more such cases as the Christiana affair will put a damper upon slave-catchers." See *Liberator*, January 2, 1852.

43. *Liberator*, April 13, 1849.

44. *Greenville Mountaineer*, December 6, 1850.

45. *The Daily Register* (Raleigh), December 10, 1850.

46. *The Mississippian*, November 15, 1850.

47. *The North Star*, December 5, 1850.

48. *Liberator*, April 6, 1849.

49. *Emancipator & Republican*, March 14, 1850.

50. Chadwick, 250–251 (first three quotations); Odell Shepard (ed.), 247. There remains some confusion regarding Parker's arming of William. By some accounts, it was a Bowie knife that Parker gave to him; other reports suggest that Parker gave William a sword. See Schwartz, 193. When the Crafts departed for England, Parker provided them with a letter of introduction to the London abolitionist James Martineau and arranged their departure to Halifax, Nova Scotia, to board the steamer bound for Liverpool.

51. Fritchman, 146 (first and second quotations); *Mississippian*, November 15, 1850 (third quotation); Collison, 96 (fourth quotation); *North Star*, January 16, 1851. William's militancy was very much in evidence when the slave catchers arrived in Boston. Upon hearing of the issuance of warrants to seize Ellen and him, he, along with Parker and other members of the Boston Vigilance Committee, arranged for Ellen's safety and then he transformed his carpenter's shop into a veritable bunker. "He armed himself with an arsenal of weapons—a revolver, pistols large and small, and knives—and insisted on going about his daily routine as usual," writes Collison, adding that after having "moved his clothing and his bed into his carpenter's shop ... [he] waited, ready to resist the officers to the death." Collison, 98.

Chapter 2

1. George Hendrick and Willene Hendrick, *Black Refugees in Canada: Accounts of Escape During the Era of Slavery* (Jefferson, NC: McFarland, 2010), 20 (first quotation). Gary Collison mentions the unusual Massachusetts

weather that year, underscoring that a Leominster abolitionist complained "a week of rain had left water shoe-deep." See Collison, *Shadrach Minkins: From Fugitive Slave to Citizen* (Cambridge, MA: Harvard University Press, 1997) 161. Second quotation from Rodney French, an antislavery ship captain who was not permitted to land in Southern ports, quoted in Fergus M. Bordewich, *Bound for Canaan: The Underground Railroad and the War for the Soul of America* (New York: HarperCollins, 2005), 323.

2. W. Freeman Galpin, "The Jerry Rescue," *New York History* 26 (Jan. 1945): 19, 30. Late in her life, Ann Bigelow suggested that Concord antislavery militants had helped, on average, one fugitive slave escape every week. Although this was likely an exaggeration, Concord was an important way-station on the Underground Railroad and militants such as the Bigelows were fearless conductors. See Collison, *Shadrach Minkins*, 151.

3. Stanley W. Campbell, *The Slave Catchers: Enforcement of the Fugitive Slave Law, 1850–1860* (New York: W.W. Norton, 1970), 98 (first two quotations); Bordewich, 323 (last quotation).

4. Collison, 132 (first quotation); Dorothy Porter Wesley and Constance Porter Uzaelac, *William Cooper Nell: Nineteenth-Century African American Abolitionist, Historian, Integrationist* (Baltimore: Black Classic Press, 2002), 274.

5. *Boston Daily Atlas*, February 20, 1851.

6. Benjamin Quarles, *Black Abolitionists* (New York: Oxford University Press, 1969), 205 (first quotation); Collison, 126 (third and fifth quotations); *Boston Investigator*, February 19, 1851 (second and fourth quotations). Collison notes that Joshua B. Smith and Lewis Hayden were the two black members of the Boston Vigilance Committee's executive committee, which was headed up by Theodore Parker. See Collison, *Shadrach Minkins*, 82

7. John White Chadwick, *Theodore Parker: Preacher and Reformer* (Boston: Houghton Mifflin, 1900), 252 (first quotation); *Boston Investigator*, February 19, 1851 (third and last quotations); *Boston Daily Atlas*, February 17, 1851 (other quotations).

8. *Liberator*, March 27, 1851 (first and second quotations); *Boston Investigator*, February 19, 1851 (third, fourth and fifth quotations); Collison, *Shadrach Minkins*, 127 (sixth and seventh quotations); The *Boston Investigator* of February 19, 1851, mentioned the presence of blacks of both sexes.

9. *Boston Daily Atlas*, February 17, 1851

(first and second quotations); Stephen Kendrick and Paul Kendrick, *Sarah's Long Walk: The Free Blacks of Boston and How Their Struggle for Equality Changed America*, 17 (third quotation); Quarles, 206 (last quotation).

10. Collison, *Shadrach Minkins*, 130. On Lovejoy, see Collison, *Shadrach Minkins*, 132.

11. Gary Collison, "'This Flagitious Offense': Daniel Webster and the Shadrach Rescue Cases, 1851–1852," *New England Quarterly* 68:4 (December, 1995), 616.

12. *Boston Investigator*, February 19, 1851 (first and second quotations); Quarles, 206 (last quotation).

13. *Boston Daily Atlas*, February 17, 1851.

14. Bordewich, 322; *Frederick Douglass' Paper*, August 26, 1853.

15. *Boston Investigator*, February 19, 1851 (first quotation); Harold Schwartz, "Fugitive Slave Days in Boston," *New England Quarterly* 27:2 (June 1954), 196.

16. *Boston Investigator*, February 19, 1851 (first quotation); Collison, 54 (other quotations). Collison reports that Shadrach's birth record does not exist and attributes his name change to either his or Martha Hutchings's embrace of the biblical story of Shadrach, Meshach, and Abednego who defied Nebuchadnezzar's order to worship a golden image instead of God. For Shadrach's experience as a slave in Norfolk, see Collison, *Shadrach Minkins*, especially 24–41.

17. In suggesting that in all likelihood Shadrach escaped by sea, Collison notes the network of antislavery activists in the Norfolk area such as Henry Lewey and Elizabeth Baines, who put fugitive slaves in contact with friendly sea captains or helped them stow away on ships. See Collison, *Shadrach Minkins*, 46–50.

18. *Frederick Douglass' Paper*, October 2, 1851 (first quotation); Collison, *Shadrach Minkins*, 65 (second quotation). On Shadrach joining the Methodist church, see Hendrick and Hendrick, 19.

19. *Boston Daily Atlas*, February 17, 1851 (first quotation); Quarles, 205 (second quotation). John Debree gave power of attorney to a Norfolk constable named John Caphart to claim Shadrach in Boston on his behalf. Caphart arrived in Boston on February 12, 1851 and requested the warrant two days later. See Collison, *Shadrach Minkins*, 110–111. When Shadrach arrived in Boston, he went sometimes by the name of Frederick Minkins and sometimes by the name of Frederick Wilkins. See *Liberator*, May 30, 1851 and *Boston Daily Atlas*, February 17, 1851.

20. Quarles, 205 (first quotation); *Boston Investigator*, February 26, 1851 (second quotation); *Liberator*, March 7, 1851 (third and fourth quotations).

21. Collison, *Shadrach Minkins*, 161. Although information on the final leg of Shadrach's escape remains sketchy, Collison cogently argues the escape route and timing set out in the text.

22. On Canada's unwillingness to extradite fugitive slaves to the U.S., see Gordon S. Barker, *The Imperfect Revolution: Anthony Burns and the Landscape of Race in Antebellum America* (Kent: Kent State University Press, 2010), 95–98; *North Star*, April 10, 1851; Collison 221–2.

23. John White Chadwick, *Theodore Parker: Preacher and Reformer* (Boston: Houghton, Mifflin, 1900), 252 (first quotation); Odell Shepard (ed.), *The Journals of Bronson Alcott* (Boston: Little, Brown, 1938), 243 (second and third quotations); *Frederick Douglass' Paper*, February 19, 1852 (fourth quotation); *Liberator*, April 4, 1851 (last quotations).

24. Vincent Y. Bowditch, *Life and Correspondence of Henry Ingersoll Bowditch* (Boston: Houghton, Mifflin, 1902) 1:212 (first quotation); *Liberator*, March 28, 1851 (second quotation); Thomas Wentworth Higginson, *Cheerful Yesterdays* (Boston: Houghton, Mifflin, 1898), 137 (third and fourth quotations); *Liberator* January 4, 1856 (fifth quotation); Schwartz, 196 (last quotation).

25. Collison, *Shadrach Minkins*, 135.

26. Campbell, 150 (first quotation); *Boston Daily Atlas*, February 20, 1851 (second quotation); *Boston Investigator*, February 26, 1851 (third and fourth quotations); Collison, *Shadrach Minkins*, 139 (other quotations).

27. Quoted in Higginson, *Cheerful Yesterdays*, 136.

28. *Liberator*, March 7, 1851.

29. Collison, *Shadrach Minkins*, 140.

30. Campbell, 150 (first quotation); *Liberator*, March 7, 1851 (last quotation).

31. *Boston Daily Atlas*, February 19, 1851 (first and second quotations); Campbell, 150 (third quotation); *Boston Daily Atlas*, March 4, 1851 (fourth and fifth quotations); Schwartz, 196.

32. Quotations from Winthrop and Lawrence in Thomas H. Connor, *Lords of the Loom: The Cotton Whigs and the Coming of the Civil War* (New York: Charles Scribner's Sons, 1968), 97.

33. Leonard W. Levy, "Sim's Case: The Fugitive Slave Law in Boston in 1851," *Journal of Negro History*, 35:1 (January, 1950), 41–42

(first, second, third quotations); The American Presidency Project, "Millard Fillmore: Second Annual Message, December 2, 1851," accessed at www.presidency.ucsb.edu/ws/index.php?pid=29492 (fourth and fifth quotations); *Liberator*, February 28 and April 4, 1851 (last two quotations).

34. For an excellent description of these legal proceedings, see Collison, "This Flagitious Offense," 609–625.

35. *Liberator*, March 7, 1851 (first and second quotations); *Boston Daily Atlas*, February 19, 1851 (third and fourth quotations).

36. *Liberator*, June 20, 1856.

37. *Boston Daily Atlas*, March 7, 1851 (first, second, third, fourth, and last quotations); Levy, 42 (fifth quotation); *Fayetteville Observer*, February 25, 1851 (sixth quotation).

38. *Boston Investigator*, April 9, 1851.

39. *Liberator*, March 7, 1851.

40. *Liberator*, May 9, 1851.

41. *Liberator*, February 28, 1851.

42. Higginson, *Cheerful Yesterdays*, 138 (first quotation); Collison, *Shadrach Minkins*, 149 (other quotations).

43. *Liberator*, March 28, 1851.

44. Campbell, 151 (first quotation); Collison, *Shadrach Minkins*, 141–2.

45. *Fayetteville Observer*, February 25, 1851 (first quotation); *Frederick Douglass' Paper*, December 22, 1854 (other quotations).

46. Collison, *Shadrach Minkins*, 82 (first quotation); *Liberator*, March 7, 1851.

47. Schwartz, 196; Shepard, 243.

48. Chadwick, 252 (first quotation); *Liberator*, March 7, 1851 (second quotation); Collison, *Shadrach Minkins* (last two quotations).

49. The American Presidency Project, "Millard Fillmore: Second Annual Message, December 2, 1851," accessed at www.presidency.ucsb.edu/ws/index.php?pid=29492 (first quotation); *Liberator*, April 4, 1851 (other quotations).

50. *Liberator*, March 14, 1851.

51. *Liberator*, March 28, 1851.

Chapter 3

1. Henry Mayer, *All on Fire: William Lloyd Garrison and the Abolition of Slavery* (New York: Norton, 1998), 411 (first quotation); *Daily Morning News* (Savannah, GA), April 10, 1851 (second quotation), April 9, 1851 (all other quotations except fifth). In the April 10 edition, the *Daily Morning News* described Sims as a "very good-looking dark mulatto." Frances Power Cobbe (ed.), *The Collected Works of Theodore Parker*, Volume VII (London: Trübner, 1864), 285 (fifth quotation). There are discrepancies in the reports of the age of Thomas Sims; some accounts said he was as young as eighteen at the time of his rendition.

2. *Trial of Thomas Sims on an Issue of Personal Liberty, on the Claim of James Potter, of Georgia, Against Him, as an Alleged Fugitive from Service* (Boston: Wm. S. Dambrell, 1851), 47 (first quotation); Leonard W. Levy, "Sims' Case: The Fugitive Slave Law in Boston in 1851," *Journal of Negro History*, 35:1 (January, 1950), 43 (second and third quotations); Cobbe, 285 (last quotation).

3. *Trial of Thomas Sims*, 47.

4. Levy, 43 (first quotation); *Monthly Law Reporter*, May 1851.

5. *Daily Morning News*, April 9, 1851 (first quotation); Levy, 43 (second quotation).

6. *Trial of Thomas Sims*, 46 (all quotations except first and second); *Daily Morning News*, April 24, 1851 (first and second quotations). Shortly after the trial of Sims, Savannah's *Daily Morning News* estimated that Potter had spent some $300, a significant sum at the time, to prepare his demand to have Sims returned. See *Daily Morning News*, April 17, 1851.

7. *Daily Morning News*, April 10, 1851.

8. Levy, 44 (first quotation); *Boston Investigator*, April 9, 1851 (second quotation); *Daily National Intelligencer* (Washington, DC), April 7, 1851 (third quotation). Wendell Phillips noted that Sims was seized on Richmond Street. *Speech of Wendell Phillips, Esq. The Sims Case — Judge Shaw — Rufus Choate — John H.P. Bigelow and Marshal Tukey ... at Faneuil Hall, Friday Evening, Jan., 1852* (American broadsides and Ephemera, Series I, 1852).

9. *Annual Report, Presented to the Massachusetts Anti-Slavery Society*, January 28, 1852, 19 (first and second quotations); *Boston Daily Atlas*, April 14, 1851 (third quotations); *Boston Investigator*, April 9, 1851 (fourth quotation); Levy, 44 (fifth quotation). It is interesting to note that when the Massachusetts Senate Committee questioned Mayor Bigelow about the arrest, he stressed that he had "ordered him [Butman] to do his best to prevent violence and bloodshed. He might have thought the arrest was complying with that order.... I would not arrest a fugitive slave, and I would not ask others to do what I would not do myself." *Boston Daily Atlas*, April 14, 1851. The *Daily Morning News* of April 7, 1851 reported that Butman suffered only "a slight wound in the thigh."

10. *Daily Morning News*, April 9, 1851 (first and second quotations); *Liberator*, May 9, 1851

(third quotation); *Daily Morning News*, April 14, 1851 (last quotations).

11. *Daily National Intelligencer*, April 7, 1851; Theodore Parker, *The Trial of Theodore Parker for the "Misdemeanor" of a Speech in Faneuil Hall Against Kidnapping* (Boston, 1855), 4; The American Presidency Project, "Millard Fillmore: Second Annual Message, December 2, 1851, accessed at www.presiden cy.ucsb.edu/ws/index.php?pid=29492; *Annual Report, Presented to the Massachusetts Anti-Slavery Society*, 19.

12. Thomas Wentworth Higginson, *Cheerful Yesterdays* (Boston and New York: Houghton, Mifflin and Company, 1899), 139–40 (first quotation); Jane H. Pease and William H. Pease, *They Who Would Be Free: Blacks' Search for Freedom, 1830–1861* (New York: Atheneum, 1974), 222 (last quotation). Marshal Devens later became famous for his antislavery sentiments. Although he was the marshal responsible for guarding Sims, "his sympathies were with the fugitive slave, [but] he felt obliged to obey the law. But he afterwards made a great effort financially and otherwise to procure freedom for Sims, and his brave career in the Civil War has been fitly recognized by naming for him the recent great soldiers' training camp at Ayer." Mary Thacher Higginson (ed.), *Letters and Journals of Thomas Wentworth Higginson, 1846–1906* (Boston: Houghton Mifflin, 1921), 157.

13. *Annual Report, Presented to the Massachusetts Anti-Slavery Society*, 19 (first quotation); *Daily National Intelligencer*, April 7, 1851 (second and fourth quotations); *Boston Investigator*, April 9, 1851 (third quotation).

14. Levy, 45 (first quotation); Cobbe (ed.), 285–6 (second quotation). Samuel Gridley Howe, one of the founders of *The Commonwealth*, stated, "Its immediate object was to reach and convince that important portion of the body politic which distrusts rhetoric and oratory, but which sooner or later gives heed to dispassionate argument and advocacy of plain issues." Laura E. (Howe) Richards, *Samuel Gridley Howe* (New York: D. Appleton-Century, 1935), 199.

15. *Speech of Wendell Phillips, Esq. The Sims Case*, 1852 (first four quotations); *Boston Daily Atlas*, April 14, 1851 (last quotation). Presumably a number of the onlookers who Levy suggests "gathered to watch the scene" moved on to the courthouse, which appears to have been an attraction for curiosity-seekers and abolitionists alike from the time of the arrest until Sims was marched to Long Wharf on his way back to slavery. Levy, 44–5.

16. *Boston Investigator*, April 16, 1851.

17. *Daily Morning News*, April 10, 1851 (first quotation) and April 9, 1851 (second quotation); *Daily National Intelligencer*, April 10, 1851.

18. Pease and Pease, *They Who Would Be Free*, 223; Jane and William Pease note the case of the sons of the black preacher Samuel Snowden "who were arrested for walking back and forth in front of the courthouse ... at least one of them armed." Pease and Pease, *They Who Would Be Free*, 223.

19. *Daily Morning News*, April 10, 1851 (first, second, and fourth quotations); Levy, 47 (third quotation).

20. *Daily Morning News*, April 12, first, second, and fourth quotations), and April 10 (third and fifth quotations).

21. Levy, 46 (first quotation); *Boston Investigator*, April 16, 1851 (second, third and fourth quotations); *Annual Report, Presented to the Massachusetts Anti-Slavery Society*, 22 (fifth quotation); Harold Schwartz, "Fugitive Slave Days in Boston," *New England Quarterly*, 27: 2 (June 1954), 201 (last quotation). Before the Massachusetts Senate Committee Inquiry, Mayor Bigelow said that he had some 1,500 volunteers, "bankers, merchants, brokers and mechanics, as respectable men as can be found in the Commonwealth" ready to participate in preserving order and ensuring the execution of the law. *Daily National Intelligencer*, April 9, 1851.

22. *Boston Investigator*, April 16, 1851 (first quotation); Austin Bearse, *Reminiscences of Fugitive-Slave Law Days in Boston* (Boston: Warren Richardson, 1880), 25.

23. Odell Shepard (ed.), *The Journals of Bronson Alcott* (Boston: Little, Brown, 1938), 243 (first, second, and third quotations); Schwartz, 197–8 (fourth quotation).

24. *Trial of Theodore Parker*, 5.

25. Higginson. *Cheerful Yesterdays*, 141.

26. *Daily Morning News*, April 24, 1851.

27. When the Boston Vigilance Committee called the meeting, the *Daily National Intelligencer*, which counseled obedience to the Fugitive Slave Law, railed against the abolitionist invitation asking Bostonians to "'come by the thousands' and prevent the execution of the law." See the *Daily National Intelligencer*, April 12, 1851. Levy, 51 (first quotation); *Daily National Intelligencer*, April 10, 1851 (second quotation); *Daily Morning News*, April 9, 1851.

28. Shepard (ed.), 244.

29. Levy, 51 (first quotation); *Daily Morning News*, April 9, 1851.

30. Levy, 52.

31. Bearse, 25–26 (first, second, third, and fourth quotations); *Daily National Intelligencer*, April 11, 1851 (fifth quotation); Samuel Longfellow (ed.), *Life of Henry Wadsworth Longfellow, with Extracts from His Journals and Correspondence* (Boston, 1936) Volume II, 192.

32. Schwartz, 198 (first quotation); Albert Réville, *The Life and Writings of Theodore Parker* (London: Simpkin, Marshall, 1865), 116 (second quotation).

33. *Annual Report, Presented to the Massachusetts Anti-Slavery Society*, 21; Levy, 44. Gary Collison notes that Charles G. Davis of Plymouth, who had been involved in the Shadrach case, also helped out. See Gary Collison, *Shadrach Minkins: From Fugitive Slave to Citizen* (Cambridge: Harvard University Press, 1997), 116.

34. *Annual Report, Presented to the Massachusetts Anti-Slavery Society*, 21 (first quotation); Mayer, 411 (second quotation); Levy, 198 (third quotation); *Daily Morning News*, April 12, 1851.

35. *Daily National Intelligencer*, April 12, 1851 (first and second quotations); *Boston Daily Atlas*, April 14, 1851 (third quotation); quoted from the *Richmond Whig* in the *Daily National Intelligencer*, April 14, 1851 (last quotation).

36. *Trial of Thomas Sims*, 1.

37. Alcott, 244 (first quotation); Collison, 194.

38. *Liberator*, May 9, 1851 (first and second quotations); *Daily National Intelligencer*, April 9, 1851 (last quotation).

39. *Daily National Intelligencer*, April 8, 1851.

40. "Petition of Thomas Sims," April 18, 1851 at www.theliberatorfiles.com (first quotation); Levy, 53 (second quotation); *Daily Morning News*, April 14, 1851 (third and fourth quotations).

41. Bruce Laurie, *Beyond Garrison: Antislavery and Social Reform* (New York: Cambridge University Press, 2005), 240 (first quotation); *Daily Morning News*, April 14, 1851.

42. Higginson, *Cheerful Yesterdays*, 142 (first quotation); Mertin L. Dillon, *The Abolitionists: The Growth of the Dissenting Minority* (DeKalb: Northern Illinois Press, 1974).

43. Bearse, 26.

44. Tilden G. Edelstein, *Strange Enthusiasm; a Life of Thomas Wentworth Higginson* (New York: Yale University Press, 1968), 162 (first quotation); *Daily Morning News*, April 14, 1851 (second quotation); Mayer, 411 (third, fourth, and seventh quotations); Higginson, *Cheerful Yesterdays*, 144 (fifth, sixth, and ninth quotations); William H. Pease and Jane H. Pease (ed.) *The Antislavery Argument* (New York: Bobbs-Merrill, 1965), lxxvii (eighth quotation).

45. John White Chadwick, *Theodore Parker: Preacher and Reformer* (Boston: Houghton, Mifflin, 1900) 253 (first and second quotations); Higginson, *Cheerful Yesterdays*, 144 (third quotation); Pease and Pease, *They Who Would Be Free*, 222 (last quotation).

46. *Trial of Thomas Sims*, 39–47.

47. Levy, 68 (first quotation); *Liberator*, May 23, 1851.

48. *Liberator*, July 24, 1857 (first and second quotations); Bearse, 27–28 (third, fourth, fifth, sixth, and seventh quotations); Bowditch, 224; Levy, 72 (last quotation).

49. Bearse, 28.

50. Bearse, 27 (first quotation); *Daily Morning News*, April 19, 1851 (second, third, and fourth quotations); Stanley W. Campbell, *The Slave Catchers: Enforcement of the Fugitive Slave Law, 1850–1860* (New York: Norton, 1968), 120.

51. Levy, 72 (quotation); details on Sims's later life from Campbell, 120.

52. Levy, 72; *Savannah Republican* quoted in *Daily National Intelligencer*, April 25, 1851. Campbell, 99–100. Pease and Pease also highlight Fillmore's relief, even joy, upon Sims's return to Georgia. See Jane H. Pease and William H. Pease, *The Fugitive Slave Law and Anthony Burns* (Philadelphia: Lippincott, 1975), 19; *Liberator*, April 25, 1851 (last two quotations).

53. *Daily Morning News*, April 16, 1851 (first, second, third, and fourth quotations) and April 17, 1851 (fifth and sixth quotations); *Daily National Intelligencer*, April 25, 1851 (last two quotations).

54. Frederick Douglass, *The Life and Times of Frederick Douglass Written by Himself* (New York: Pathway Press, 1941), 312 (first quotation); Donald M. Jacobs, (ed.), *Courage and Conscience: Black and White Abolitionists in Boston* (Indianapolis: Indiana University Press, 1993), 184 (second quotation); Quarles, 207 (other quotations).

55. Samuel Ringgold Ward, *Autobiography of a Fugitive Negro* (New York: Arno Press, 1969), 115.

56. Bowditch, 215; A.W. Plumstead and William H. Gilman (ed.) *The Journals and Miscellaneous Notebooks of Ralph Waldo Emerson* (Cambridge, Belknap Press of Harvard University Press, 1975), Volume 9, 362 and 352.

57. Bearse, 29 (first, second, fifth and sixth

quotations); *Boston Investigator*, April 16, 1851 (third and fourth quotations).

58. Bowditch, 218 (first quotation); Ralph L. Rusk, (ed.), *The Letters of Ralph Waldo Emerson* (New York: Columbia University Press), Volume 9, 249.

59. Michael Fellman, "Theodore Parker and the Abolitionist Role in the 1850s," *Journal of American History*, 61:3 (December, 1974), 673.

60. Cobbe (ed.), 290.

61. Michael Fellman, 667–8 (first, second, third quotations); Bowditch, 218; Edelstein 157, 162; *Frederick Douglass' Paper*, February 19, 1852.

Chapter 4

1. Frederick Douglass, *Life and Times of Frederick Douglass Written by Himself* (New York: Pathway Press, 1941), 313; Yuval Taylor, ed., *I Was Born a Slave: An Anthology of Classic Slave Narratives* (Chicago: Lawrence Hill Books, 1999), 742 (last quotation). See also Johnathan Katz, *Resistance at Christiana: The Fugitive Slave Rebellion, Christiana, Pennsylvania, September 11, 1851* (New York: Thomas Y. Crowell, 1974), 139.

2. Taylor (ed.), 743 (first quotation); Douglass, *Life and Times*, 312 (second and third quotations); *Frederick Douglass' Paper*, October 2, 1851 (last quotation). See also Thomas P. Slaughter. He compares the Christiana Riot to the Stamp Act crisis in the way it "galvanized public opinion." Slaughter, *Bloody Dawn: The Christiana Riot and Racial Violence in the Antebellum North* (New York: Oxford University Press, 1991), ix–xii.

3. Fergus M. Bordewich, *Bound for Canaan: The Underground Railroad and the War for the Soul of America* (New York: HarperCollins, 2005), 332 (first quotation). In describing the flight of Parker and his friends, Bordewich stresses that it was "one of the great moments in the history of the Underground Railroad." Bordewich, 332. *Fayetteville Observer*, September 23, 1851 (second quotation); *Raleigh Register*, September 20, 1851 (third quotation); *Vermont Watchman and State Journal*, September 25, 1851, and *Liberator*, October 24, 1851 (fourth quotation).

4. C. Peter Ripley (ed.), *Black Abolitionist Papers* (Chapel Hill: University of North Carolina Press, 1991) 4: 264 (first and second quotations); *Frederick Douglass' Paper*, December 11, 1851 (third quotation); Douglass, *Life and Times*, 312.

5. Frederick Douglass, *Narrative of the Life of Frederick Douglass* (New York: Dover Pub-

lications, 1995), 1 (first quotation); Taylor (ed.), 747–55 (other quotations).

6. Carol Wilson, *Freedom at Risk: The Kidnapping of Free Blacks in America, 1780–1865* (Lexington: University Press of Kentucky, 1994), 53 (first quotation); Marion Gleason McDougall, *Fugitive Slaves, 1619–1865* (New York: Bergman, 1967), 50. For the Lancaster black population estimate and information on the Gap Tavern, see Slaughter, 20 and 45. For additional background information on the impact of the Fugitive Slave Law on kidnapping in the Free states, see Gordon S. Barker, *The Imperfect Revolution: Anthony Burns and the Landscape of Race in Antebellum America* (Kent: Kent State University Press, 2010), 87–91.

7. Taylor (ed.), 755–7 (first and second quotations); McDougall, 50 (third quotation); Bordewich, 327 (fourth and seventh quotations); Slaughter, 47 (fifth quotation); Katz, 33 (sixth quotation). Carol Wilson emphasizes that, "The activities of Parker and his gang show the degree to which blacks, those legally free and those who had freed themselves, defended each other, even at the risk of their own lives." Wilson, 115. Katz notes that Eliza's experience in slavery had been even more bitter than Parker's. See Katz, 29.

8. *Daily Ohio Statesman*, September 16, 1851 (first quotation); Slaughter, 5 (second quotation; *Boston Daily Atlas*, September 16, 1851 (third quotation). There are varying reports of Gorsuch's age. I have used that provided by W.U. Hensel. See Hensel, *The Christiana Riot and the Treason Trials of 1851, An Historical Sketch* (Lancaster: Press of the New Era Printing Company, 1911), 20.

9. Hensel, 20 (first quotation); Bordewich, 325 (second quotation); *Frederick Douglass' Paper*, September 25, 1851 (third quotation). Bordewich lists the names of the slaves; for the provision in Gorsuch's father's will, see Taylor, note 16, page 787, and Hensel, 20. Slaughter emphasizes Gorsuch's concern with his honor. See Slaughter, 14.

10. Hensel, 25 (first quotation); Roderick W. Nash, "William Parker and the Christiana Riot," *Journal of Negro History*, 46:1 (1961), 27 (second quotation); *Cleveland Herald*, December 22, 1851 (third quotation); Bordewich, 326 (fourth quotation).

11. There is much confusion about which Gorsuch slaves were in the house. Most scholars accept that Nelson Ford was there; Hensel suggests Joshua Hammond was also there, which implies that Samuel Thompson was Joshua Hammond. Contemporary reports

provide descriptions suggesting that Noah Buley may have been Gorsuch's killer, which would place him near the house at the time of the riot. See *Vermont Watchman and State Journal*, September 18, 1851. For comments on this confusion, see Slaughter, 214, n33. Hensel notes Abraham Johnson may even have been Abe Johnson of Baltimore County implicated in the theft of Gorsuch's wheat. See Hensel, 29.

12. Taylor, 766, 771 (first, second, and fifth quotations). Slaughter, 60 (third and fourth quotations).

13. Slaughter, 60 (first quotation); Taylor, 771 (other quotations).

14. Taylor, 771–772 (first five quotations); Slaughter, 61 (sixth and seventh quotations); Hensel, 30 (last quotation).

15. Slaughter 62 (first, second, and fourth quotations); Taylor, 772 (third and fifth quotations); Hensel, 31 (last quotation). Elijah Lewis was also the local postmaster. See Katz, 92.

16. Katz, 94.

17. *Frederick Douglass' Paper*, September 25, 1851 (first quotation); Member of the Philadelphia Bar, *History of the Trial of Castner Hanway and Others for Treason* (Philadelphia: Uriah Hunt, 1852), 36–7 (second and fifth quotations); *Boston Daily Atlas*, September 13, 1851, and *Vermont Watchman and State Journal*, September 18, 1851; *Daily Ohio Statesman*, September 16, 1851; Slaughter, 66.

18. Taylor, 774–777 (first, third, and sixth quotations); *History of the Trial of Castner Hanway and Others*, 37 (second, fourth quotations); Hensel, 33 (fifth quotation). For a detailed account of events from the time Nelson Ford announced the slave catchers' arrival to the end of the shooting, see Slaughter, 59–75.

19. Hensel, 36 (first quotation); Taylor, 777–781 (second, fourth, sixth, seventh quotations); *History of the Trial of Castner Hanway and Others*, 42 (third quotation); Slaughter, 77 (fifth quotation).

20. Albert J. Von Frank, *The Trials of Anthony Burns: Freedom and Slavery in Emerson's Boston* (Cambridge, MA: Harvard University Press, 1998), xiii (first quotation); *History of the Trial of Castner Hanway and Others*, 38–9 (second, third, and fourth quotations); Taylor, 757 (fifth quotation); Slaughter, 85 (sixth quotation); *Liberator*, November 21, 1851, and October 3, 1851 (other quotations).

21. Samuel Ringgold Ward, *Autobiography of a Fugitive Negro* (New York: Arno Press, 1969), 117.

22. *History of the Trial of Castner Hanway and Others*, 38–9 (first, second, and fourth quotations); Slaughter, 105 (third quotation); *Daily National Intelligencer*, September 24, 1851 (fifth and sixth quotations); *Annual Report of the Massachusetts Anti-Slavery Society 1952*, 30–31 (last two quotations).

23. Hensel, 41–2.

24. *History of the Trial of Castner Hanway and Others*, 39 (first, second, and third quotations); *Frederick Douglass' Paper*, October 23, 1851 (fourth quotation); *Liberator*, September 19, 1851 (fifth quotation); *Fayetteville Observer*, September 23, 1851 (sixth and seventh quotations) and September 30, 1851 (last three quotations); Katz, 138 (eighth and ninth quotations); *Hinds County Gazette*, February 26, 1852 (tenth and eleventh quotations). Many Marylanders who went to Lancaster County demonstrated "a deep-seated and burning desire for revenge." See *Liberator*, October 3, 1851. The men who spoke to the Baltimore meeting included John H.T. Jerome, Z. Collins Lee, Coleman Yellot, Francis Gallagher, Samuel H. Taggart, and Col. George W. Hughes. See *History of the Trial of Castner Hanway and Others*, 39.

25. *Liberator*, October 24, 1851, and November 21, 1851 (last two quotations). Perhaps the ugliest reactions to the Christiana affair was the demand of some racist whites to exclude blacks from the Free states. See letter from the *New York Express* reprinted in *The Raleigh Register*, October 11, 1851.

26. Katz, 169. Katz also notes that the Christiana treason indictments, which eventually totaled forty-one, represented the largest collective indictment for treason in American history.

27. *American Law Journal*, April, 1852, 459 (first quotation); *Pennsylvanian* quoted in *Liberator*, September 26, 1851 (second and third quotations); *Boston Atlas*, September 16, 1851 (fourth, fifth, sixth, and seventh quotations); *Cleveland Herald*, December 3, 1851 (eighth and ninth quotations); *Frederick Douglass' Paper*, October 23, 1851 (other quotations).

28. *Frederick Douglass' Paper*, October 23, 1851 (first quotation); *Liberator*, October 17, 1851 (second quotation); *Vermont Chronicle*, October 28, 1851 (third and fourth quotations).

29. *Liberator*, October 17, 1851 (first quotation), October 24, 1851 (second, third, and fourth quotations), November 21, 1851 (other quotations except last); Katz, 141 (last quotation). It is clear that authorities were very

much aware that many Americans regarded the trial as a spectacle and that all eyes were on Philadelphia. One observer commented, "For this occasion the room had been refitted. Gas fixtures of the chastest [sic] designs had been erected, in anticipation of evening sessions. Ventilators of the most appropriate patterns had been placed in the ceiling, controlled by cords terminating at the bench of the Judges, so that a uniform temperature could be preserved. Nothing was wanting but space to promote the ease and comfort of those who were to figure in the solemn investigation about to take place." *History of the Trial of Castner Hanway and Others*, 52.

30. Katz, 140–1 (first and second quotations); *Frederick Douglass' Paper*, October 9, 1851 (other quotations).

31. *Annual Report Massachusetts Anti-Slavery Society, 1852* (first and second quotations); *Frederick Douglass' Paper*, February 19, 1852 (other quotations).

32. *Frederick Douglass' Paper*, November 27, 1851.

33. *History of the Trial of Castner Hanway and Others*, 80; Katz, 142–3 (second quotation), 147 (third quotation).

34. *Frederick Douglass' Paper*, October 2, 1851 (first quotation) and November 13, 1851 (second and third quotation); *Liberator*, January 9, 1852.

35. Katz, 152–3 (first and second quotations); *Liberator*, January 2, 1852 (other quotations).

Chapter 5

1. *Syracuse Post-Standard*, February 13, 2000. For discussion of the Iroquois or *Haudenosaunee* creation stories, the Cosmogonic Myth and the Deganawidah Epic, see Daniel Richter, *The Ordeal of the Longhouse: The Peoples of the Iroquois League in the Era of European Colonization* (Chapel Hill: University of North Carolina Press, 1992). Jayme Sokolow emphasizes the importance of the New England ancestry in the "burned-over district" of western New York, including how it helped set the stage for the Jerry rescue. See Jayme Sokolow, *Journal of American Studies*, 16:3 (1982), 429–30.

2. Earl E. Sperry, *The Jerry Rescue* (Syracuse: Onondaga Historical Association, 1924), 18 (first and fifth quotations); *Syracuse Post Standard*, March 30, 1924 (second quotation) and July 18, 2007 (third quotation); [Thomas James Mumford], *Memoir of Samuel Joseph May* (Boston: Roberts Brothers, 1873), 218

(fourth quotation); Ella B. Moffet, "Jerry Rescued—The Story," *Syracuse Herald*, October 1, 1899 (last quotation). Loguen and his wife Caroline lived on East Genesee Street in the heart of the city and their home became a refuge for fleeing bondspersons on their way to Canada. For a firsthand account of the Harriet Powell case, see William M. Clarke's unpublished manuscript on Harriet Powell, dated 1875 and held by the Syracuse Public Library. Harriet finished her life in Kingston, Ontario, where she married and raised a family.

3. Sokolow, 430 (first quotation); Mumford, 218 (second quotation); Aaron M. Powell, *Personal Reminiscences of the Anti-Slavery and Other Reforms and Reformers* (Westport, CT: Negro Universities Press, 1970), 67 (third and fourth quotations); Evamaria Hardin, *Syracuse and the Underground Railroad* (Syracuse: Erie Canal Museum, 1989), 3. In his in-depth analysis, Donald Yacovone emphasizes that up until this point in time, "May had proven the most consistent of the antislavery pacifists." See Yacovone, *Samuel Joseph May and the Dilemma of Liberal Persuasion, 1797–1871* (Philadelphia: Temple University Press, 1991), 143–144.

4. Sokolow, 430 (first, second, and fourth quotations); Moffet (third quotation); Earl Ofari, "Let Your Motto Be Resistance": The Life and Times of Henry Highland Garnett (Boston: Beacon Press, 1972), 61 (fifth, sixth, seventh, and eighth quotations).

5. Frederick Douglass, *The Life and Times of Frederick Douglass* (New York: Pathway Press, 1941), 313–314 (first quotation). Douglass suggested that the Christiana and Jerry rescue dramas "inflicted fatal wounds on the fugitive slave bill ... [making it] almost a dead letter." Moffet, "Jerry Rescued—The Story" (second quotation); Samuel J. May, *Some Recollections of Our Antislavery Conflict* (Boston: Fields, Osgood, 1869), 374 (third quotation); W. Freeman Galpin, "The Jerry Rescue," *New York History* 26:1, 19 (fourth quotation); Sperry, 21 (last quotation). The initial vigilance committee included Charles A. Wheaton, Dr. Lyman Clary, Vivus W. Smith, C.B. Sedgewick, Hiram Putnam, E.W. Leavenworth, Abner Bates, George Barnes, P.H. Agan, the Reverend J.W. Loguen, John Williams, the Reverend R.R. Raymond, and John Thomas. See Sperry, 19.

6. Sokolow, 432 (first quotation); Samuel Joseph May, *The Fugitive Slave Law, and Its Victims: Anti-Slavery Tracts No. 18*, 7–14 (other quotations). After his May 26 speech, Syracuse

abolitionists referred to Daniel Webster as "Black Dan"; his name — at least for them — was mud. See, for example, *Syracuse Standard*, October 19, 1851. Because of Webster's threat and later knowledge that James Lear, Mc-Reynold's agent, had been in Syracuse for about a month, rumors abounded that the administration had carefully planned Jerry's arrest for the day of the Liberty Party convention. Officials consistently denied this. See *Syracuse Journal*, October 3, 1851.

7. *Syracuse Standard*, October 7, 1851 (first and second quotations); *Syracuse Post-Standard*, October 14, 1914 (third and fourth quotations); Sokolow, 433 (fifth quotation).

8. See Galpin, 22, n10.

9. Sperry, 30. For discussion of Jerry's escape from slavery, see Galpin and Moffet. Moffet notes that in their defense for having aided Jerry in his escape, some of Jerry's rescuers used the fact that Jerry's master had taken him to free soil in Illinois, where he had been "beyond the power of a United States Marshal."

10. Sperry, 30.

11. *Syracuse Journal*, October 3, 1851 (first quotation); *Syracuse Post-Standard*, September 2010 (second quotation). It would appear that Syracuse's salt works had provided gainful employment for blacks, fugitive slaves and free blacks, for several decades. Evamaria Hardin writes, "The New York Senate recorded in 1823 that as early as 1774, two black men, likely runaway slaves, were boiling salt in the Onondaga salt works. Their only customers were the neighboring Indians." Hardin, 1.

12. Moffet, "Jerry Rescued — The Story" (first and fifth quotations); *Syracuse Post-Standard*, October 11, 1941 (second and third quotations); *Syracuse Standard*, October 2, 1851.

13. *Syracuse Standard*, October 2 (first quotation) and October 3, 1851 (third quotation); Sokolow, 433 (second quotation); Moffet, "Jerry Rescued — The Story," (fourth quotation). Moffett mentions May suggesting the Congregational Church or city hall as alternatives; Yacovone alludes to the myth that May's offering of the Congregational Church as a place to continue the hearings was a "pre-arranged signal" for an attempted rescue. See Yacovone, 144.

14. *Syracuse Standard*, October 20, 1851.

15. Moffett "Jerry Rescued — The Story" (first, fourth, and ninth quotations); *Syracuse Standard*, October 2, 1851 (second quotation); Sokolow (third and sixth quotations); *Post-Standard*, October 6, 1946 (fifth quotation); May, *Some Recollections*, 375 (eighth quota-tion); Jane H. Pease and William H. Pease, *They Who would be Free: Blacks' Search for Freedom, 1830–1861* (New York: Atheneum, 1974), 224 (seventh quotation). Moffett indicates that Jerry suffered two cracked or broken ribs during the fight. Some accounts of Jerry's first escape suggest that he was "hoisted" and carried by the crowd. See Yacovone, 144–5.

16. *Syracuse Journal*, October 9, 1851.

17. May, *Some Recollections*, 375–6 (first, fourth, and fifth, quotations); J.W. Loguen, *The Rev. J.W. Loguen as a Slave and as A Free-man: A Narrative of Real Life* (Syracuse: J.G. Truair, 1859), 404 (second and third quota-tions); Galpin, 28 (last quotation).

18. Loguen, 406 (first quotation); May, *Some Recollections*, 376. For additional discussion of the countermanding of the militia, see Galpin, 28–9, and Sokolow, 434–436.

19. Samuel Ringgold Ward, *Autobiography of a Fugitive Negro* (New York: Arno Press, 1969), 118–9.

20. *Syracuse Journal*, October 2, 1851 (first quotation); Sperry, 33 (second quotation); Moffett, "Jerry Rescued — The Story" (third and fourth quotations); *Jefferson County Jour-nal* (Adams, NY), November 1, 1882 (fifth quotation); Ralph Volney Harlow, *Gerrit Smith: Philanthropist and Reformer* (New York: Henry Holt, 1939), 298 (other quotations). The following were among those at Hoyt's office: Hiram Hoyt, Gerrit Smith, Dr. Fuller, Dr. R.W. Pease, the Rev. Samuel Joseph May, Charles A. Wheaton, the Rev. Samuel Ring-gold Ward, the Rev. Jermain W. Loguen, Caleb Davis, the Rev. R.R. Raymond, Montgomery Merrick, Abner Bates, James Davis, J.W. Clapp, James Baker, Jason Hoyt, Edward K. Hunt, George Carter, Peter Hallenbeck, James Parsons, Lemuel Field, William Gray, Samuel Thomas, L.P. Noble and Washington Stickney.

21. [Mumford], 220.

22. Loguen, 408 (first quotation); Moffett, "Jerry Rescued — The Story" (second and third quotations); Sokolow, 435 (fourth quo-tation); Galpin, 30 (fifth quotation).

23. *Syracuse Standard*, October 2, 1851 (first, sixth, seventh, eighth, and thirteenth quota-tions); Loguen, 414 (second and twelfth quo-tations); Galpin, 30 (third, fourth, and fifth quotations); Moffett, "Jerry Rescued — The Story" (ninth, tenth, eleventh quotations). Moffett recounts that as the mob impeded the rescuers from getting to the carriage, James Davis screamed "Fire" which had the effect of momentarily dispersing the crowd so that they could carry him through. For Loguen's esti-mate of the crowd, see Loguen, 408.

24. Moffett, "Jerry Rescued — The Story" (first quotation); Loguen, 418–19 (second, third, and fourth quotations); *Liberator*, October 10, 1851, reprint from the *Worcester Spy* (fifth quotation) *Syracuse Journal*, October 3, 1851 (last three quotations) and March 20, 1939 (sixth quotation); Sokolow, 436 (seventh quotation). On Susan Watson's death, the *Syracuse Journal* published an obituary commenting on her involvement in removing Jerry's shackles. See *Syracuse Journal*, January 11, 1911. Moffett notes the location of Davis's house.

25. The Ames House at 3339 Main St. in the town of Mexico, NY, is the only house associated with the Jerry Rescue that has survived. See *Syracuse Post-Standard*, September 28, 2001.

26. *Mexico Independent*, Centennial Issue, 1861–1961 (first quotation); *Syracuse Post-Standard*, January 30, 2005, and September 28, 2001.

27. *Daily Morning News* (Savannah, GA), October 8, 1851.

28. *Raleigh Register*, October 11, 1851 (first and second quotations); *Liberator*, November 12, 1851 (other quotations).

29. *Frederick Douglass' Paper*, October 9, 1851 reprint from *New York Courier & Enquirer* (first, second, and third quotations); *Montreal Gazette*, October 6, 1851, reprint from *Syracuse Star* (fourth quotation); *Syracuse Star*, October 15, 1851 (fifth, sixth, and seventh quotations) and October 20, 1851 (last quotation).

30. *Syracuse Standard*, October 7, 1851, Reprints from *Albany Register* and *Journal of Commerce*, and October 16, 1851 (third quotation); Albert Von Frank, *The Trials of Anthony Burns* (Cambridge: Harvard University Press, 1998), xiii (fourth quotation); *Religious Recorder*, October 1852 (last two quotations). The threat of reducing import duties on salt was again mentioned in the month of November when the *Syracuse Journal* stated, "When 'Jerry' was unceremoniously set adrift, the *New York Express* insisted that Congress should open our ports to foreign salt in order to punish Syracuse salt Boilers!" *Syracuse Journal*, November 20, 1851.

31. *Syracuse Standard*, October 9, 1851 (first and second quotations); *Syracuse Journal* October 16, 1851 (other quotations).

32. *Syracuse Journal*, October 14, 1851 (first and second quotations); Yacovone, 148 (third and sixth quotations); Harlow, 300 (fourth and fifth quotations); *Syracuse Standard*, October 6, 1851. On November 13, a witness tes-tifying to the grand jury in Buffalo informed the *Syracuse Standard* that United States Attorney Lawrence "expressed a strong determination to pursue Mr. Lisle, the colored preacher, into Canada, and obtain him by a requisition upon the Governor General." See *Syracuse Standard*, Buffalo November 15, 1851. For the British stance on extradition, see Gordon S. Barker, *The Imperfect Revolution: Anthony Burns and the Landscape of Race in Antebellum America* (Kent: Kent State University Press, 2010), 94–101. The Northern press, voicing law-and-order sentiments, vehemently attacked May and other preachers for their antislavery sermons. The *Albany Register*, for example, reprinted the following from the *Syracuse Star*: "The ministry and the politicians bore a conspicuous part in getting up the rescue riot and outrage; and some of the former gentry, not satisfied with what they had done in the streets, took the subject in their pulpits on Sunday, and not only desecrated the day by fulminating their treasonable doctrines of resistance to the execution of the laws, but disgraced their sacerdotal robes by assuming the character of political demagogues, and endeavoring to stir up sedition against the government and laws, among their congregations." *Syracuse Journal*, October 17, 1851.

33. *Syracuse Journal*, October 18, 1851. The *Syracuse Journal* of October 21, 185 listed the women who journeyed to Auburn first in a single column; the men were listed separately afterward in two columns.

34. *Syracuse Journal*, October 9, 1851 (first and second quotations); *Syracuse Journal*, October 4, 1851.

35. Samuel J. May, *Speech of Rev. Samuel J. May, to the Convention of Citizens of Onondaga County, in Syracuse on the 14th of October, 1851* (Syracuse: Agan & Summers, 1851), 18.

36. *Syracuse Journal*, October 15, 1851. The term pocket revolution is used by Von Frank.

37. *Syracuse Journal*, October 13, 1851.

38. Gerrit Smith, *Address of the Convention Held for the Purpose of Celebrating the Rescue of the Man Jerry*, Gerrit Smith Broadside and pamphlet Collection, Special Collections Research Center, Syracuse University Library (first four quotations); *Liberator*, November 28, 1851 (fifth quotation) and September 24, 1851 (sixth quotation); *Syracuse Standard*, October 13, 1851 (seventh quotation).

Chapter 6

1. Ruby West Jackson and Walter T. McDonald, *Finding Freedom: The Untold Story of*

Joshua Glover, Runaway Slave (Madison: Wisconsin Historical Society Press, 2007), 38–39 (first and second quotations); Joseph Schafer, "Stormy Days in Court: The Booth Case," *Wisconsin Magazine of History*, 20:1, 89 (third quotation). H. Robert Baker notes that Glover had gained a reputation as "a skilled carpenter" by selling his "handcrafted goods" in Racine. See Baker, *The Rescue of Joshua Glover: A Fugitive Slave, the Constitution, and the Coming of the Civil War* (Athens: Ohio University Press, 2006), 2. It is quite possible that the rumors of a relationship between Glover and Turner's wife are unfounded and that Turner, like too many other unscrupulous individuals in antebellum America, simply sought to cash in on his knowledge of a fugitive slave's whereabouts.

2. Jackson and McDonald, 4–8, 25, 27. For the best discussion of Glover's escape, see Jackson and McDonald, 25–28.

3. Jackson and McDonald, 38–9 (first, second, and third quotations); Stanley W. Campbell, *The Slave Catchers: Enforcement of the Fugitive Slave Law, 1850–1860* (New York: Norton, 1970), 157 (fourth quotation).

4. Jackson and McDonald, 40 (first and fifth quotations); Schafer, 89 (second quotation); Baker, 2 (third, fourth, and seventh quotations); *Frederick Douglass' Paper*, March 24, 1854 (sixth quotation).

5. *Milwaukee Daily Sentinel*, April 1, 1854 (first quotation); *Frederick Douglass' Paper*, March 24, 1854 (second and third quotations).

6. Schafer, 90 (first quotation); *Frederick Douglass's Paper*, March 24, 1854 (second and third quotations).

7. Schafer, 90.

8. Schafer, 90.

9. Baker, 6 (first quotation); Jackson and McDonald, 43 (second quotation); Schafer, 90 (last quotation).

10. Jackson and McDonald, 43 (first quotation); *Milwaukee Daily Sentinel*, March 22, 1854 (second and third quotations); Baker, 8 (fourth quotation).

11. Jackson and McDonald, 21–2.

12. Quoted in Jeffrey Schmitt, "Rethinking *Ableman v. Booth* and States' Rights in Wisconsin," *Virginia Law Review* 93:1, 1324–5.

13. *Milwaukee Daily Sentinel*, March 22, 1854 (first and second quotations); Baker, 10 (third quotation); Schafer, 91 (fourth and fifth quotations); *Liberator*, March 24, 1854 (last quotation).

14. Baker, 10 (first quotation); Schmitt, 1324 (second quotation); *Milwaukee Daily Sentinel*,

March 22, 1854 (third quotation); *Liberator*, March 24, 1854 (last quotation). For Baker's discussion of crowd action and the expression of popular sovereignty in antebellum America, see Baker, 12–17.

15. *Liberator*, March 24, 1854 (first quotation); Baker, 21 (second quotation); Schmitt, 1324 (last quotations).

16. *Liberator*, March 24, 1854 (first and second quotations); Baker, 20 (third quotation); Campbell, 158 (fourth quotation).

17. Baker, 18–19 (first and second quotations); Campbell, 158 (last quotation).

18. *Milwaukee Daily Sentinel*, March 24, 1854 (first, fifth, and sixth quotations); Jackson and McDonald, 47 (second quotation); Baker, 22–23 (third, seventh, eighth quotations); Schmitt, 1325 (fourth quotation). In later court proceedings, some people estimated the crowd at about five thousand. See Baker, 87.

19. Jackson and McDonald, 48–9.

20. Jackson and McDonald, 58, 70 (first and last quotation); *Liberator*, March 31, 1854 (second and third quotations). For the known details of Glover's final days on the Underground Railroad in Wisconsin, see Jackson and McDonald, 59–70.

21. *Liberator*, March 31, 1854 (second, third, fourth quotations); Baker, 24 (third quotation); Schmitt, 1327. For an excellent summary of the issues of slavery and comity in antebellum America, see also Paul Finkelman, *An Imperfect Union: Slavery, Federalism, and Comity* (Chapel Hill: University of North Carolina Press, 1981), especially 3–19. Schmitt also points out that Wisconsinites were moved by the Kansas-Nebraska Bill's repeal of the Missouri Compromise. See Schmitt, 1327.

22. *Liberator*, March 31, 1854.

23. Baker, 85–88.

24. Schmitt, 1329–30 (first and second quotations); Baker, 94 (last quotations).

25. Baker, 114–119 (first, second, third, fourth, fifth quotations); Schmitt, 1331 (sixth quotation); *Richmond Enquirer*, June 16, 1854.

26. Baker, 119–122. For Justice Samuel Crawford's dissent from the majority opinion, see Baker, 125.

27. *Daily National Intelligencer*, January 24, 1855 (first and second quotations); *Daily Chronicle & Sentinel*, January 28, 1855 (third quotation); *Unconstitutionality of the Fugitive Slave Act. Decisions of the Supreme Court of Wisconsin in the Cases of Booth and Ryecraft* (Milwaukee: Rufus King, 1855), 155 (fourth quotation); Baker, 132 (last quotation).

28. Baker, 154–5.

Chapter 7

1. William W. Brown, *Lecture Delivered Before the Female Anti-Slavery Society of Salem*, reprinted in *Four Fugitive Slave Narratives* (Reading, MA: Addison-Wesley, 1969), 83 (first quotation); Charles Emery Stevens, *Anthony Burns: A History* (Boston: John P. Jewett, 1856), 174–5 (second quotation). For a more comprehensive discussion of the Anthony Burns drama and its consequences, see Gordon S. Barker, *The Imperfect Revolution: Anthony Burns and the Landscape of Race in Antebellum America* (Kent, Ohio: Kent State University Press, 2010). On Gabriel's Rebellion, see Douglas Egerton, *Gabriel's Rebellion: The Virginia Conspiracies of 1800 and 1802* (Chapel Hill: University of North Carolina Press, 1993).

2. Barker, 6–7 (first, third, and fourth quotations); Stevens, 179 (second quotation).

3. Jane H. Pease and William H. Pease, *The Fugitive Slave Law and Anthony Burns: A Problem in Law Enforcement* (Philadelphia: J.B. Lippincott, 1975), 28 (first quotation); Stevens, 16 (second quotation); *Boston Slave Riot, and Trial of Anthony Burns* (Northbrook, IL: Metro Books, 1972), 5 (third quotation).

4. Stephen Kendrick and Paul Kendrick, *Sarah's Long Walk: The Free Blacks of Boston and How Their Struggle for Equality Changed America* (Boston: Beacon Press, 2004), 17 (first quotation); Howard N. Meyer, *Colonel of the Black Regiment: The Life of Thomas Wentworth Higginson* (New York: W.W. Norton, 1967), 83 (second and fourth quotations); quoted in Charles Johnson, Patricia Smith, and WGBH Series Research Team, *African Americans in America: America's Journey Through Slavery* (New York: Harcourt Brace, 1998), 399 (fifth quotation); Thomas Wentworth Higginson, "Massachusetts in Mourning, A Sermon Preached in Worcester, on Sunday, June 4, 1854" (Boston: James Munroe, 1854), 12 (sixth and seventh quotations).

5. Robert F. Lucid (ed.), *The Journal of Richard Henry Dana Jr.* (Cambridge, MA: Belknap Press of Harvard University Press, 1968), 2:625–6.

6. Leonard W. Levy, "Sims's Case: The Fugitive Slave Law in Boston in 1851," *Journal of Negro History* 35:1 (1950), 44 (first quotation); Stevens, 252 (second, third, and fourth quotations) and 24 (fifth and ninth quotations); *Journal of Richard Henry Dana Jr.*, 626 (sixth, seventh, and eighth quotations).

7. James Brewer Stewart, *Wendell Phillips: Liberty's Hero* (Baton Rouge: Louisiana State University Press, 1986), 168 (first and second quotations); Meyer, 84 (third quotation); Gary Collison, "The Boston Vigilance Committee: A Reconsideration," *Historical Journal of Massachusetts* 12:2 (1984), 109 (fourth and fifth quotations); Barker, 12.

8. Stevens, 50, 56.

9. Henry Steele Commager, *Theodore Parker: Yankee Crusader* (Boston: Beacon Press, 1960), 233 (first quotation); Albert J. Von Frank, *The Trials of Anthony Burns: Freedom and Slavery in Emerson's Boston* (Cambridge, MA: Harvard University Press, 1998), 9 (second and third quotations); *Boston Slave Riot*, 19 (last quotation).

10. *Boston Slave Riot*, 7–8 (first, third, fourth and fifth quotations); *Boston Evening Transcript*, May 27, 1854 (second quotation); *Boston Morning Journal*, May 27, 1854 (sixth and seventh quotations).

11. Stevens, 35.

12. Von Frank, 56 (first quotation); Barker, 11 (second quotation).

13. *Boston Slave Riot*, 8–9; Stevens, *Anthony Burns*, 39; *Frederick Douglass' Paper*, June 9, 1854; *Boston Morning Journal*, May 27, 1854; Von Frank, 57–8, 61.

14. *Boston Slave Riot*, 9–11; Stevens, 39–41; *Boston Morning Journal*, May 27, 1854.

15. *Boston Slave Riot*, 10 (first quotation); *Boston Morning Journal*, May 27, 1854.

16. Stevens, 42.

17. Barker, 13 (first quotation); *Boston Morning Journal*, May 27, 1854; *Boston Evening Transcript*, May 27, 1854; Stevens, 44; Von Frank, 70, 217.

18. Vincent Y. Bowditch, *Life and Correspondence of Henry Ingersoll Bowditch* (Boston: Houghton, Mifflin, 1902), 1:265–66. See also Barker, 47–48.

19. Stevens, 35 (first quotation); Harold Schwartz, "Fugitive Slave Days in Boston," *New England Quarterly*, 27: 2 (1954), 209–10.

20. Stevens, 289–91.

21. *Boston Morning Journal*, June 3, 1854 (first and second quotations); Meyer, 83 (last quotation). On Harriet Beecher Stowe, see Von Frank, 54, 193–4.

22. Stevens, 61.

23. Collison, 110 (first quotation); James Freeman Clarke, *The Rendition of Anthony Burns: Its Causes and Consequences: A Discourse on Christian Politics Delivered in Williams Hall, Boston on Whitsunday, June 4, 1854* (Boston: Crosby, Nichols and Prentiss & Sawyer, 1854), 16–20 (other quotations).

24. *Liberator*, June 9, 1854 (first and second

quotations); Levy, 41–2 (last). For further discussion of how law-and-order Bostonians invoked their Revolutionary heritage in the Burns drama, see Barker, especially xviii, 122–3.

25. Stevens, 43–44 (first quotation); *Boston Morning Journal* May 27, 1854 and *Boston Evening Transcript*, May 27, 1854. As I have noted in *The Imperfect Revolution*, after the door broke open and Batchelder cried out he had been stabbed, blood gushed from his groin. His fellow guards rushed him into an adjacent room where he died within minutes. There was much confusion about his death until a coroner's inquest ruled that he died of a knife wound to his femoral artery. Attackers who had fired pistol shots, notably Higginson and Stowell, did not know until then that they had not killed Batchelder. See Barker, n37, 130.

26. *Boston Slave Riot* (first and second quotations); Stevens, 43 (third quotation); Barker, 13 (last quotation).

27. Roy Franklin Nichols, *Franklin Pierce: Young Hickory of the Granite Hills* (Philadelphia: University of Pennsylvania Press, 1969), 361. See also, *Richmond Enquirer*, June 2, 1854; Commager, *Theodore Parker*, 236–7; Barker, 13; *Journal of Richard Henry Dana*, 629.

28. Monthly Law Reporter, August 1854, 181–2 (first quotation); *Boston Slave Riot*, 13 (other quotations).

29. *Boston Evening Transcript* May 29, 1854; See also, *Richmond Enquirer*, June 2, 1854.

30. In *The Imperfect Revolution*, I argue that Grimes's inability to fund this purchase or to come up with funds later when Burns had been returned to Virginia and Suttle was willing to sell him reflect the Boston establishment's lack of support for the antislavery cause. See Barker, 52–3.

31. Stanley Shapiro, "The Rendition of Anthony Burns," *Journal of Negro History* 44: 1 (1959), 41 (first quotation); *Monthly Law Reporter*, August, 1854, 182 (other quotations).

32. *Monthly Law Reporter*, August 1854, 188.

33. *Frederick Douglass' Paper*, June 9, 1854 (first quotation); *Boston Slave Riot* (other quotations).

34. Stevens, 125 (first and second quotations), and 141 (fifth and sixth quotations); *Boston Slave Riot*, 76 (third quotation); Barker, 17 (fourth quotation).

35. *Boston Evening Transcript*, May 31, 1854 (first quotation). See also Barker, 17. *Journal of Richard Henry Dana Jr.*, 632 (second quotation); Stevens, 113 (third, fourth, and fifth quotations).

36. *Boston Slave Riot*, 77.

37. Stevens, 114.

38. John White Chadwick, *Theodore Parker: Preacher and Reformer* (Boston: Houghton, Mifflin, 1900), 263.

39. *Monthly Law Reporter*, August 1854, 203–7. For additional discussion of Loring's opinion, see Barker, 17–18.

40. *Monthly Law Reporter*, August 1854, 207–10.

41. *Boston Slave Riot*, 83 (first quotation); *Monthly Law Reporter*, August 1854, 209–10.

42. *Boston Slave Riot*, 77 (first quotation); Barker, 19 (second quotation); *Frederick Douglass' Paper*, June 9, 1854 (third quotation); Arthur S. Bolster, *James Freeman Clarke: Disciple to Advancing the Truth* (Boston: Beacon Press, 1954), 236 (fourth and fifth quotations).

43. *Boston Evening Transcript*, June 3, 1854 (first quotation); Shapiro, 45 (second quotation); Bolster, 236 (third quotation); Commager, *Theodore Parker*, 241 (fourth quotation); Ray Allen Billington (ed.), *The Journal of Charlotte L. Forten: A Free Negro in the Slave Era* (New York: Collier Books, 1961), 46 (fifth quotation); Von Frank, 135 (sixth quotation); *Boston Slave Riot*, 76 (seventh quotation); *Richmond Enquirer*, June 6, 1854 (eighth quotation); *Boston Evening Transcript*, June 2, 1854.

44. Barker, 41 (first quotation); Stacey M. Robertson, *Parker Pillsbury: Radical Abolitionist, Male Feminist* (Ithaca: Cornell University Press, 2000), 129 (second, third fourth, and fifth quotations); Deborah Anna Logan (ed.), *Writings on Slavery and the American Civil War: Harriet Martineau* (Dekalb: Northern Illinois University Press, 2002), 94–97 (other quotations).

45. Barker, 56 (first quotation); *Liberator*, June 23, 1854 (second quotation); Albert Réville, *The Life and Writings of Theodore Parker* (London: Simpkin, Marshall, 1865), 116 (third quotation); *Frederick Douglass' Paper*, August 1854 (fourth quotation); John W. Blassingame (ed.), *The Frederick Douglass Papers* (New Haven: Yale University Press, 1985), 3:3, 123.

46. Anthony Burns, letter published in *Liberator*, August 13, 1858 (first quotation); G. Carter Woodson (ed.), *The Mind of the Negro as Reflected in Letters Written During the Crisis, 1800–1860* (New York: Russell and Russell, 1969), 661.

47. David M. Potter, *The Impending Crisis* (New York: Harper & Row, 1976), 128 (first quotation); *Southern Literary Messenger*, November 1850 (second and third quotations).

48. *Raleigh Daily Register*, June 14, 1854 (first

quotation); Richard K. Crallé (ed.), *The Works of John C. Calhoun* (New York, 1854), 4:542, 550 (second and third quotations); *Richmond Enquirer*, June 2, 1854 (last quotation).

49. Barker, 73 (first and third quotations); *Charleston Mercury*, January 8, 1854 (second quotation); *Richmond Enquirer*, June 7, 1854 (last quotation).

50. *Frederick Douglass' Paper*, June 30, 1854. For further discussion of this issue, see also Barker, 84–5.

51. John Greenleaf Whittier, "The Rendition" in *The Complete Poetical Works of John Greenleaf Whittier*, W. Garret Horder, ed. (New York: Oxford University Press, 1920), 344.

Chapter 8

1. Leverett Wilson Spring, *Kansas: The Prelude to War for the Union* (Boston: Houghton, Mifflin, 1885), 102 (first quotation); *Daily Cleveland Herald*, February 28, 1856 (second quotation); *Liberator*, May 16, 1856 (third quotation); Cynthia Griffin Wolff, "'Margaret Garner': A Cincinnati Story," *Massachusetts Review* 32: 3 (1991), 417–40. The most comprehensive study of the Margaret Garner case is Steven Weisenburger's *Modern Medea: A Family Story of Slavery and Child-Murder from the Old South* (New York: Hill and Wang, 1998).

2. Mark Reinhardt, *Who Speaks for Margaret Garner?* (Minneapolis: University of Minnesota Press, 2010), 11 (first and third quotations); *Daily Cleveland Herald*, January 31, 1856 (second quotation); Fergus M. Bordewich, *Bound for Canaan: The Underground Railroad and the War for the Soul of America* (New York: HarperCollins, 2005), 401 (fourth quotation); *Liberator*, February 28, 1854 (fifth quotation). On Daughtery's slaves, see *Daily Cleveland Herald*, January 30, 1856. For a description of Margaret, see Coffin, 562–3 or Griffin Wolff, 417–440. As noted, Steven Weisenburger argues convincingly that Archibald Gaines abused Margaret. See Weisenburger, especially 44–48, 156–58, and 278–79.

3. *Daily Cleveland Herald*, January 30, 1856 (first quotation); Coffin, 558 (second and third quotations); *Inter Ocean* (Chicago), December 6, 1874 (fourth quotation); Bordewich, 401 (fifth quotation). The purchase of Joe Kite's liberty is mentioned in Coffin, 558, and in the *Milwaukee Daily Sentinel*, February 4, 1856. Weisenburger reports that Elijah's liberty was purchased for $50, "a generously low price." See Weisenburger, 69.

4. *Daily Cleveland Herald*, January 30, 1856 (first and second quotations); Weisenburger, 67 (third quotation) and 72 (fourth quotation). On Cincinnati's population and demographic profile, see Weisenburger, 83 and Reinhardt, 17.

5. *Daily Evening Bulletin*, March 26, 1870.

6. *Liberator*, February 8, 1856 (first quotation); Reinhardt, 3 (third quotation); *Cincinnati Daily Enquirer*, January 29, 1856; Weisenburger, 6.

7. *Cincinnati Daily Enquirer*, January 29, 1856; Weisenburger, 6; *Milwaukee Daily Sentinel*, February 4, 1856 (other quotations). That Clinton Butts was the first man through the door is reported in the article "A Reminiscence of Slavery" published in *Daily Evening Bulletin*, March 26, 1870.

8. *Liberator*, February 8, 1856 (first, second, and third quotations) and April 29, 1864 (fourth quotation); *Cincinnati Daily Enquirer*, January 29, 1856 and quoted in Griffin (fifth and sixth quotations).

9. *Liberator*, February 8, 1856 (first, second, and fifth quotations); *Cincinnati Daily Enquirer*, February 29, 1856 and quoted in Griffin and in Bordewich, 403 (third and sixth quotations); *Milwaukee Daily Sentinel*, February 4, 1856 (fourth quotation). There are several different versions of the murder scene in the literature; in the text, I have included the most commonly accepted one. Mark Reinhardt notes: "Margaret either was or was not found with a knife in hand. She did or did not use the knife on her boys. She did or did not ask her mother-in-law Mary to help her kill the children, and Mary did or did not respond by refusing and hiding under a bed. Margaret's husband, Robert, either was or was not 'screaming as if bereft of reason' and did not urge Margaret to do the killing." See Reinhardt, 8–9.

10. Reinhardt, 215, 217–8.

11. *Cincinnati Daily Enquirer*, January 30, 1856 and quoted in Griffin (first quotation); *Liberator*, February 8, 1856 (second and fourth quotations); Bordewich, 403 (third quotation). In describing the black response during the Garner affair, Reinhardt identifies a number of black organizations and notes that only scanty information is available on them. This is perhaps not overly surprising as these groups constantly violated the Fugitive Slave Law's prohibition of aiding runaways and would have kept their activities secret if only to avoid heavy fines. See Reinhardt, 17. On the fugitive slave Louis's escape, see Weisenburger, 104–5.

12. Coffin, 569 (first quotation); *Milwaukee Daily Sentinel*, February 4, 1856 (second quotation).

13. *Liberator*, February 8, 1856 (other quotations); Coffin, 568 (fifth quotation); Reinhardt, 5–6 (fourth quotation).

14. *Liberator*, February 8, 1856 (first quotation); *Daily Cleveland Herald*, January 31, 1856 (second quotation).

15. *Daily Cleveland Herald*, January 31, 1856 (first, second, and third quotations); Reinhardt, 6 (fourth quotation); Weisenburger, 117 (last quotation).

16. *Daily Cleveland Enquirer*, January 30, 1856 (first quotation); Weisenburger, 75 (second quotation); *Cincinnati Post*, March 30, 2002 (third quotation). On this argument, see also Reinhardt, 14. For an interesting look at women in the Old South, see Victoria E. Bynum, *Unruly Women: The Politics of Social and Sexual Control in the Old South* (Chapel Hill: University of North Carolina Press, 1992).

17. *Liberator*, April 11, 1856 (first, second and third quotations); Reinhardt 221 (last quotation). In such passages, Lucy Stone and others did — as we now say — speak for Margaret Garner in a variety of ways. Although scholars may at times criticize the way they sought to spin her story, it should also be pointed out that the mid-nineteenth century print culture effectively allowed the tale of an ordinary person to occupy center stage in national discourse and thus to help shape the nation's fate.

18. Griffin Wolff, 417–440; *The Ripley Bee*, February 23, 1856 (last two quotations).

19. *Liberator*, February 29, 1856.

20. *Liberator*, February 29, 1856.

21. Wendell W. Brown, "A Lecture Delivered Before the Female Anti-Slavery Society of Salem" in *Four Fugitive Slave Narratives* (Reading, MA: Addison-Wesley, 1969), 84.

22. *Daily Cleveland Herald*, January 31, 1856.

23. *Daily Cleveland Herald*, February 13, 1856 (first quotation) and January 31, 1856 (third quotation); *Ripley Bee*, February 9, 1856. Levi Coffin later described Joliffe saying, "His heart was quick to respond to the needs of the fugitives, and no sacrifice of time, strength, talent, or business reputation was too great to be willingly and cheerfully rendered in behalf of the oppressed." See Coffin, 548. On the crowd outside the building, see Weisenburger, 110.

24. *Daily Cleveland Herald*, February 13, 1856; Weisenburger, 141 (last quotation).

25. Coffin, 561–2; Weisenburger, 119 (last quotation). Joliffe also later argued that commissioners assumed powers that the Constitution accorded only to judges.

26. *Daily Cleveland Herald*, February 28, 1856.

27. *Liberator*, June 10, 1864. Apparently the Sarsefield Guards and Shield Guards waited in the wings and were "armed with repeating rifles." See Weisenburger, 195.

28. Stanley W. Campbell, *The Slave Catchers: Enforcement of the Fugitive Slave Law, 1850–1860* (New York: W.W. Norton, 1968), 146 (first quotation); *Liberator*, May 23, 1856 (second quotation).

29. For criticism of Chase, see *Liberator*, June 19, 1857, August 3, 1860, and June 10, 1864; *Milwaukee Daily Sentinel*, December 28, 1863; Weisenburger, 214–218.

30. *Liberator*, March 21, 1856 (first quotation); *Cleveland Daily Herald*, December 4, 1874 (second quotation).

31. Weisenburger, 220–223.

32. *Liberator*, March 21, 1856 (first and second quotations); *Boston Daily Atlas*, July 8, 1856 (third, fourth, and fifth quotations); *Ripley Bee*, April 19, 1856 and *Liberator*, May 2, 1856 (sixth quotation); *New York Herald*, January 8, 1858 (last quotation).

33. *Daily Evening Bulletin*, March 26, 1870.

34. Bordewich, 405 (first and second quotations); Stacey M. Robertson, *Hearts Beating for Liberty: Women and Abolitionists in the Old Northwest* (Chapel Hill: University of North Carolina Press, 2010), 115 (other quotations). Evidently Ernst believed newspaper reports suggesting that she was happy that her child had drowned when the *Henry Lewis* collided with another riverboat.

35. Reinhardt, 215–218.

36. *Liberator*, November 30, 1860.

37. *Liberator*, April 22, 1859, September 19, 1856, and February 12, 1858.

38. Weisenburger, 268.

39. *Liberator*, October 27, 1856, August 3, 1860, July 20, 1860, and August 10, 1857.

40. Weisenburger, 7–8.

Bibliography

Aptheker, Herbert. *The Negro in the American Revolution*. New York: International, 1940.

Baker, H. Robert. *The Rescue of Joshua Glover: A Fugitive Slave, the Constitution, and the Coming of the Civil War*. Athens: Ohio University Press, 2006.

Bancroft, George. *History of the United States from the Discovery of the American Continent*. Boston: Little Brown, 1854.

Barker, Gordon S. *The Imperfect Revolution: Anthony Burns and the Landscape of Race in Antebellum America*. Kent: Kent State University Press, 2010.

_____. "Secession and Slavery as a Positive Good: The Impact of the Anthony Burns Drama in Boston on Virginia," *Virginia Magazine of History and Biography* 118:2 (2010).

Bearse, Austin. *Reminiscences of Fugitive-Slave Law Days in Boston*. Boston: Warren Richardson, 1880.

Berlin, Ira. *Many Thousands Gone: The First Two Centuries of Slavery in America*. Cambridge: Harvard University Press, 1998.

Billington, Ray Allen, ed. *The Journal of Charlotte L. Forten: A Free Negro in the Slave Era*. New York: Collier Books, 1961.

Blassingame, John W. *The Slave Community: Plantation Life in the Antebellum South*. New York: Oxford University Press, 1972.

_____, John R. McKivigan, and Peter P. Hinks, eds. *The Frederick Douglass Papers*. New Haven: Yale University Press, 1999.

Blight, David W. *Beyond the Battlefield: Race Memory, and the American Civil War*. Amherst: University of Massachusetts Press, 1997.

_____, and Brooks D. Simpson, eds. *Union and Emancipation: Essays on Politics and Race in the Civil War*. Kent: Kent State University Press, 1997.

Bolster, Arthur S., Jr. *James Freeman Clarke: Disciple to Advancing Truth*. Boston: Beacon Press, 1954.

Bordewich, Fergus M. *Bound for Canaan: The Underground Railroad and the War for the Soul of America*. New York: HarperCollins, 2005.

Boston Slave Riot and the Trial of Anthony Burns Containing the Report. Northbrook, IL: Metro Books, 1972.

Bowditch, Vincent Y. *Life and Correspondence of Henry Ingersoll Bowditch*. Boston: Houghton, Mifflin, 1902.

Brown, Henry Box. *Narrative of the Life of Henry Box Brown, Written by Himself*. Manchester: Lee & Glynn, 1851.

Brown, Richard D. *Major Problems in the Era of the American Revolution, 1760–1791*. Boston: Houghton Mifflin, 2000.

Brown, Wendell W. "A Lecture Delivered Before the Female Anti-Slavery Society of Salem," *Four Fugitive Slave Narratives*. Reading, MA: Addison-Wesley, 1969.

Bynum, Victoria E. *Unruly Women: The Politics of Social and Sexual Control in the Old South*. Chapel Hill: University of North Carolina Press, 1992.

Campbell, Stanley W. *The Slave Catchers:*

Enforcement of the Fugitive Slave Law, 1850–1860. New York: W.W. Norton, 1970.

Chadwick, John White. *Theodore Parker: Preacher and Reformer.* Boston: Houghton, Mifflin, 1900.

Clarke, James Freeman. *The Rendition of Anthony Burns: Its Cause and Consequences: A Discourse on Christian Politics Delivered in Williams Hall on Whitsunday, June 4, 1854.* Boston: Crosby, Nichols and Prentiss & Sawyer, 1854.

Cobbe, Frances Power, ed. *The Collected Works of Theodore Parker.* London: Trübner, 1863.

Collison, Gary. "The Boston Vigilance Committee: A Reconsideration." *Historical Journal of Massachusetts* 12:2 (1984).

_____. *Shadrach Minkins: From Fugitive Slave to Citizen.* Cambridge: Harvard University Press, 1997.

_____. "'This Flagitious Offense': Daniel Webster and the Shadrach Rescue Cases, 1851–1852." *New England Quarterly* 68:4 (1995).

Commager, Henry Steele. *Theodore Parker: Yankee Crusader.* Boston: Beacon Press, 1960.

Connor, Thomas H. *Lords of the Loom: The Cotton Whigs and the Coming of the Civil War.* New York: Charles Scribner's, 1968.

Craft, William. *Running a Thousand Miles for Freedom: the Escape of William and Ellen Craft from Slavery.* Athens: University of Georgia Press, 1999.

Crallé, Richard K., ed. *The Works of John C. Calhoun.* New York: D. Appleton, 1851.

Cunningham, Valerie, and Mark Sammons. *Black Portsmouth: Three Centuries of African-American Heritage.* Durham: University of New Hampshire Press, 2004.

Dillon, Merton L. *The Growth of a Dissenting Minority.* DeKalb: Northern Illinois University Press, 1974.

Donald, David Herbert. *Charles Sumner and the Rights of Man.* New York: Knopf, 1970.

Douglass, Frederick. *Life and Times of Frederick Douglass.* New York: Macmillan, 1962.

_____. *Narrative of the Life of Frederick Douglass.* New York: Dover Publications, 1995.

Drew, Benjamin. *The Refugee, or The Narratives of the Fugitive Slaves in Canada, Related by Themselves, with an Account of the History and Condition of the Colored Population of Upper Canada.* Boston: John P. Jewett, 1856.

Edelstein, Tilden G. *Strange Enthusiasm: A Life of Thomas Wentworth Higginson.* New York: Yale University Press, 1968.

Egerton, Douglas R. *Death or Liberty: African Americans and Revolutionary America.* New York: Oxford University Press, 2009.

_____. *Gabriel's Rebellion: The Virginia Conspiracies of 1800 and 1802.* Chapel Hill: University of North Carolina Press, 1993.

Elkins, Stanley M. *Slavery: A Problem in American Institutional and Intellectual Life.* Chicago: University of Chicago Press, 1976.

Ely, Melvin Patrick. *Israel on the Appomattox: A Southern Experiment in Black Freedom.* New York: Alfred A. Knopf, 2004.

Faust, Drew Gilpin, ed. *The Ideology of Slavery: Proslavery Thought in the Antebellum South, 1830–1860.* Baton Rouge: Louisiana State University Press.

Fellman, Michael. "Theodore Parker and the Abolitionist Role in the 1850s." *Journal of American History* 61:3 (1974).

Fields, Barbara Jeanne. *Slavery and Freedom on the Middle Ground: Maryland During the Nineteenth Century.* New Haven: Yale University Press, 1985.

Finkelman, Paul. *An Imperfect Union: Slavery, Federalism, and Comity.* Chapel Hill: University of North Carolina Press, 1981.

Foner, Philip S. *History of Black Americans: From the Compromise of 1850 to the End of the Civil War.* Westport, CT: Greenwood Press, 1983.

Frey, Sylvia. *Water from the Rock: Black Resistance in a Revolutionary Age.* Princeton, NJ: Princeton University Press, 1991.

Fritchman, Stephen Hole. *Men of Liberty: Ten Unitarian Pioneers.* Port Washington, NY: Kennikat Press, 1944.

Galpin, W. Freeman. "The Jerry Rescue." *New York History* 26:1 (1945).

Gara, Larry. *The Liberty Line: The Legend of the Underground Railroad.* Lexington: University Press of Kentucky, 1996.

Gross, Robert A. *The Minutemen and Their World.* New York: Hill and Wang, 17.

Hardin, Evamaria. *Syracuse and the Underground Railroad.* Syracuse: Erie Canal Museum, 1989.

Harlow, Ralph Volney. *Gerrit Smith: Philanthropist and Reformer.* New York: Henry Holt, 1939.

Hendrick, George, and Willene Hendrick. *Black Refugees in Canada: Accounts of Escape During the Era of Slavery.* Jefferson, NC: McFarland, 2010.

Hensel, W.U. *The Christiana Riot and the Treason Trials of 1851, an Historical Sketch.* Lancaster, PA: Press of the New Era Printing, 1911.

Higginson, Mary Potter Thacher, ed. *Letters and Journals of Thomas Wentworth Higginson, 1846–1906.* Boston: Houghton Mifflin, 1921.

Higginson, Thomas Wentworth. *Cheerful Yesterdays.* Boston: Houghton, Mifflin, 1898.

_____. *Massachusetts in Mourning: A Sermon Preached in Worcester, on Sunday June 4, 1854.* Boston: James Munroe, 1854.

Hill, Daniel G. *The Freedom Seekers: Blacks in Early Canada.* Toronto: Stoddart, 1992.

Hodges, Graham. *David Ruggles: A Radical Black Abolitionist and the Underground Railroad in New York City.* Chapel Hill: University of North Carolina Press, 2010.

Horder, W. Garret, ed. *The Complete Poetical Works of John Greenleaf Whittier.* New York: Oxford University Press, 1920.

Horton James Oliver, and Lois E. Horton. *Slavery and the Making of America.* New York: Oxford University Press, 2005.

Isaac, Rhys. "Preachers and Patriots: Popular Culture and the Revolution in Virginia." *The American Revolution: Explorations in the History of American Radicalism.* Edited by Alfred F. Young. Dekalb: Northern Illinois Press, 1976.

Jackson, Ruby West, and Walter T. McDonald. *Finding Freedom: The Untold Story of Joshua Glover, Runaway Slave.* Madison: Wisconsin Historical Society Press, 2007.

Jacobs, Donald M. *Courage and Conscience: Black and White Abolitionists in Boston.* Indianapolis: Indiana University Press, 1993.

Johnson, Charles, Patricia Smith, and WGBH Series Research Team. *African Americans in America: America's Journey Through Slavery.* New York: Harcourt Brace, 1998.

Johnson, Walter. *Soul by Soul: Life Inside the Antebellum Slave Market.* Cambridge: Harvard University Press, 1999.

Katz, Jonathan. *Resistance at Christiana: The Fugitive Slave Rebellion, Christiana, Pennsylvania, September 11, 1851.* New York: Thomas Y. Crowell, 1974.

Kendrick, Stephen, and Paul Kendrick. *Sarah's Long Walk: The Free Blacks of Boston and How Their Struggle for Equality Changed America.* Boston: Beacon Press, 2004.

Kerber, Linda. *Women of the Republic: Intellect and Ideology in Revolutionary America.* Chapel Hill: University of North Carolina Press, 1980.

Knadler, Stephen. "At Home in the Crystal Palace: African American Transnationalism and Aesthetics of Representative Democracy." *ESQ: A Journal of the American Renaissance* 56:4 (2010).

Kolchin, Peter. *American Slavery, 1619–1877.* New York: Hill and Wang, 2003.

Laurie, Bruce. *Beyond Garrison: Antislavery and Social Reform.* New York: Cambridge University Press, 2005.

Leichtle, Kurt E., and Bruce G. Carveth. *Crusade Against Slavery: Edward Coles, Pioneer of Freedom.* Carbondale: Southern Illinois Press, 2011.

Levy, Leonard W. "Sims' Case: The Fugitive Slave Law in Boston in 1851." *Journal of Negro History*, 35:1 (1950).

Linebaugh, Peter, and Marcus Rediker. *"Many Headed Hydra": Sailors, Slaves, Commoners, and the Hidden History of the Revolutionary Atlantic.* Boston: Beacon Press, 2000.

Litwack, Leon. *North of Slavery: The Negro in the Free States, 1790–1860.* Chicago: University of Chicago Press, 1961.

Logan, Deborah Anna, ed. *Writings on Slavery and the American Civil War: Harriet Martineau*. Dekalb: Northern Illinois University Press, 2002.

Loguen, J.W. *The Rev. J.W. Loguen as a Slave and as a Freeman: A Narrative of Real Life*. Syracuse: J.G. Truair, 1859.

Longfellow, Samuel, ed. *Life of Henry Wadsworth Longfellow, with Extracts from His Journals and Correspondence*. Boston: Ticknor, 1886.

Lucid, Robert F., ed. *The Journal of Richard Henry Dana Jr*. Cambridge, MA: Belknap Press of Harvard University Press, 1968.

MacLeod, Duncan J. *Slavery, Race and the American Revolution*. London: Cambridge University Press, 1974.

Magol, Edward. *The Antislavery Rank and File: A Social Profile of the Abolitionists' Constituency*. Westport, CT: Greenwood Press, 1986.

Malcolm, Joyce Lee. *Peter's War: A New England Slave Boy and the American Revolution*. New Haven: Yale University Press, 2009.

May, Samuel J. *Some Recollections of Our Antislavery Conflict*. Boston: Fields, Osgood, 1869.

_____. *Speech of Rev. Samuel J. May, to the Convention of Citizens of Onondaga County, in Syracuse on the 14th of October, 1851*. Syracuse: Agan & Summers, 1851.

Mayer, Henry. All *on Fire: William Lloyd Garrison and the Abolition of Slavery*. New York: Norton, 1998.

McCardell, John. *The Idea of a Southern Nation: Southern Nationalists and Southern Nationalism, 1830–1860*. New York: Norton, 1979.

McCaskill, Barbara. "'Yours very truly': Ellen Craft — the Fugitive as Text and Artifact." *African American Review* 28 (1994).

McDougall, Marion Gleason. *Fugitive Slaves, 1619–1865*. New York: Bergman, 1967.

Member of the Philadelphia Bar. *History of the Trial of Castner Hanway and Others for Treason*. Philadelphia: Uriah Hunt, 1852.

Meyer, Howard N. *Colonel of the Black Regiment: The Life of Thomas Wentworth Higginson*. New York: W.W. Norton, 1967.

Mumford, Thomas James, ed. *Memoir of Samuel Joseph May*. Boston: Roberts Brothers, 1873.

Nash, Gary B. *Race and Revolution*. Madison, WI: Madison House, 1990.

Nash, Roderick W. "William Parker and the Christiana Riot." *Journal of Negro History*, 46:1 (1961).

Nelson, Scott Reynolds, and Carol Sheriff. *A People's War: Civilians and Soldiers in America's Civil War, 1854–1877*. New York: Oxford University Press, 2008.

Nelson, Truman, ed. *Documents of Upheaval: Selections from William Lloyd Garrison's the Liberator, 1831–1865*. New York: Hill and Wang, 1966.

Nichols, Roy Franklin. *Franklin Pierce: Young Hickory of the Granite Hills*. Philadelphia: University of Pennsylvania Press, 1969.

Norton, Mary Beth. *Liberty's Daughters*. Boston: Little, Brown, 1980.

Oates, Stephen B. *The Fires of Jubilee: Nat Turner's Fierce Rebellion*. New York: Harper, 1990.

Ofari, Earl. *"Let Your Motto Be Resistance": The Life and Thought of Henry Highland Garnet*. Boston: Beacon Press, 1972.

Parker, Theodore. *Trial of Theodore Parker for the Misdemeanor of a Speech in Faneuil Hall Before the Circuit Court of the United States*. Boston, N.p., 1855.

Pease, Jane H., and William H. Pease. *Bound Them in Chains: A Biographical History of the Antislavery Movement*. Westport, CT: Greenwood Press, 1972.

_____. *The Fugitive Slave Law and Anthony Burns: A Problem in Law Enforcement*. Philadelphia: Lippincott, 1975.

_____. *They Who Would Be Free: Blacks' Search for Freedom, 1830–1861*. New York: Athenum, 1974.

Pease, William H., and Jane H. Pease, eds. *The Antislavery Argument*. Indianapolis: Bobbs-Merrill, 1965.

Phillips, E. Wendell. *Speech of Wendell Phillips, Esq. The Sims Case*. Boston, 1852.

_____. *Speeches, Lectures, and Letters*. Boston: J. Redpath, 1863.

[Phillips, E. Wendell]. *No Slave Hunting*

in the Old Bay State: An Appeal to the People and Legislature of Massachusetts in Anti-Slavery Tracts Series 2: No. 1–14. Westport: Negro Universities Press, 1970.

Plumstead, A.W., and Gilman William H., eds. The Journals and Miscellaneous Notebooks of Ralph Waldo Emerson. Cambridge: Belknap Press of Harvard University Press, 1975.

Potter, David M. The Impending Crisis. New York: Harper & Row, 1976.

Powell, Aaron M. Personal Reminiscences of the Anti-Slavery and Other Reforms and Reformers. Westport: Negro Universities Press, 1970.

Pybus, Cassandra. Epic Journeys of Freedom: Runaway Slaves of the American Revolution and Their Global Quest for Liberty. Boston: Beacon Press, 2006.

Quarles, Benjamin. Black Abolitionists. New York: Oxford University Press, 1969.

_____. The Negro in America. Chapel Hill: University of North Carolina Press, 1996.

Quincy, Josiah. Address Illustrative of the Nature and Power of the Slave States; Delivered at the Request of the Inhabitants of the Town of Quincy, Mass., on Thursday, June, 1856. Boston: Ticknor and Fields, 1856.

Rasmussen, Daniel. American Uprising: The Untold Story of America's Largest Slave Revolt. New York: HarperCollins, 2011.

Reinhardt, Mark. Who Speaks for Margaret Garner? Minneapolis: University of Minnesota Press, 2010.

Reville, Albert. The Life and Writings of Theodore Parker. London: Simpkin, Marshall, 1865.

Richards, Laura E. (Howe). Samuel Gridley Howe. New York: D. Appleton-Century, 1935.

Richter, Daniel K. The Ordeal of the Longhouse: The Peoples of the Iroquois League in the Era of European Colonization. Chapel Hill: University of North Carolina Press, 1992.

Ripley, C. Peter, ed. Black Abolitionist Papers. Chapel Hill: University of North Carolina Press, 1991.

Robertson, Stacey M. Hearts Beating for Liberty: Women Abolitionists in the Old Northwest. Chapel Hill: University of North Carolina Press, 2010.

_____. Parker Pillsbury: Radical Abolitionist, Male Feminist. Ithaca, NY: Cornell University Press, 2000.

Rosenberg, Norman. "Personal Liberty Laws and Sectional Crisis: 1850–1860." Civil War History 17:1 (1971).

Ruchames, Louis, ed. The Letters of William Lloyd Garrison: From Disunion to the Brink of War, 1850–1860. Cambridge, MA: Belknap Press of Harvard University, 1975.

Rusk, Ralph L., ed. The Letters of Ralph Waldo Emerson. New York: Columbia University Press, 1939.

Schmitt, Jeffrey. "Rethinking Ableman v. Booth and States' Rights in Wisconsin." Virginia Law Review 93:1 (2007).

Schwartz, Harold. "Fugitive Slave Days in Boston." New England Quarterly, 27: 2 (1954).

Shanks, Henry T. The Secession Movement in Virginia, 1847–1861. New York: Da Capo, 1970.

Shapiro, Stanley. "The Rendition of Anthony Burns." Journal of Negro History 44: 1 (1959).

Shepard, Odell, ed. The Journals of Bronson Alcott. Boston: Little, Brown, 1938.

Sherwin, Oscar. Prophet of Liberty: The Life and Times of Wendell Phillips. New York: Bookman Associates, 1958.

Siebert, Wilbur H. The Underground Railroad from Slavery to Freedom. North Stratford, NH: Ayer, 2000.

Slaughter, Thomas P. Bloody Dawn: The Christiana Riot and Racial Violence in the Antebellum North. New York: Oxford University Press, 1991.

Smith, Gerrit. Address of the Convention Held for the Purpose of Celebrating the Rescue of the Man Jerry. Gerrit Smith Broadside and Pamphlet Collection, Special Collections Research Center, Syracuse University Library.

Sokolow, Jayme A. "The Jerry McHenry Rescue and the Growth of Northern Antislavery Sentiment During the 1850s." Journal of American Studies 16: 3 (1982).

Sperry, Earl E. The Jerry Rescue. Syracuse: Onondaga Historical Association, 1924.

Spring, Leverett Wilson. *Kansas: The Prelude to War for the Union.* Boston: Houghton, Mifflin, 1885.

Stampp, Kenneth M. *The Peculiar Institution: Slavery in the Ante-Bellum South.* New York: Vintage Books, 1956.

Stevens, Charles Emery. *Anthony Burns: A History.* Boston: John P. Jewett, 1856.

Stewart, James Brewer. *Wendell Phillips: Liberty's Hero.* Baton Rouge: Louisiana State University Press, 1986.

Stowe, Harriet Beecher. *Uncle Tom's Cabin.* New York: Airmont Books, 1967.

Switla, William J. *Underground Railroad in Pennsylvania.* Mechanicsburg: Stackpole Books, 2001.

Taylor, Yuval, ed. *I Was Born a Slave: An Anthology of Classic Slave Narratives.* Chicago: Lawrence Hill Books, 1999.

Tweed, Paul. "'A Brave Man's Child': Theodore Parker and the Memory of the American Revolution." *Historical Journal of Massachusetts* 29:2 (2001).

Voegeli, V. Jacque. *Free but Not Equal: The Midwest and the Negro During the Civil War.* Chicago: University of Chicago Press, 1967.

Von Frank, Albert J. *The Trials of Anthony Burns: Freedom and Slavery in Emerson's Boston.* Cambridge: Harvard University Press, 1998.

Ward, Samuel Ringgold. *Autobiography of a Fugitive Negro.* New York: Arno Press, 1969.

Waugh, John C. *On the Brink of Civil War: The Compromise of 1850 and How It Changed the Course of American History.* Wilmington, DE: Scholarly Resources, 2003.

Weisenburger, Steven. *Modern Medea: A Family Story of Slavery and Child-Murder in the Old South.* New York: Hill and Wang, 1998.

Wesley, Dorothy Porter, and Constance Porter Uzelac, eds. *William Cooper Nell: Nineteenth-Century African American Abolitionist, Historian, Integrationist.* Baltimore: Black Classic Press, 2002.

White, Deborah Gray. *Ar'n't I a Woman?: Female Slaves in the Plantation South.* New York : Norton, 1985.

Williams, George W. *History of the Negro Race in America 1619–1880.* New York: Arno Press, 1968 (originally published in 1885).

Wilson, Carol. *Freedom at Risk: The Kidnapping of Free Blacks in America, 1780–1865.* Lexington: University Press of Kentucky, 1994.

Winks, Robin. *The Blacks in Canada: A History.* New Haven: Yale University Press, 1971.

Wolff, Cynthia Griffin. "'Margaret Garner': A Cincinnati Story." *Massachusetts Review* 32: 3 (1991).

Wood, Gordon S. *Radicalism of the American Revolution.* New York: Vintage Books, 1993.

Woodson, Carter G. *The Negro in Our History.* Washington, D.C.: Associated, 1927.

_____, ed. *The Mind of the Negro as Reflected in Letters Written During the Crisis, 1800–1860.* New York: Russell and Russell, 1969 (originally published in 1926).

Woodward, C. Vann. *American Counterpoint: Slavery and Racism in the North-South Dialogue.* Boston: Little, Brown, 1971.

Yacovone, Donald. *Samuel Joseph May and the Dilemmas of the Liberal Persuasion, 1797–1871.* Philadelphia: Temple University Press, 1991.

Young, Alfred F. *The Shoemaker and the Tea Party: Memory and the American Revolution.* Boston: Beacon Press, 1999.

Index

Numbers in *bold* italics indicate pages with photographs.

Ableman, Stephen 131
Ableman v. Booth 134–135; *see also* Taney, Roger
Acorn 68, 71
acquisition of Texas 24, 97, 98
Adams, John 2, 3, 4, 20, 74, 94, 169
Adams, John Quincy 3
"Address from the Freemen of Onondaga" 115
Agan, John 83
Age of Andrew Jackson 4
Aitken 56
Albany Journal 91
Albany Register 111
Alberti, George 81
Alby, William 119, 120–121
Alcott, Abby 52; *see also* women and fugitive slave crises
Alcott, Bronson 12, 36, 60–61, 62, 66, 144; *see also* Boston Vigilance Committee; "Give Me Liberty or Give Me Death" ideology
Allen, Henry W. 103–105, 108–109
Alvaro Lamphir 42
American Antiquarian Society 1
American Antislavery Society 100, 164, 169
American Civil War 182
American Revolution 3–7, 181–182
Ames, Cephas J. 55, 66
Ames, Orson 109–110
Andrew, John 11, 153
Angove, James 128
Anti-Slave-Catchers' Mass Convention 131
Anti-Slavery Sewing Society 166, 178; *see also* Ernst, Sarah women and fugitive slave crises
Anti-Slavery Standard 88
Antoinette 28; *see also* "Give Me Liberty or Give Me Death" ideology

Appeal in Four Articles 14
Aptheker, Herbert 6
Arnold, Jonathan E. 120, 121, 130
Ashmead, John 88–92, 94
Attucks, Crispus 14, 70

Bacon, John B. 56, 66
Bacon, Winchel D. 129
Baines, Elizabeth 192*n*17
Baker, Robert H. 126
Bancroft, George 3–7; *see also* periodization of the Revolution; Whig interpretation
Barnett, Edward 56
Bassett, P.C. 165, 178
Batchelder, James 78, 147, 149, 203*n*25
Bates, Abner 103, 105, 113
Battle of Vicksburg 177
Bearse, Austin 63, 64, 68, 70, 73, 74; *see also* Boston Vigilance Committee
Beckley, Jesse 175; *see also* Life Guards
Beckley, William 171
Beebe, Asa 110
Beecher, Henry Ward 170
Beloved 180
Bemis, Deputy Marshal 103, 106
Bennet, George 163–167
Bibb, Henry 15, *79*
Bielfield, Abram H. 126
Bigelow, Ann 37–38, 41–42, 43, 191*n*2
Bigelow, Francis Edwin 37–38, 41–42, 43, 191*n*2
Bigelow, John P. 46, 57, 59, 63, 193*n*9, 194*n*21
Bishop, Francis 25
Bishop's University Crossing Borders Research Cluster 1
Bishop's University Library 1
Bishop's University Research Office 1

Bishop's University Vice-Principal Academic 1
Black laws 110
Blassingame, John W. 185n13
Bleeding Kansas crisis 78
"Bleeding Kansas" speech 160; *see also* Sumner, Charles
Bleeding Sumner–Bleeding Kansas 161, 177; *see also* Sumner, Charles
Bolding, John 101
Bonham, Dewitt Clinton 177
Booth, Sherman 17, 118, 124, **125**, 126–135, 188n63
Boston Artillery 147
Boston Athenaeum 1
The Boston Atlas 90
Boston Courier 46, 47
The Boston Daily Atlas 32, 41, 48
Boston Herald 72
Boston Investigator 74
Boston Light Dragoons 147
Boston Light Infantry 147
Boston Massacre 14
Boston Public Library 1
Boston Transcript 72
Boston Vigilance Committee 23, 32, 36, 39, 43, 49, 52, 58, 59, 62, 63–64, 66–68, 71, 73, 76, 139–142, 144, 145, 191n51, 191n6, 194n27
Bowditch, Henry Ingersoll 44, 70, 73, 75, 76, 141, 145
Bowen, John 98
Brashears, Gazoway 167, 174–175
Brent, William 139, 140, 149–150
Bristol and Clifton Ladies Anti-Slavery Society 29; *see also* women and fugitive slave crises
Broadbent, Dana 1
Brogdon, David "Master Mack" 80
Brogdon, William 80
Brooks, Preston 78, 161
Brown, Henry "Box" 27, 30, 31
Brown, John 11, 78, 161, 177, 187n39; *see also* Harpers Ferry Raid; Secret Six
Brown, William Wells 2, 5, 8, 27, 73, 77, 189n6, 189n11
Buckeye State 101
Buckingham, Jeffrey 167
Bucktown 162
Buley, Noah 83, 85–86, 197n11
Burgoyne, John 167, 175
Burns, Anthony 7, 8, 9, 11–12, 19–20, 135, 136–155, **156**, 157–159; *see also* "Give Me Liberty or Give Me Death" ideology; *The Imperfect Revolution: Anthony Burns and the Landscape of Race in Antebellum America*
Burton, Alexander P. 47

Bushnell, H. 178
Butler, Andrew Pickens 160
Butman, Asa O. 57, 65, 139, 151, 168, 193n9
Butts, Clinton 163–164, 176–177

Calhoun, John C. 26, 157; *see also* Southern Nationalists
Caphart, John 192n19
Cayuga 97
Chadwick, John White 25
Chambers, Francis T. 171, 172
Chase, Salmon P. 175–176, 177
Child, Lydia Maria 178
Childs, Michael 1
Christiana riot 11, 15, 78–80, 84–95, 191n42, 197n26
Cincinnati Enquirer 163
Civil War 14, 44, 78, 177, 180, 181, 182
Clarke, James Freeman 12, 146, 153; *see also* "Give Me Liberty or Give Me Death" ideology
Clarke, Olive 110
Clarke, Sidney 110
Clarke, William M. 98
Clay, Henry 3, 45, 49
Clemens, Jeremiah 45
Clement, Charles 122–124, 130; *see also* *Racine Advocate*
The Cleveland Herald 32, 90, 190n19
Clifford, John H. 142
Clinton, Sir Henry 5
Cluer, John 76
Coates, Lindley 82
Cobb, Ira 108
Coburn, John P. 47
Coffin, Levi 162–163, 167, 172
Coleman, Lucy N. 179
Coles, Edward 186n19
College of William and Mary 1
Collins, Robert 22, 31–32, 190n37
Collinson, Gary 141
Colver, Nathaniel 62–63; *see also* Boston Vigilance Committee
The Commonwealth 39, 45, 47, 58, 142, 153, 194n14; *see also* Wright, Elizur
Compromise of 1850 22, 31, 37–38, 47, 90, 98, 99, 110, 177
Concord Underground Railroad 41
Confederate ideology 157
Congress of Freedom 114
"Congress of Freedom" 107
Conkling, Alfred 101, 113
Constitutional Amendments 131
Cook, W.A. 98
Coombs, Henry 68
Cooper, Joseph 176
Cornwallis, Lord 4

Cotton, Charles G. 120–121, 122, 124, 125, 127–128, 130
Cotton Whigs 34, 35, 46, 72
Courthouse Riot 146, 158
Cox, James 168
Craft, Ellen 7, 9, 11, 17, 20, 21–26, **27**, 28–36, 95, 181 189*n*12, 190*n*19, 190*n*27, 190*n*42, 191*n*50. 191*n*51; *see also* women and fugitive slave crises
Craft, William 7, 9, 11, 17, 20, 21–26, **27**, 28–36, 95, 181 189*n*12, 190*n*19, 190*n*27, 190*n*42, 191*n*50. 191*n*51; *see also* women and fugitive slave crises
Crandall, William L. 96, 103, 113, 114, 117; Syracuse Vigilance Committee
Critical Period 4
Crystal Palace 21, 23, 29
Curtis, George Ticknor 39, 43, 46, 56, 63–69

Daily Morning News 57–58, 60, 72, 110
Daily National Intelligencer 58, 66, 72, 194*n*11, 194*n*27
Daily Republican 161
Dana, Richard Henry, Jr. 140, 148, 150, 151
Daniel 101
Daughters of Samaria 166; *see also* women and fugitive slave crises
Daughtery, Levi F. 163
Davenport, J. 98
Davis, Caleb 109
Davis, Charles G. 39, 43, 47, 48
Davis, James 109
Dawn Settlement 9
Debree, John 39, 42
Declaration of Independence 2, 12, 14, 16, 20, 53, 92, 106, 115, 117, 123, 178, 181, 182, 186*n*17
"*Declaration of Sentiments of the Colored Citizens*" 14, 15, 21, 36
Deganawidah 97
Delany, Martin 9–10; *see also* "Give Me Liberty or Give Me Death" ideology
Delyon, M.S. 56, 66
Democratic Party 97
Derrick, W.S. 88
Deslondes, Charles 7, 186*n*16
Devens, Charles 57, 58, 65, 194*n*12
Douglas, Stephen A. 122, 139, 142
Douglass, Frederick 10, 24, 27, 29, 31, 35, 42, 44, 51, 73, 77, **78**, 79, 80, 82, 87, 91, 94–95, 100, 154, 188*n*56, 198*n*5
Dover Morning Star 49
Drake, Francis 43
"The Dreadful Slave Tragedy" 164; *see also* Garner, Margaret
Drew, George 150
Dunmore, Lord 4

Earl Gregg Swem Library 1
Eclipse 177
Edward Howard 176
Egerton, Douglas R. 6, 186*n*15
eighteenth-century women's history 4
Eldridge, Captain 55
Elkins, Stanley 185*n*13
Ellis, Charles 140, 148, 150, 151
Ely, Melvin Patrick 1
Emancipation Bill 43
Emancipation Proclamation 182
emancipation proclamations 5
Emancipator & Republican 35
Emerson, Ralph Waldo 44, 52, 73, 75
Empire of Liberty 3
Erie Canal 3
Ernst, Sarah 13, 178; *see also* Anti-Slavery Sewing Circle; Ohio Ladies Education Society; women and fugitive slave crises
Evening Transcript 151

Fairmount Theological Seminary 178
fancy trade 28, 98, 137
Faran, James 167
Fayetteville Observer 89–90
Federalist Era 3
Fellman, Michael 75
Fifteenth Amendment 186*n*14
Fillmore, Millard 19, 25, 30, 38, 43, 45–46, 48–52, 58, 71–72, 89, 92, **93**, 99–100, 112–114, 177, 195*n*52
Finkelman, Paul 129
Finnell, John W. 171
First Amendment 172
Fitzhugh, George 157
Five Nations 97
Foote, Charles C. 106
Ford, Lewis 27
Ford, Nelson (Joshua Kite) 83–85, 196*n*11
Fort Sumter 78
Forten, Charlotte 12, 153; *see also* women and fugitive slave crises
Foster, Abby Kelley 12, 32, **33**, 146; *see also* "Give Me Liberty or Give Me Death" ideology; women and fugitive slave crises
Foster, Stephen 32, 33
Founding Fathers 4, 147, 157, 180, 186*n*19; *see also* Adams, John; Henry, Patrick; Jefferson, Thomas; Washington, George
Fourteenth Amendment 185*n*14
Foye (Noye), John 47, 50
Frank, Albert Von 87
Franklin, John Hope 6
Frederic Morell's cooperage shop 102
Frederick Douglass' Paper 80
Free Soil Party 52
Freeman, Watson 12, 139, 141, 147, 148

Index

Frey, Sylvia 6
Fugitive Slave Law 9, 10, 11, 14, 17, 19, 21, 22, 25, 30, 31, 32, 34–36, 37–39, 41, 43, 45, 47–53, 55, 57–60, 62–66, 69, 72–74, 76, 81, 82, 83, 89, 90, 94, 96, 99–100, 106, 110–115, 118, 122–124, 127, 129, 130–135, 138, 139, 142, 145, 147, 150–154, 157–158, 163, 166, 168, 172–173, 177, 188n69, 196n6

Gaines, Abner Legrand 176, 177
Gaines, Archibald Kinkhead 161–164, 168–169, 176–177
Gaines, Benjamin 176, 177
Gaines, John P. 161–162
"Gap Gang" 81
Gap Tavern 81, 196n6
Gardiner, William C. 105, 111
Garland, Benammi Stone 119–122, 124, 127, 130–131, 135
Garner, Margaret 7, 8, 9, 13, 14, 160–172, 173, 174–180, 181, 204n9; see also "Give Me Liberty or Give Me Death" ideology; women and fugitive slave crises
Garner, Mary 161–172, 175–177, 201n1, 204n11, 205n17
Garner, Priscilla 161–167, 169, 171, 175–177
Garner, Robert 161–172, 175–177
Garner, Samuel 161–167, 169, 171, 175–177
Garner, Simon 161–168, 170–172, 175–177
Garner, Thomas 161–167, 169, 171, 175–177
Garrison, William Lloyd 10, 29, 31, 35, 46, 50, 52, 57, 66 74, 75, 82, 91–92, 94, 95, 100, 110, 169, 178, 181; see also "Garrisonian pacifism"; "Give Me Liberty or Give e Death" ideology
"Garrisonian pacifism" 13, 76; see also Garrison, William Lloyd
Gibbs, Leonard 104, 107
Giddings, Joshua R. 149
General Warren 14, 15
Gentry, Joshua 102
Georgia Citizen 48
Georgia Platform 47, 56, 89, 111, 157
Gitchell, James 171
"Give Me Liberty or Give Me Death" ideology 8–17, 19, 20, 25, 28, 36, 40, 69, 80, 118, 124, 155, 160, 170, 180, 181, 186n20; see also Alcott, Bronson; Andrew, Governor John; Antoinette; Burns, Anthony; Clarke, James Freeman; Delany, Martin; Douglass, Frederick; Foster, Abby Kelly; fugitive slave crises; Garner, Margaret; Garrison, William Lloyd; Henry, Patrick; Henson, Josiah; Higginson, Thomas Wentworth; Howe, Samuel Gridley; Jerry; Johnson, Lewis; Loguen, Jermain W.; May, Samuel Joseph; Minkins, Shadrach; Parker, Theodore; Parker,

William; Quincy, Josiah; Sims, Thomas; Smith, Gerrit; Smith, Joshua B; Ward, Samuel Ringgold
Glen, C.M.K. 16
Glenn, Thomas 42
Glover 16–17
Glover, Joshua 7, 17, 118–120, 121, 122, 123, 124–135, 201n1
Golden Trumpet 25, 63, 144; see also Phillips, Wendell
"Good Feelings" 3
Gorsuch, Dickinson 83–86
Gorsuch, Edward 16, 78, 82–86, 93, 196n8, 196n9, 196–197n11
Gorsuch, Joshua 83–84, 86
Gorsuch, J.S. 89
Gray, William 108
Great Debates of 1850 47
Great Exhibition of the Works of Industry of All Nations 21–23, 27
Great League of Peace and Power 97
Greeley, Horace 92–93
Grier, Robert C. 88
Griffing, Josephine 179
Griffiths, Julia 12, 94; see also women and fugitive slave crises
Grimes, Leonard A. 43, 68, 73, 138, 139, 140, 146, 149, 155, 203n30

Hackett, Nelson 44
Hallenbeck, Peter 108
Hallett, Benjamin F. 65, 149
Hamlet, James 50
Hammond, George 83
Hammond, Jabez D. 16
Hammond, James 157
Hammond, Joshua (Samuel Thompson) 83–84, 86, 196n11
Hanway, Castner 85–87, 90–91, 93, 94, 113, 197n29
Harper, William 162
Harpers Ferry Raid 177, 187n39; see also Brown, John
Harris, Chester 110
Hartford Republican 49
Haudenosaunee 97
Hayden, Lewis 9, 25, 32, 36, 39–44, 47, 50, 51, 57, 58, 60, 73, 144, 146, 147, 154, 186n26, 189n14, 191n6; see also Boston Vigilance Committee; "Give Me Liberty or Give Me Death" ideology; "Nigger Hill"
Hayes, Joseph K. 47
Hebard, William Wallace 179
Henry, Patrick 8, 9–10, 14–15, 17, 19–20, 21, 24, 25, 28, 36, 40, 80, 118, 124, 135, 155, 160, 170, 180, 181, 186n20, 188n64; see also "Give Me Liberty or Give Me Death" ideology

216

Henry, William 102
Henry Lewis 176
Henson, Josiah 9, 15; *see also* "Give Me Liberty or Give Me Death" ideology
Higgins, John A. 42
Higginson, Thomas Wentworth 11, 17, 18, 19, 33, 44–45, 49, 57, 58, 61, 67–68, 76, 136, 139–140, 141 143–147, 151, **182**, 187*n*39, 188*n*69, 203*n*25; *see also* Boston Vigilance Committee; "Give Me Liberty or Give Me Death" ideology; *Massachusetts in Mourning* sermon; Secret Six
Hillis, D.D. 107
History of the United States 3–7
Hornbeck, John 108
Houghton, Daniel F. 120–121
Hovey, Alfred H. 99; *see also* Vigilance Committee
Howard, Eliza Ann Elizabeth 82, 84, 87; *see also* women and fugitive slave crises
Howe, Samuel Gridley 11–12, 52, 53, 62, 67, 141, 143, 145, 187*n*39, 194*n*14; *see also* Boston Vigilance Committee; "Give Me Liberty or Give Me Death" ideology
Hoyte, Hiram 106, 113
Hoyte, Jason 109
Hughes, Willis H. 22, 31–32, 34, 36
Humphrey, Zebulon 123
Hutchings, Martha 42
Hutchins, Calvin 39
Hutchins, Nicholas 83, 86
Hutchinson Family 167

The Imperfect Revolution: Anthony Burns and the Landscape of Race in Antebellum America 16, 187*n*48, 203*n*25, 203*n*30; *see also* Burns, Anthony
Imperial Emancipation Bill 25
Ingrham, Edward 83
Iroquois 97
Ivens, Barkley 22

Jackson, Francis 64; *see also* Boston Vigilance Committee
Jackson, Henry R. 56
Jackson, James 90
Jackson, Prince 104
James A. Gibson Library of Brock University 1
Jefferson, Thomas 2–4, 20, 24, 131, 170
Jenkins, Charles 124–125, 127–128
Jerry 7, 8, 9, 10, 15–16, 18, 96–117, 181, 199*n*9, 199*n*15, 199*n*23, 200*n*25 *see also* "Give Me Liberty or Give Me Death" ideology
Jerry Rescue Celebration 116
Jerry Rescue Statue *116*
John Taylor 152

Johnson, Abraham 78, 84, 87, 197*n*11
Johnson, Lewis 118, 124; *see also* "Give Me Liberty or Give Me Death Ideology"
Johnson, William F. 89
Joliffe, John 168, 171–175, 205*n*23, 205*n*25
Jones, Edward 30
Jones, William 138, 150
Journal of Commerce 90, 112

Kane, John K. 88
Kansas-Nebraska Bill 122, 127, 138–139, 142, 201*n*21
Kearney, John 120–121
Kemp, William 76
Kentucky Resolutions 131
Kerber, Linda K. 4
Keyes, Senator 66
Kingston, Ontario 77, 110
Kinney, Martin Palmer 129
Kite, Elijah 162–165
Kite, Joe 162–165
Kite, Sarah 162–165
Kline, Henry H. 83–86
Knight, John 22, 31–32, 34, 36
Kook 7, 186*n*16
Kossuth, Louis 95, 115

Laurie, Bruce 16
Lawrence, Amos 46
Lawrence, James R. 103–104
Lear, James 103
Leary, John F. 34
Leavitt, Court Judge Humphrey 175
Lewey, Henry 192*n*17
Lewis, Elijah 85–87, 90, 93, 197*n*15
The Liberator 30, 35, 37, 160
Liberty or Death!; or, Heaven's Infraction of the Fugitive Slave Law 13, 179; *see also* women and fugitive slave crises
Liberty Party 114
Liberty Party State Convention 96, 102
Library of Congress 1
Life Guards 166, 175; *see also* Beckley, Jesse
Lilly, Peter 109
Lincoln, Abraham 182
Linebaugh, Peter 5
Loguen, Jermain W. 9, 98–99, 100, 105, 108–109, 113, 115, 188*n*69, 198*n*2 *see also* "Give Me Liberty or Give Me Death" ideology; Syracuse Vigilance Committee
Longfellow, Henry Wadsworth 63
Loomis, Joseph 103–104
Loring, Charles G. 64–66, 75
Loring, Edward Greely 139, 140, 148–152
Loring, Ellis Gray 22
Louis 165
Lovejoy, Elijah 41
Lovejoy, Joseph C. 41

Index

Lowe, E. Louis 88
Lowell, Russell 105
Lumpkin, Robert 137, 154
Lyon G. Tyler Department of History 1

M & J.C. Gilmore 54–55, 66
Madison, James 131
Magol, Edward 16
Malcolm, Joyce Lee 6
"Manifest Destiny" 3
Mann, Daniel 179
Mann, Horace 53, 67
"Many Headed Hydra": Sailors, Slaves, Commoners, and the Hidden History of the Revolutionary Atlantic 5
Maplewood Plantation 161, 162, 169
Marshall, James 161, 163
Marshall, John 91
Marshall, Thomas 163–164, 166
Martin, Valerie 1
Martineau, Harriet 19, 136, 154; see also women and fugitive slave crises
masculinity discourse 188n69
Massachusetts Anti-Slavery Society 10, 13, 18–19, 30–31, 33, 76, 93
Massachusetts Historical Society 1
Massachusetts in Mourning sermon 49, 140; see also Burns, Anthony; Higginson, Thomas Wentworth
Mattapan Iron Works 138, 150
May, Samuel Joseph 7, 10, 18, 31, 32–33, 48–49, 52, 96–97, 98, 99–100, 103–107, 111–115, 122, 139, 178, 198n3, 200n32; see also "Give Me Liberty or Give Me Death" ideology; Syracuse Vigilance Committee
Mayo, A.D. 178
McGill University Library 1
McQuerry, George Washington 165
McReynolds, John 102–104
Menzies, Dr. John 165, 167
Merrick, Charles 104
Messenger, John 128
Mexican War 24, 98
Milita Act of July 1862 182
Miller, Andrew Galbraith 120, 121, 124, 127, 130, 133–134
Millspaugh 137, 149
Milwaukee Free Democrat 124, 129; see also Booth, Sherman
Milwaukee vigilance committee 127–128
Minkins, Shadrach 7, 11, 37–53, 181, 192n16, 192n17, 192n18, 192n19, 192n21; see also "Give Me Liberty or Give Me Death" ideology
The Mississippian 34
Mississippian and State Gazette 86
Missouri Compromise 3, 122, 139

M'Keehan, Hattia 13, 179; see also women and fugitive slave crises
Moby Dick 63
"The Modern Medea" 180; see also Garner, Margaret
Moffat, Windsor 15
Mohawks 97
Monroe, James 3
Monroe Doctrine 3
Montreal, Canada 43–44
Morehouse, Charles 176
Morgan, Leroy 107
Morris 152
Morris, Robert 39, 43, 47
Morris, Timothy D. 121, 130
Morrison, Toni 180
Murphy, William B. 163–164
Murray, Thomas 41

Nash, Gary 4, 185n7
National Era 88
natural rights ideology 7, 13, 169, 186n19
The Negro in Our History 185n7
The Negro in the American Revolution 6
Nell, William Cooper 5, 15, 178, 187n26; see also "Declaration of Sentiments of the Colored Citizens"
Nelson, Nathan 83, 86
Nelson, Samuel 133
New England Anti-Slavery Society 154
New National Era 4, 7
New York Courier and Enquirer 111
New York Daily Advertiser 111
New York Evening Post 103
New York Herald 57
New York Journal of Commerce 46
New York Tribune 92, 103
New York Weekly Herald 190n34
"Nigger Hill" 25, 41, 139
Nineteenth Amendment 186n14
"No Slave Hunting in the Empire State" 178
Noble, Thomas 180
North American and United States Gazette 32
Northwest Ordinance of 1787 172
Norton, Mary Beth 4
Nottingham, Abram 98

Oates, Stephen 186n17
Oberlin College 155
Ohio Ladies Education Society 178; see also Ernst, Sarah
Oneida 97
Onondaga 97
O'Sullivan, John 3

Padgett, William 83, 84
Paine, Byron 127–128, 132, 133

Paine, James 124–127, 130–133
Palfrey, John G. 67
Panic of 1819 3
Panic of 1837 97
Parker, Edward 140, 149, 152
Parker, Theodore 2, 7, 11, 17–18, 22, 24, 25, 32, **35**, 36, 37, 44, 48–50, 54–59, 61–62, 66, 68–69, 71, 74–75, 76, 140–143, 145–146, 149, 152, 170, 187*n*39, 191*n*50, 191*n*6; *see also* Boston Vigilance Committee; "Give Me Liberty or Give Me Death" ideology
Parker, William 7, 8, 10, 12, 15, 16, 77–95, 181, 196*n*7; *see also* Christiana riot; "Give Me Liberty or Give Me Death" ideology
Patterson, John 164
Pearce, Thomas 83, 86
Pellet, Sarah 12, 145–146; *see also* women and fugitive slave crises
Pendery, John L. 163, 166–167, 170–175
Pennsylvania Freeman 11, 93
Pennsylvanian 90
periodization of the Revolution 4–6, 182, 183; *see also* Bancroft, George; *History of the United States*
Phillips, Wendell 2, 12, 13–14, 25, 26, 30–31, 35, 57, 59, 60, 62–63, **64**, 66, 68, 74, 79, 110, 136, 139, 141, 143–145, 176, 187*n*49; *see also* Boston Vigilance Committee; Golden Trumpet
Pierce, Franklin 123, 147, **148**, 158, 160
Pillsbury, Parker 18, 154, 160, 178–179, 190*n*34
Pinckney, Alexander 78, 84, 86, 87
Pinckney, Hannah 84
Pitts, Coffin 138–139
Pottawatomie Massacre 161, 177
Potter, James 56, 71, 73
Powell, Harriet 98, 198*n*2; *see also* fancy trade
Powell, William P. 95
Pownall, Levi 88
Pownall, Mrs. Levi 87
Prigg v. Pennsylvania 64, 68, 98
Prosser, Gabriel 7, 82, 137; *see also* slave revolts
Prudence Crandall's school for black children 96
Purvis, Robert 24

Quamana 7, 186*n*16
Quarles, Benjamin 5–6
Quincy, Josiah 12, 69; *see also* "Give Me Liberty or Give Me Death" ideology

Race and Revolution 4
Racine Advocate 118, 121, 122–123; *see also* Clement, Charles

Radicalism of the American Revolution 4
The Raleigh Register 86, 110
Rantoul, Robert 64, 65–66, 68–69, 132, 150
Rasmussen, Daniel 186*n*16
Rediker, Marcus 5
Reed, Enoch 108, 114
Religious Recorder 112
Remond, Charles Lenox 10, 24, 36, 73, 95, 154, **155**
Remond, Sarah 178; *see also* women and fugitive slave crises
republican experiment 3–4, 16, 35, 147, 154
Retreat Farm 82, 83
Revolutionary Generation 2–4, 74, 143
revolutionary Haiti 186*n*16
Revolutionary legacy 3
Richmond Dispatch 111
Richmond Enquirer 133, 157, 158
Riley, Elizabeth 41; *see also* women and fugitive slave crises
Riley, Patrick 43, 58–59, 71
Roberts, Anthony E. 87
Robertson 164
Robinson, Hiram 163, 166, 171, 175
Ruffin, Edmund 157
Russell, George E. 142
Rust, Benjamin S. 101
Ryecraft, John 133–134

Sabine, Joseph F. 10, 103–104, 107–108
Sack of Kansas 177
Sack of Lawrence 161
St. Catharines, Ontario 155
Salmon, William L. 104, 108
Sambo thesis 185*n*13
Sanborn, Franklin 187*n*39
Savannah Republican 48, 71
Scarlett, Joseph 85, 90
Schmitt, Jeffrey 129–130, 201*n*21
Scott, Dred 160, 177
Scott, James 47, 50
Second Great Awakening 13, 28, 97, 102
Secret Six 11; *see also* Brown, John; Higginson, Thomas Wentworth
Semi-Weekly Raleigh Register 189*n*12
Seneca 97
Seventeenth Annual Meeting of Massachusetts Anti-Slavery Society 30, 31, 33; *see also* Brown, Henry "Box"; Craft, Ellen; Craft, William; Douglass, Frederick; Massachusetts Anti-Slavery Society; May, Samuel Joseph; Phillips, Wendell; Stearns, Charles
Sewall, Samuel E. 53, 58–59, 63–65, 67, 141–142, 145; *see also* Boston Vigilance Committee
Seward, William 113

Sharpstein, U.S. District Attorney 131
Shatuck, William 94
Shaw, Lemuel 64–65, 66, 133, 142, 152
Shay's Rebellion: The Making of an Agrarian Insurrection 4
Sheldon, Henry 107
Sims, Henry 86
Sims, Thomas 7, 8, 9, 12, 17, 18–19, 35, 53, 54–73, **74**, 75–76, 83, 139, 146, 152, 168, 175, 181, 193*n*1, 193*n*6, 193*n*8, 194*n*15; *see also* "Give Me Liberty or Give Me Death" ideology
"*Sims Brigade*" 60; *see also* Sims, Thomas
Sinclair, Duncan 118
Slaughter, Thomas 86
"the Slave Catcher of Dover" 120
The Slave Community: Plantation Life in the Antebellum South 185*n*13
slave revolts 7; *see also* Prosser, Gabriel; Turner, Nat; Vesey, Denmark
Sleeper, Alfred 57
Smith, Abram 132–134
Smith, Gerrit 10, 52, 74, 93, 98, 103–104, 106, **107**, 113, 116, 187*n*39 *see also* "Give Me Liberty or Give Me Death" ideology; Syracuse Vigilance Committee
Smith, H.K. 101
Smith, Jerome V.C. 147–149, 151, 152
Smith, John J. 38–39, **40**, 41–42
Smith, Joshua B. 14, 39, 191*n*6; *see also* "Give Me Liberty or Give Me Death" ideology
Smith, Samuel 103
Smith, Thomas Paul 47
Smith, Winfield 121, 130–131
social history 4
Sons of Liberty 126, 166
Southern Literary Messenger 157
Southern Nationalists 56, 83, 157
Sprague, Peleg 65
Stearns, Charles 33
Stearns, George Luther 187*n*39
Stevens, Charles Emory 151
Still, William 84
Stone, Lucy 32–33, 160, 169, **170**; *see also* women and fugitive slave crises
Story, Joseph 64, 68, 91, 133
Stowe, Harriet Beecher 13, 26, 28, 74, 145, 170; *see also* Uncle Tom's Cabin
Stowell, Martin 16, 109, 139–141, 143–145, 147, 151, 203*n*25
Strader et al. v. Graham 174; *see also* Taney, Roger
"*Sub Libertate Quietem*" 188*n*49
Sumner, Charles 22, 60, **61**, 65, 74, 78, 110, 160; *see also* "Bleeding Kansas" speech; Bleeding Sumner-Bleeding Kansas
Sumner, Moses 108

surrender at Yorktown 4, 6; *see also* Bancroft, George; *History of the United States*
Suttle, Charles 137, 138–140, 146, 149–152, 154, 157
Suttle, John 137
Swift, John L. 142, 145
Syracuse Journal 105, 109, 112, 114
Syracuse Standard 103, 112, 113
Syracuse Star 111
Syracuse Vigilance Committee 10, 100, 103, 105–108, 198*n*5, 199*n*20; *see also* Bates, Abner; Crandall, William L.; Hovey, Alfred H.; Jerry (William Henry); Loguen, Jermain W.; Smith, Gerrit; Ward, Samuel Ringgold; Wheaton, Charles
Syracuse's Congregational Church 96; *see also* May, Samuel Joseph
Szatmary, David P. 4

Taft's Cornhill Coffee House 43
"A Tale of Horror" 164; *see also* Garner, Margaret
Taney, Roger 134–135, 174; *see also* *Ableman v. Booth*; *Strader et al. v. Graham*; *United States v. The Ship Garonne*
Taylor, Ira 22
Taylor, Zachary 24, 162
Tenth Amendment 172
Thirteenth Amendment 7
Thomas, Seth J. 43, 64, 140, 149–150, 152
Thompson, George 52
Thompson, John L. 89
Thompson, John Reuben 157
Thompson, Samuel 109
Thompson, Zeke 85
Tichenor, Moses 129
Treaty of Paris 4, 6
Tukey, City Marshal 57, 60, 63
Tully, Thomson 83
Turner, Nat 7, 80, 186*n*17; *see also* slave revolts
Turner, Nelson 119–121, 201*n*1
Twelfth Baptist Church 43, 138, 139, 149; *see also* Grimes, Leonard A.
Twentieth Massachusetts Anti-Slavery Society Meeting 76; *see also* Massachusetts Anti-Slavery Society
Two Years Before the Mast 140; *see also* Dana, Richard Henry, Jr.

Uncle Tom's Cabin 13, 26, 28, 74, 190*n*24; *see also* Stowe, Harriett Beecher
Underground Railroad 41–42, 84, 99, 110, 128–129, 136, 162, 191*n*2, 196*n*3, 201*n*20; *see also* Ames, Orson; Bacon, Winchel D.; Bigelow, Ann; Bigelow, Francis

Edwin; Clarke, Olive; Clarke, Sidney; Coffin, Levi; Concord Underground Railroad; Loguen, Jermain W.; May, Samuel Joseph; Underground Railroad song
Underground Railroad song 136
United States Constitution 3, 4, 35, 37, 46, 48, 51, 58, 62, 65–66, 68–69, 127, 131–135, 147, 150, 152, 157, 172
United States v. The Ship Garonne 174; *see also* Taney, Roger

Vanderburgh, Colonel Origen 105, 111
Vermont Anti-Slavery Society 178
The Vermont Chronicle 91
Vesey, Denmark 7, 80, 82, 186*n*17; *see also* slave revolts
Vesper 42
Virginia Resolutions 131
Voice of the Fugitive 15, 79

Wakarusa War 160
Walker, David 14
Wall, Samuel T. 171
Wallace, Jarrett 83
Ward, Reverend Samuel Ringgold 9, 15–16, 17, 19, 73, 88, 96, 100, 105–106, 115, 181, 182, 188*n*56; *see also* "Give Me Liberty or Give Me Death" ideology; Syracuse Vigilance Committee
Washburn, Emory 141
Washington, George 2, 38, 147
Washington Hotel 162
Washington Republic 90
Watkins, Charles 128, 130, 132
Watkins, James 154, 155
Watkins, Susan (Autnie) 109; *see also* women and fugitive slave crises
Way, Peter 105
Webb, Seth, Jr. 141
Webster, Daniel 30, 35, 38, 45–46, 66, 71, 90, 100–101, 111, 147, 199*n*6
Weisenburger, Steven 180
Western Anti-Slavery Society 178
Weymouth antislavery convention 44

Wheaton, Charles 103, 105, 113; *see also* Syracuse Vigilance Committee
Whig interpretation 4; *see also* Bancroft, George; *History of the United States*
Whipple, Prince 15
Whipple, William 15
Whittier 74
Williams, George Washington 5, 185*n*7, 185*n*12
Williams, Samuel 84, 90–91
Willis, Hamilton B. 149
Williston, Charles F. 102–103
Willow Grove Plantation 177
Wilmot, David, proviso 98
Wilson, Henry 67, 74
Winthrop, Robert C. 46
Wisconsin Historical Society 1
Wisconsin Personal Liberty Law 135
Wolcott, Edward B. 126, 128
women and fugitive slave crises 12–13, 61, 62, 86, 108, 113–114, 145, 146, 151, 159, 181; *see also* Alcott, Abby; Anti-Slavery Sewing Society; Bristol and Clifton Ladies Anti-Slavery Society; Christina riot; Craft, Ellen; Craft, William; Daughters of Samaria; Ernst, Sarah; Forten, Charlotte; Foster, Abby Kelly; Garner, Margaret; Griffiths, Julia; Howard, Eliza Ann Elizabeth; *Liberty or Death!; or, Heaven's Infraction of the Fugitive Slave Law*; Martineau, Harriet; M'Keehan, Hattia; Pellet, Sarah; Remond, Sarah; Riley, Elizabeth; Stone, Lucy; Watkins, Susan (Auntie)
Wood, Gordon S. 4
Woodbury, Justice 65, 69
Woodruff, Jason 109
Woodson, Carter G. 185*n*7
Wright, Elizur 39, 45, 47, 48, 49, 59, 142; *see also* Boston Vigilance Committee; *The Commonwealth*
Wright, Henry C. 40, 44, 47, 48, 50, 77, 94, 116, 169–170, **171**, 189*n*5, 189*n*8

Zion Baptist Church 155